MODERN HUMANITIES RESEARCH ASSOCIATION
TUDOR AND STUART TRANSLATIONS
VOLUME 28

GENERAL EDITORS
ANDREW HADFIELD
NEIL RHODES

THE FIRST ENGLISH *PASTOR FIDO* (1602)

MODERN HUMANITIES RESEARCH ASSOCIATION
TUDOR AND STUART TRANSLATIONS

General Editors
Andrew Hadfield (University of Sussex)
Neil Rhodes (University of St Andrews)

Associate Editors
Guyda Armstrong (University of Manchester)
Fred Schurink (University of Manchester)
Louise Wilson (Liverpool Hope University)

Advisory Board
Warren Boutcher (Queen Mary, University of London)
Colin Burrow (All Souls College, Oxford)
A. E. B. Coldiron (Florida State University)
Patricia Demers (University of Alberta)
José María Pérez Fernández (University of Granada)
Robert S. Miola (Loyola College, Maryland)
Alessandra Petrina (University of Padua)
Anne Lake Prescott (Barnard College, Columbia University)
Quentin Skinner (Queen Mary, University of London)
Alan Stewart (Columbia University)

For details of published and forthcoming volumes please visit our website:

www.tudor.mhra.org.uk

The First English *Pastor Fido* (1602)

Edited by
Massimiliano Morini

Modern Humanities Research Association
Tudor and Stuart Translations 28

2024

Published by

The Modern Humanities Research Association
Salisbury House
Station Road
Cambridge CB1 2LA
United Kingdom

© Modern Humanities Research Association, 2024

Massimiliano Morini has asserted his right under the Copyright, Designs and Patents Act 1988 to be identified as the author of this work. Parts of this work may be reproduced as permitted under legal provisions for fair dealing (or fair use) for the purposes of research, private study, criticism, or review, or when a relevant collective licensing agreement is in place. All other reproduction requires the written permission of the copyright holder who may be contacted at rights@mhra.org.uk.

First published 2024

ISBN 978-1-781889-91-6 (paperback)
ISBN 978-1-781889-92-3 (hardback)

Typeset in Minion Pro by Allset Journals & Books, Scarborough, UK

CONTENTS

General Editors' Foreword	vi
Acknowledgements	vii
List of Abbreviations	viii
Note on this Edition	ix
Introduction	1
The Faithful Shepherd (1602)	29
Bibliography	204

GENERAL EDITORS' FOREWORD

The aim of the *MHRA Tudor & Stuart Translations* is to create a representative library of works translated into English during the early modern period for the use of scholars, students and the wider public. The series will include both substantial single works and selections of texts from major authors, with the emphasis being on the works that were most familiar to early modern readers. The texts themselves will be newly edited with substantial introductions, notes, and glossaries, and will be published both in print and online.

The series aims to restore to view a major part of English Renaissance literature which has become relatively inaccessible and to present these texts as literary works in their own right. For that reason it will follow the same principle of modernisation adopted by other scholarly editions of canonical literature from the period. The series will have a similar scope to that of the original *Tudor Translations* published early in the last century, and while the great majority of the works presented will be from the sixteenth century, like the original series it will not be rigidly bound by the end-date of 1603. There will, however, be a very different range of texts with new and substantial scholarly apparatus.

The *MHRA Tudor & Stuart Translations* will extend our understanding of the English Renaissance through its representation of the process of cultural transmission from the classical to the early modern world and the process of cultural exchange within the early modern world.

Andrew Hadfield
Neil Rhodes

ACKNOWLEDGEMENTS

This edition has grown out of a more than decade-long interest in the first English *Pastor fido* — though the idea of proposing it for the MHRA Tudor and Stuart Translations Series was suggested to me by Alessandra Petrina. The latter, therefore, has the greatest share of direct responsibility, though some of it must also be assigned to all those who have welcomed my papers and articles on the subject in these last few years: Giovanni Iamartino and Massimo Sturiale, Brenda Hosington and Marie-Alice Belle, Francesca Lorandini, Pavel Drábek and Klára Škrobánková, *Theatralia* and the *Cahiers Élisabéthains*. I would also like to mention some people and institutions that were only indirectly involved: Jeremy Munday and the people at Bloomsbury (who published my 2022 *Theatre Translation*), Iolanda Plescia and the IASEMS association (for providing the ideal platform from which to discuss early modern translation). Andrew Hadfield, Neil Rhodes and Gerard Lowe warmly accepted my proposal for the series and gave me a number of very useful suggestions on how to carry out my task. Simon Davies astounded me with his Argus-like ability to spot the smallest of misprints and incongruities.

LIST OF ABBREVIATIONS

Donno — *Three Renaissance Pastorals: Tasso-Guarini-Daniel*, ed. by Elizabeth Story Donno (Binghamton: Medieval & Renaissance Texts & Studies, 1993)

EEBO — *Early English Books Online* <https://search.proquest.com/eebo>

ODNB — *Oxford Dictionary of National Biography* <https://www.oxforddnb.com>

OED — *Oxford English Dictionary* <https://www.oed.com>

Selmi — Battista Guarini, *Il pastor fido*, ed. by Elisabetta Selmi, with an introduction by Guido Baldassarri (Venezia: Marsilio, 1999)

S1591 — Battista Guarini / Torquato Tasso, *Il Pastor Fido: Tragicomedia Pastorale* […] *Aminta: Favola Boschereccia* (London: John Wolfe for Giacomo Castelvetro, 1591)

T1602 — *Il Pastor fido: Or The faithfull Shepheard. Translated out of Italian into English* (London: Simon Waterson, 1602)

T1633 — *Il Pastor fido: Or The faithfull Shepheard. Translated out of Italian into English* (London: William Sheares, 1633)

NOTE ON THIS EDITION

There are two seventeenth-century editions of this translation: T1602 is in the quarto format, while T1633 is a duodecimo.[1] T1602 was entered in the Stationers' Register by Simon Waterson on 16 September 1601; T1633 was entered by William Sheares on 6 September 1633. The National Art Library of London holds a copy of T1602, while the British Library has one of T1633. I have worked on the electronic versions available on *EEBO* (these are derived from copies of T1602 and T1633 kept at the Huntington Library), and checked a number of unclear passages in the two London copies. The differences between the two editions are minor, generally involving spelling and punctuation; and it is not necessarily the case that the later version modernizes the earlier one. Here, for instance, are the two non-modernized versions of the beginning of Act 1, Scene 1, which exhibit only slight variations in spelling (Go/Goe; me/mee):

T1602	T1633
Go you that haue enclos'd the dreadfull beast,	Go you that haue enclos'd the dreadfull beast,
And giue the signe that's vsuall to our hunting,	And giue the signe that's usuall to our hunting,
Go swell your eyes and hearts with hornes and shoutes,	Goe swell your eyes and hearts with hornes and shouts.
If there be any swaine of *Cinthia's* troupe	If there be any swaine of *Cinthia's* troupe
In all *Arcadia*, delighted in her sports,	In all *Arcadia*, delighted in her sports,
Whose generous affects are stung with care,	Whose generous affects are stung with care,
Or glory of these woods: let him come forth	Or glory of these woods: let him come forth,
And follow me, where in a circle small	And follow mee, where in a circle small
(Though to our valure large) inclosed is	(Though to our valure large) inclosed is
The ougly Bore, monster of nature & these woods.	The ougly Boare, monster of nature & these woods,

The present edition generally follows T1602; the few significant differences between the two versions are indicated in the footnotes (rather than in a separate section on variants). All minor differences are made irrelevant by the fact that the text as presented here is modernized and standardized in spelling and punctuation. More specifically, as regards spelling: 'v' is turned into 'u' whenever it stands for the vowel (see 'vsuall' above); the final -e is eliminated when no

[1] The 'T' in the abbreviations stands for 'target (text)', or 'translation'; the 'S' in S1591 stands for 'source'. The modern critical edition of the Italian text published by Marsilio in 1999 is referred to by its editor's name (Selmi), as is the English collection of Renaissance pastorals which includes an edited version of the translation presented here (Donno).

longer in use (see 'signe' above, but also 'vaine', 'beare', 'hee', 'shee', 'mee'); -ll terminations are normalized when necessary ('vsuall'); old-fashioned expanded spellings are contracted when this does not affect the syllabic count ('lippes' turns into 'lips'); outmoded variants are replaced unless the substitution causes prosodic problems ('infortunate' becomes 'unfortunate'); common nouns are de-capitalized ('Bore' / 'Boare' becomes 'boar'); and proper names are given in roman rather than italics (see *Cinthia's*, above).

A separate note is necessary for all past forms terminating with -ed. In this case, both T1602 and T1633 have e.g. 'seemed' indicating a disyllabic reading, and 'seem'd' (or, with other forms, 'mixt') when the word is to be read as a monosyllable. This edition follows modern usage, and has therefore 'seemed' for the monosyllable, 'seemèd' for the disyllable.

On occasion, the original spelling or contraction of a word or phrase has been kept for prosodic reasons (e.g. 'worser'; 'ta'n' for 'taken'; 'th'adder'; or 'go'w' for 'let us go'). Certain old-fashioned variants of second-person verbs have been kept for the sake of euphony (e.g. 'wert', 'wouldst'). In order to read Dymock's verse correctly, the reader should keep in mind that words with v and w sounds in central positions are often meant to be mentally contracted (i.e., 'power' sometimes scans as 'powr', 'heaven' as 'heavn').

Some use has been made of the only twentieth-century book which employs the Dymock version to present Guarini's play to English-speaking readers (Donno). The prefatory materials in that selection of *Three Renaissance Pastorals* are very useful, and the footnotes to the present edition make occasional reference to Elizabeth Story Donno's textual choices in presenting the 1602/1633 *Faithfull Shepheard*. Those choices, however, are the product of a rather odd mixture of modernization and mere replication that is apt to leave the contemporary reader confused. Donno, for instance, keeps the original spelling 'then' for the comparative particle: this means that in certain passages, readers have to retrace their steps and re-interpret, or decide for themselves whether the word has a comparative or temporal value. The present edition has the purpose of making the first English translation of *Il pastor fido* as readable as possible — though it also attempts to do so by preserving the metre and prosody of Dymock's text.

Since there is very little difference between the various Italian editions which Dymock might have had at his disposal, and considering that on the few occasions on which he might have been led astray by early modern Italian spelling and punctuation it is impossible to point at a single source for reference, the translation has been read in parallel with Selmi — and that modern critical edition has been compared with S1591 (the only Italian version printed in early modern England) whenever it seemed significant to do so; though given Daniel and Edward Dymock's travels, recounted in the Introduction, they could have brought home any of a number of Italian editions.

INTRODUCTION

Tragical-Comical-Pastoral: An Outmoded Genre

At the risk of alienating the reader's benevolence from the very beginning, an admission needs to be made: the text being presented here is a forgotten English translation of an outmoded Italian original. Without specialist mediation, it would be very difficult for anyone not versed in the European Renaissance to derive any pleasure or knowledge from it.[1] This introduction is dedicated to the task of explaining why that is, and why, conversely, a mediated reading can be both pleasurable and illuminating.

If one looks at its present diffusion, there is no doubt that Giovanni Battista Guarini's pastoral tragicomedy *Il pastor fido* (1589) exercises very little fascination on contemporary theatregoers and readers. In its native Italy there are only two printed editions of the work in commercial circulation, both of them relatively hard to find.[2] By comparison, there are at least six available books currently in print featuring Torquato Tasso's pastoral play *Aminta*, of which Guarini's tragicomedy was partly a rewriting. A similar balance obtains in anthologies and literary histories for secondary schools, where Tasso is treated as a canonical author, Guarini as little more than a footnote. As regards their theatrical afterlife, it must be said that neither Tasso's nor Guarini's plays have proved particularly appealing to contemporary audiences; though in the case of *Aminta*, at least one recent experimental adaptation testifies to a niche cultural value.[3]

Its current neglect would not feel at all extraordinary were it not for the febrile interest that *Il pastor fido* aroused in Guarini's contemporaries. Even before it was published or staged, its fame had spread throughout Italy, and various potentates had tried to acquire the rights to its courtly premiere — to use an anachronism that gives one an idea of the excitement the play generated. Guarini began to write this complex pastoral tragicomedy in the early 1580s, less than a decade after the first staging of Tasso's simpler dramatic fable. *Il pastor fido* was not completed before 1585/1586, yet even in its unfinished state it was commented on and extravagantly praised in the courtly and intellectual circles of northern

---

[1] Walter F. Staton and William E. Simeone, the twentieth-century editors of Richard Fanshawe's 1647 translation, also begin their introduction on a rather apologetic note: 'the play', they opine, 'though not great, is rather good'; Battista Guarini, *A Critical Edition of Sir Richard Fanshawe's 1647 Translation of Giovanni Battista Guarini's 'Il Pastor Fido'*, ed. by Walter F. Staton Jr. and William E. Simeone (Oxford: Clarendon Press, 1964), p. ix.

[2] One of them is the critical edition used as reference here (Selmi). The other is Battista Guarini, *Il pastor fido*, ed. by Ettore Bonora (Milano: Mursia, 1977).

[3] A re-elaboration directed by Antonio Latella, with four actors and an electric guitarist on stage, toured Italy between 2018 and 2019.

Italy. Around 1586, Guarini asked the Florentine humanist Lionardo Salviati to help him 'purify' its language along Tuscan lines, and also begged the assistance of his friend and literary associate Scipione Gonzaga in the final process of revision.[4] The play was finally printed by the Venetian Giovanni Battista Bonfadino in 1589, and it was first performed a few years later.[5]

Nor did the official appearance of the pastoral tragicomedy in the public arena exhaust the interest it had aroused; if anything, that interest grew to a paroxysm after 1589, and rapidly extended to the rest of Europe. Between that year and 1602, when Guarini published an authoritative edition with his own annotations and the apologetic *Compendio della Poesia Tragicomica*, around twenty Italian editions were printed, in Italy and elsewhere.[6] Translations sprouted all over the continent for the European readers who did not understand Italian, penned by writers who wished to produce a pastoral tragicomedy in their own language. Even where a vernacular translation was already available, other practitioners would decide to try their hand at their own *Pastor fido*. Before the end of the seventeenth century, there existed no less than five complete versions in French, three in Spanish, four in German and four in English — not to mention those in Latin, Dutch, Polish, modern Greek, the dialects of Naples and Bergamo, as well as a plethora of partial translations and imitations.[7] In short, for at least a

---

[4] On the period of composition, see Vittorio Rossi, *Battista Guarini ed il pastor fido: Studio biografico-critico* (Torino: Loescher, 1886), pp. 55-89, 179-89; Walter W. Greg, *Pastoral Poetry & Pastoral Drama: A Literary Inquiry, with Special Reference to the Pre-Restoration Stage in England* (London: A. H. Bullen, 1906), pp. 206-10; the prefatory materials to Selmi, pp. 28-32; Lisa Sampson, *Pastoral Drama in Early Modern Italy: The Making of a New Genre* (Abingdon: The Modern Humanities Research Association and Routledge, 2006), p. 130.

[5] Possibly in 1593, though 1595 or 1596 is a more likely date. On the early Italian stagings, see Rossi, *Battista Guarini*, pp. 104-21, 223-35; Luigi Ammirati, *Nola nella luce della Rinascenza: La prima rappresentazione del Pastor Fido col Prologo di G. B. Marino nel 1599* (Nola: G. Scala, 1980); Lisa Sampson, 'The Mantuan Performance of Guarini's *Pastor fido* and Representations of Courtly Identity', *Modern Language Review*, 98.1 (2003), 65-83; Sampson, *Pastoral Drama*, pp. 183-89; Francesco Pozzi, 'La prima rappresentazione del "Pastor Fido" di Battista Guarini a Crema: Carnevale 1595 o 1596', *Insula Fulcheria*, 36 (2006), 265-82.

[6] Guarini's authoritative edition of 1602, printed by Ciotti in Venice, is presented on its title page as the twentieth edition, and a later 1602 impression of the same as the twenty-seventh. While these numbers may be rough estimates, there is no reason to believe that they were gross exaggerations. These claims seem to have been accepted by most commentators (see for instance Rossi, *Battista Guarini*, p. 236; Sampson, *Pastoral Drama*, p. 130).

[7] This is not an exhaustive list, and is only meant to give readers an idea of Guarini's immense popularity. On the European translations, see Daniela Dalla Valle, *Pastorale barocca: Forme e contenuti dal Pastor Fido al drama pastorale francese* (Ravenna: Longo, 1973), pp. 23-38; Laurence Giavarini, 'La reception du *Pastor Fido* en France au XVIIe siecle: bref état des lieux de la recherche', *Études Épistémè*, 4 (2003); Battista Guarini, *El Pastor Fido de Battista Guarini*, Ediciones de Nápoles 1602 y Valencia 1609, trans. by Cristóbal Suárez de Figueroa, ed. by Enrique Suárez Figaredo (Madrid: Centro Virtual Cervantes, 2006-2007); Rosilie Hernández-Pecoraro, 'Cristóbal Suárez de Figueroa and Isabel Correa: Competing Translators of Battista

century after its first Italian publication, there was hardly a moment when a version of Guarini's play was not in print somewhere, in one language or other.

A condensed history of the English editions and translations will suffice as a more specific illustration of the point, if one bears in mind that similar chronicles could be drawn up for all the major European cultures. As early as 1591 John Wolfe, printer of Italian books in London, published for Giacomo Castelvetro a volume collecting Guarini's and Tasso's dramatic pastorals. 1602 saw the first impression of the English translation that is presented here. Between 1604 and 1605, a Latin *Fidus pastor* was performed in Cambridge. The 1602 translation was reprinted in 1633. In the 1630s, Jonathan Sidnam began his own version of the tragicomedy, which he later decided not to print because another successful edition had meanwhile entered circulation.[8] That edition was the work of Richard Fanshawe: originally published in 1647, his *Faithfull Shepherd* was reprinted several times in the translator's lifetime and beyond (in 1648, 1664, 1676, 1694 and 1736, not counting twentieth-century critical editions). In the 1670s, Elkanah Settle adapted Fanshawe's translation for the stage: this theatrical version appeared in print in 1677, and was itself reprinted twice. In 1712, Georg Friedrich Händel presented his three-act operatic version at the Queen's Theatre in the Haymarket, London.[9] Again, to appreciate the extraordinary nature of the interest aroused by *Il pastor fido*, it may be useful to point out that Tasso's *Aminta* was admired by a much smaller coterie of English readers.[10]

Most of these versions testify not only to the popularity of Guarini's play, but to the Italian author's canonical status. The very idea of re-translating a text that is already in circulation demonstrates its value as cultural capital — in that

Guarini's *Il Pastor Fido*', *Romance Notes*, 46.1 (2005), 97–105; Encarnación Sánchez García, '"Salientes acquae". Due edizioni poetiche napoletane in lingua spagnola: "El pastor fido" di Cristóbal Suárez (1602) e le "Obras" di Garcilaso de la Vega (1604)', in *Cancioneros del Siglo de Oro: Forma y formas / Canzonieri dei Secoli d'oro: Forma e forme*, ed. by Andrea Baldissera (Como: Ibis, 2019), pp. 183–204; Alba Schwartz, *Der Teutsch-redende treue Schäfer: Guarinis 'Pastor fido' und die Übersetzungen von Eilger Mannlich 1619, Statius Ackermann 1636, Hofmann von Hoffmannswaldau 1652, Assmann von Abschatz 1672* (Bern: Peter Lang, 1972); Christiane Caemmerer, 'Die Schäferliteratur und die Frauen', in *'Wenn sie das Wort ich gebraucht': Festschrift für Barbara Becker-Cantarino*, ed. by John Pustejovsky and Jacqueline Vansant (Amsterdam: Rodopi, 2013), pp. 221–47; P. E. L. Verkuyl, *Battista Guarini's 'Il pastor fido' in de Nederlandse dramatische literatuur* (Assen: Van Gorcum, 1971); Andrea Lazzarini, 'Una polemica attorno al *Pastor fido in lingua Napolitana* di Domenico Basile', *Studi secenteschi*, 44 (2013), 187–203. A critical edition of Isabella Correa's 1694 Spanish version (ed. by Noelia Pousada-Lobeira) is forthcoming in the MHRA's European Translations series.

[8] See G. W. Pigman III, 'Pastoral Drama', in *The Oxford History of Literary Translation in English, vol. 2: 1550–1660*, ed. by Gordon Braden, Robert Cummings and Stuart Gillespie (Oxford: Oxford University Press, 2010), pp. 293–98 (p. 296).

[9] Händel's opera was not well received in 1712, but it was successfully revived more than two decades later. See Duncan Chisholm, 'The English Origins of Händel's "Pastor fido"', *The Musical Times*, 115.1578 (1974), 650–54.

[10] Greg, *Pastoral Poetry*, p. 238.

connection, the numerous complete and partial versions of the *Aeneid* spring to mind.[11] In addition, it is normally only the most important works in a culture that end up being translated into Latin: three decades earlier, for instance, the same honour had been conferred in England to Castiglione's *Cortegiano*.[12] As a further testimony of respect, all English versions keep close enough to their source, with the very partial exception of the first and the understandable exception of Settle's play. However, even the Restoration dramatist had to pay homage to the Italian author whose work he had rather ruthlessly abridged. When Settle published his 'Pastoral' play in 1677, he prefaced it with a dedication in which he declares that since he is 'a Stranger to the Italian', he has worked directly on a previous poetic translation. About this process he is completely unapologetic (and he fails to mention Fanshawe), but in the same passage he respectfully says that his work 'borrows its Value from the Esteem'd *Guarini*'; and in his tongue-in-cheek prologue he refers (seriously) to the Italian author's 'Sacred Dust'.[13]

While any attempt at following the vagaries of canon may ultimately be futile, it is possible to envisage a set of reasons for this steep decline from instant popularity to present near-oblivion. Some of these may have to do with the genre itself — pastoral drama in verse, today, being even more outmoded than pastoral lyric poetry. Others may be connected with Guarini's peculiar style as a pastoral playwright, as well as the historical period in which he was composing, revising and defending his work. After all, as seen above, Tasso's *Aminta* has not been eclipsed quite in the same manner as the *Pastor fido*.

The first reason may be political, in the widest sense of the term. From its origins in the second half of the fifteenth century, Italian pastoral verse (dramatic or lyric) had been conceived of as courtly entertainment. Whether it was eclogues or full-blown plays, to be presented in a banquet hall, in the open or

---

[11] For the application of Pierre Bourdieu's notion of 'cultural capital' to Translation Studies, see André Lefevere, 'Translation practice(s) and the Circulation of Cultural Capital: Some *Aeneids* in English', in *Constructing Cultures: Essays on Literary Translation*, ed. by Susan Bassnett and André Lefevere (Clevedon: Multilingual Matters, 1998), pp. 41–56; see also Massimiliano Morini, 'Virgil in Tudor Dress: In Search of a Noble Vernacular', *Neophilologus*, 97.3 (2013), 591–610.

[12] On the practice of and reasons for translating from the vernacular (especially Italian) into neo-Latin, see Peter Burke, 'Translations into Latin in Early Modern Europe', in *Cultural Translation in Early Modern Europe*, ed. by Peter Burke and Ronnie Po-Chia Hsia (Cambridge: Cambridge University Press, 2007), pp. 65–80; and Andrew Taylor, 'Introduction: The Translations of Renaissance Latin', *Canadian Review of Comparative Literature / Revue Canadienne de Littérature Comparée*, 41.4 (2014), 329–53. On the specific issue of neo-Latin translation as a marker of cultural capital, see Massimiliano Morini, 'The Superiority of Classical Translation in Sixteenth-Century England: Thomas Hoby and John Harington', *Philological Quarterly*, 98.3 (2019), 273–95 (p. 275).

[13] Battista Guarini, *Pastor Fido: Or, the Faithful Shepherd*, trans. by Elkanah Settle (London: William Cademan, 1677), sigs A2ᵛ, A4ʳ.

on a stage, during the day or at night,¹⁴ all the poems and fables by Poliziano, Castiglione and many others were written for courtly audiences, and therefore reflected the interests and preoccupations of their courts. This was true thematically, in the sense that most pastoral verse and drama can be read as a celebration of, commentary on or even critique of courtly life (as will be seen in Guarini's *Pastor fido*). It was also true in compositional terms, because pastoral drama at its highest degree of evolution came to incorporate all the kinds of spectacle which were appreciated at Italian and European courts — verse, music, song, dancing and (lavish) scenography. From this very general perspective, it was inevitable that the genre would become obsolete with the waning of the *ancien régime*: in the late eighteenth century, and even more in the nineteenth, the audience for this kind of entertainment was no longer there, or was no longer rich and powerful enough to give it sustenance.¹⁵

There is another sense in which pastoral drama is inextricably linked with the period in which it flourished, first in Italy and then in the rest of Europe. Though it is difficult to recapture the sense of its novelty today, this was a decidedly modern genre, following Virgil and Theocritus in poetic and thematic terms but having no precedent in classical theatre. Since they were working in a new, third form, pastoral dramatists could afford to innovate in ways which were not available to those writing neo-classical comedy or tragedy. Perhaps the most important of these innovations was the introduction of the tragicomic plot — which had already been in existence in the classical world, but had been denounced as illegitimate by sixteenth-century Aristotelians. Practitioner-theoreticians such as Giraldi Cinthio and, later and most famously, Guarini himself, used the pastoral setting to create tragedies with happy endings, and/or to combine a tragic plot with a comic sub-plot.¹⁶ Furthermore, being new,

---

¹⁴ On the variability of pastoral stagecraft, see Marzia Pieri, *La scena boschereccia nel Rinascimento italiano* (Padova: Liviana Editrice, 1983), pp. 211–26; 'Selve e giardini nella scena europea di Ancien Régime', *Italies*, 8 (2004), 189–207; Sampson, *Pastoral Drama*, pp. 172–83.

¹⁵ See Sampson, *Pastoral Drama*, p. 233: 'The taste for this kind of drama persisted in Europe as long as the court system and academies that patronized it survived'. Clubb (*Italian Drama in Shakespeare's Time* (New Haven: Yale University Press, 1989), p. 125) marvels at the fate of a genre 'that flourished intensely into the seventeenth century and then disappeared so effectively as to leave Dr. Johnson without a clue to *Lycidas*'. Nicolas J. Perella (*The Critical Fortune of Battista Guarini's "Il pastor fido"* (Firenze: Olschki, 1973), p. 6) is more optimistic in fixing the beginning of the decline to the late eighteenth century.

¹⁶ Cinthio attempted to interpret Aristotle in order to defend his own practice of writing tragedies that did not end tragically (see Daniel Javitch, 'Introduction to Giovan Battista Giraldi Cinthio's "Discourse or Letter on the Composition of Comedies and Tragedies"', *Renaissance Drama*, 39 (2011), 197–206). Guarini, for his part, had to impose a model that was tragicomic in a much more 'mixed' sense, in that it combined two plots of differing decorum. Like Cinthio, he defended the claims of modern use; more specifically, he pointed out that Aristotle had not recognized the validity of certain genres simply because, at his time, they were not in existence. See Elisabetta Selmi, *'Classici e Moderni' nell'officina del 'Pastor Fido'*

pastoral drama allowed for the inclusion of elements which were normally excluded from comedy and tragedy, such as romantic and even sensual love. Elsewhere in Europe, playwrights such as William Shakespeare and many others seized on the structure and themes of pastoral tragicomedy, even more than on its setting.[17] And after its early diffusion, once tragicomedy was recognized as a viable choice, the pastoral garb was no longer needed: subsequent centuries saw the development of other 'mixed' forms, most notably bourgeois drama.

As noted above, however, even when the general obsolescence of pastoral drama has been accounted for, there are aspects of the *Pastor fido* that do nothing to endear this particular play to contemporary audiences. Guarini was a very learned writer, who knew the tradition of Italian vernacular poetry inside out and had a strong grounding in the Greek and Latin classics. When he turned his powers to the task of writing *Il pastor fido*, he considered the brief tradition of the genre, and produced the pastoral play to end all pastoral plays. He looked to Tasso, Giraldi Cinthio and the Ferrarese tradition, as well as to the pastoral verse and drama which had been produced at other Italian courts — but he created something that was far more complex, with a double tragicomic plot, a tangled moral, religious overtones, and a web of dynastic homage and courtly satire. Having created this multi-layered structure, Guarini proceeded to fill it with harmonious verse which is always reminiscent of some illustrious predecessor or other in the great Graeco-Latin-Italian tradition, as he himself pointed out painstakingly in his 'annotationi' to the 1602 Ciotti edition. Again, this kind of learned bricolage was much appreciated in late sixteenth-century Europe, where marginal notes were still largely used in printed books to indicate the provenance of phrases and poetic lines. In post-Romantic times, however, no reader can fail to notice that just as Tasso's *Aminta* is simpler in ethics and mood, it is more direct in its poetic diction.[18] There is

---

(Alessandria: Edizioni dell'Orso, 2001), pp. 11–74. On a related note, a very interesting study of how Italian pastoral drama revises Aristotle's notion of catharsis (and therefore of the ethic value of the genre, and of Tasso's and Guarini's plays in particular) is Federico Schneider's *Pastoral Drama and Healing in Early Modern Italy* (Farnham: Ashgate, 2010).

[17] See Clubb, *Italian Drama*, pp. 153–162; Robert W. Leslie, 'Shakespeare's Italian Dream: Cinquecento Sources for *A Midsummer Night's Dream*', *Comparative Drama*, 29.4 (1995–1996), 454–65; Robert Henke, *Pastoral Transformations: Italian Tragicomedy and Shakespeare's Late Plays* (Newark: University of Delaware Press, 1997); Richard Andrews, '*A Midsummer Night's Dream* and Italian Pastoral', in *Transnational Exchange in Early Modern Theater*, ed. by Robert Henke and Eric Nicholson (Aldershot: Ashgate, 2008), pp. 49–62. Two decades after *Italian Drama*, Clubb convincingly argued for Italian pastoral drama not only as a novel form embracing novel modes, but also as a convenient repository of new themes which could hardly be accommodated in comedy and tragedy ('Pastoral Jazz from the Writ to the Liberty', in *Italian Culture in the Drama of Shakespeare & his Contemporaries: Rewriting, Remaking, Refashioning*, ed. by Michele Marrapodi (Aldershot: Ashgate, 2007), pp. 15–26).

[18] It must be noted here that already, a few decades after Guarini's death, various European commentators noted that the artificiality of his language sometimes marred its dramatic

nothing in the whole *Pastor fido*, for instance, to equal the affective appeal of this line and a half:

> Il mondo invecchia,
> e invecchiando intristisce.[19]

The distance in immediacy between the two pastoral playwrights is nowhere more evident than in the famous 'Golden Age' chorus which concludes Act I of *Aminta* and — in Guarini's revised version — Act IV of *Il pastor fido*. Tasso's chorus expresses a nostalgia for a mythical time when the unploughed earth used to give fruit, honour was nobody's concern and love was not a sin: in that world, young virgins walked around completely naked, and it was lawful to do everything one pleased ('s'ei piace, ei lice').[20] In Guarini's golden age, by contrast, young women and men only show themselves naked to their spouses. It is 'Hymenaeus' that dictates their pleasure, and their motto is exactly the opposite of Tasso: love is pleasant only if lawful ('piaccia, se lice').[21] 'Honour' is still reviled, but only if it is in inverted commas — because true honour consists in knowing instinctively what is due to marital love and womanly discretion. If Tasso's chorus is a piece of sensual, courtly daydreaming, Guarini's prelapsarian rewriting reads as a rebuke. It also reads less smoothly, because its point is more complex and — the poet having to tread in another man's footsteps — a bit convoluted. On first reading it, today's readers and audiences might feel confused about what exactly is being held up as good and bad. Most decisively, they might also feel that they would not want to live in Guarini's golden age, where social norms appear to be foregrounded much more than idleness and pleasure.

This leads one to the last, perhaps most general reason why Guarini's *Pastor fido* is no longer appreciated as much as it used to be — the fact that it is, in inspiration and purpose, a product of the Counter-Reformation. While Guarini was composing and revising it, Tasso himself was having his own religious scruples about his great Christian epic. As a result, *La Gerusalemme liberata* is a very strange poem in ethical terms — sensual yet devout, melodious and tortured. Completed a few years before and covering very different ground, *Aminta* is mercifully free from such contradictions: like its famous chorus, it is in essence a sensual divertissement for powerful people in their leisure hours. Guarini's *Pastor fido*, however, incorporates the impulses of the

efficacy. See for example Nicolas J. Perella, 'Amarilli's Dilemma: The *Pastor Fido* and Some English Authors', *Comparative Literature*, 12.4 (1960), 348–59; Dalla Valle, *Pastorale Barocca*, pp. 47–55.

[19] 'The world is getting older, | and as it does it gets sadder'. Torquato Tasso, *Aminta* (Torino: Einaudi, 1963), p. 30. Staton and Simeone write, very much from the point of view of post-Romantic criticism, that 'The *Aminta* is certainly better poetry; we hear in Tasso's plea for freedom to love an authentic heart's cry'; Guarini, *A Critical Edition*, ed. by Staton and Simeone, p. xii.

[20] Tasso, *Aminta*, p. 23.

[21] Selmi, p. 229.

Counter-Reformation in the erotic context of pastoral drama. It shows all the allure of sexual attraction, but subjugates it to the requirements of religious devotion and patriarchal rule.[22] It titillates at the same time as it chastises. Again, the impression is that this would have felt familiar to late sixteenth-century readers, whether Catholic or Protestant; today, however, Guarini's pastoral morals may seem perverse.

The Pastoral Play to End All Pastoral Plays

The section above might give rise to the mistaken impression that Tasso's *Aminta* and Guarini's *Pastor fido* were the only pastoral plays of the second half of the sixteenth century — isolated dramatic revisions of a rich poetic output. On the contrary, as twentieth-century critics have been at pains to point out, these were only two episodes in a vital tradition, which continued to produce works until the end of the century and beyond.[23] If anything, in fact, the two Ferrarese plays can be said to be slightly aberrant with respect to that tradition, even though paradoxically they ended up representing it for posterity. *Aminta* is almost alone in being constructed as a tragedy with a superimposed happy ending, and as a simple paean to love.[24] *Il pastor fido* is an attempt at subsuming all the elements of the genre, and at the same time an attempt to blunt and normalize them in the light of a supposedly superior ethical and Christian vision. It is also, as evidenced both by its tone and plot and by Guarini's attendant critical writings, an attempt at demonstrating that the pastoral play could be made to fit in the mould of classical drama and Aristotelian theory.[25]

If the *Pastor fido* is viewed in the context of the Italian pastoral tradition, as well as of the sixteenth-century debate on Aristotle's *Poetics* and the viable forms that theatrical writing could take, it becomes evident that Guarini was trying to have the last word on pastoral drama. As noted above, most of the features of previous pastorals are present, though the magical spells, creatures and transformations favoured by many predecessors are expunged in the interests of verisimilitude. Pastoral characters and topoi, however, are made to fit into a classical plot that is loosely based on Sophocles' *Oedipus Rex* — minus the incest and the tragic ending, and with the addition of a providential design, a

---

[22] See Sampson, *Pastoral Drama*, p. 45: 'However, later in the century and particularly with Guarini's *Pastor fido* [...] pastoral drama became marked by an increased emphasis on paternal and patriarchal authority, as the moral imperatives of the Counter-Reformation became unavoidable also in this genre.' See also Clubb, *Italian Drama*, pp. 110–12.

[23] The first complete survey of the genre was Enrico Carrara, *La poesia pastorale* (Milan: Vallardi, 1909), pp. 297–382. See also Pieri, *La scena boschereccia*, pp. 151–80; Clubb, *Italian Drama*, p. 97.

[24] Clubb, *Italian Drama*, pp. 96–98.

[25] The most complete exposition of the composite critical nature of *Il pastor fido* is the first chapter of Selmi, *'Classici e Moderni'*, pp. 11–74.

comprehensive Christian explanation for all the suffering Arcadia has had to endure.[26] Under the influence of Terence and contemporary *commedia grave*, Guarini adopts a language that is rather monotonously formal, but sweet rather than grandiloquent.[27] Wanting to create the *Gesamtkunstwerk* of the pastoral scene, and enlisting the help of professionals in other arts, the Ferrarese author includes choruses, music, and choreographed scenes which make an unabridged version of the play extremely difficult and expensive to stage.[28] The result is at once elaborate, sensual, formal, spectacular and religious — again, a very strange and unpalatable mixture for modern audiences.

The plot in its bare bones has been summarized perfectly by Louise George Clubb:

> Guarini's Arcadia is under a curse brought on by a nymph's infidelity to a shepherd. To remove the curse the oracle says that two scions of divine stock must marry and a faithful shepherd must cancel out the old infidelity. The only scions known are Amarilli and Silvio, who do not love each other. Amarilli is loved by Mirtillo, and Silvio (Guarini's variation on Tasso's hardhearted Silvia) by Dorinda. Through the machinations of Corisca, who lusts after Mirtillo and wants Amarilli out of the way, the lovers are brought close to death, but at last it is discovered that Mirtillo, the faithful shepherd, is the long-lost elder brother of Silvio, and through his marriage with Amarilli the oracle is fulfilled and the ancient curse removed.[29]

Such a short summary makes the *Pastor fido* seem simple — but the complexity of the play resides in its multiplicity of moods, motifs and techniques, rather than the complications of its *fabula*. One notable example of this is the way in which the main Sophoclean plotline is interwoven with a number of stereotypical pastoral situations and set pieces (as well as characters) which look somewhat out of place in an Arcadia that is suffering under a divine curse. Silvio, for instance, is the young shepherd whose projected wedding with Amarilli should cure all wrongs: but he is also the clichéd enemy of love (and lover of hunting) whom an older servant vainly tries to convert, and who is in the end converted when he strikes Dorinda by mistake with an arrow. Carino, Mirtillo's putative father, is the character who makes the final anagnorisis possible, and thus sets in motion the events which will lead to the happy ending: yet he is also a disillusioned former courtier who is made to rehash some old adages on the envy festering in princely palaces (some of his complaints, incidentally, reflect

---

[26] It can be said that in terms of anagnorisis, Guarini's play reverses Sophocles' — in that the discovery that Mirtillo is Montano's son lifts the curse and stops the former's execution.

[27] See Selmi, 'Classici e Moderni', pp. 67, 70, 86, on the centrality of Terence in Guarini's comedic view, and pp. 27-29 on the late-Petrarchan style of *Il pastor fido*.

[28] See Sampson, 'The Mantuan Performance', p. 66; *Pastoral Drama*, p. 187; Laura Riccò, *'Ben mille pastorali': L'itinerario dell'Ingegneri da Tasso a Guarini e oltre* (Roma: Bulzoni, 2004), pp. 219-86. See also Selmi, 'Classici e Moderni', pp. 179-99, on the structural significance of Guarini's choruses.

[29] Clubb, *Italian Drama*, p. 131.

the author's own grudges). Corisca, as hinted at in the summary above, is the Judas-like figure who, for her own vile reasons, ends up facilitating the resolution: she is also, however, the expert city dweller and courtly lover, and her soliloquies give the pastoral writer scope for some traditional satire on the wiles and tricks of women.

As for variety of mood, the fictional world of the play is fundamentally split in half. On one side there stand all the characters from Greek tragedy — the old shepherd-priests like Montano, Titiro and the blind seer Tirenio, whose discourse is invariably serious and religious. Montano, who is Silvio's father and will discover that Mirtillo is his lost first child, is the very emblem of this seriousness, in his Abraham-like readiness to sacrifice even his own progeny to appease the gods. On the other side of the divide, the young people live in a separate world of love-sickness and amorous dallying, and give life to a very different set of situations. Again, the erotic encounters in the play are mostly set pieces of pastoral drama: there is a near-rape scene featuring Corisca and the Satyr, for instance;[30] while Mirtillo and Amarilli are involved in a couple of stolen-kiss encounters (one recounted by Mirtillo, one seen on stage) that are heavily charged with sexual attraction. The attempted rape is averted, while Mirtillo and Amarilli's irrepressible feelings turn out to be the harbingers of chaste married love. Nonetheless, these titillating scenes contribute to the general atmosphere of the play, and no final hymeneal celebration will fully dispel their aftertaste.

It is in the communal scenes of Act v that Guarini finally manages to join these two worlds together. Here, and particularly in the trial and sacrifice scenes (4, 5, 6), one cannot help admiring the author's ability in combining the erotic potential of pastoral comedy with the high religious seriousness of classical tragedy. However, one also cannot help feeling that these two worlds have not really been harmonized with one another. When Mirtillo is about to be ritually slaughtered by his own biological father, his attitude and discourse become very devout — even as he reiterates his faithful love to Amarilli. More generally, in the course of these serious scenes the voices of the young lovers are almost silenced, only to re-emerge when the truth is out and the wedding about to be celebrated. In this sense, rather than as a real marriage of pastoral lightness and weighty classicism, *Il pastor fido* ultimately reads as a subjection of the former to the latter. In the very last scene of the play, Amarilli and Mirtillo are briefly allowed to speak in amorous tones (v. 10), but then the final chorus succinctly draws a moral for 'mortal' readers.

This does not mean, however, that *Il pastor fido* is a disjointed piece of dramatic writing. On the contrary, Guarini's ability in tightening up all the

---

[30] On Guarini's transformation of the stereotypical figure of the satyr (as a symptom of his revision of the genre), see Gabriele Niccoli, 'Modalità metamorfiche nella figura e funzione del maggior satiro ferrarese del tardo Cinquecento', *Quaderni d'Italianistica*, 29.2 (2008), 5–16.

narrative strands, his punctiliousness in making every single character and scene serve his overall design, ends up producing a strikingly cohesive plot. Also, as can be deduced from the text itself and the author's 1602 annotations, the same kind of cohesiveness is created in theatrical terms. Guarini sets out to write the definitive pastoral play by trying to employ all the multimedia resources developed in the course of at least a century, and in five decades of experiments at the court of Ferrara. He includes music, singing and dancing, for instance, for the scene in which Mirtillo kisses the unwitting Amarilli during a game of blind man's buff (III. 2): but the whole thing, involving in its realization a dancing master and a musical composer, is not conceived as a mere spectacular addition to the performance of the play. This episode has a crucial narrative function, as it brings the two lovers together and helps precipitate the events which will eventually lead to their sacred union. It is also figuratively central to the whole play, as the game on which it is based mirrors the blindness of human desire and the high priests' myopic reading of divine signs. Finally, it is performed during Act III — which places it at the material centre of the play as well.[31] On this and countless other occasions, Guarini manages to harness all the strengths of this young dramatic and theatrical tradition with the evident purpose of becoming its most significant exponent.

European and English Faithful Shepherds

The diffusion of *Il pastor fido* in seventeenth-century Europe has been sketched above. What has been left unsaid is that the popularity of Guarini's play was for the most part literary, rather than theatrical — the huge quantity of editions, translations and imitations being in no way matched by a comparable number of performances. This was partly the consequence of a sharp decline for the whole genre as stage entertainment. After 1600, pastoral modes, set-pieces and motifs migrated in many traditions and took various other forms (including baroque poetry, Shakespearean drama and musical opera); but full-fledged pastoral works in Giraldi Cinthio's, Tasso's or Guarini's mould were performed less and less often.[32] In some ways, Guarini's play and its attendant critical writings, or Angelo Ingegneri's 1598 summative treatise *Della poesia rappresentativa e del modo di rappresentare le favole sceniche* ('On stageable poetry, and how to stage theatrical fables'), were themselves celebrations of a vanishing world. When Ingegneri dedicated his book to Cesare d'Este, his dedicatee's former dukedom of Ferrara — where so much of the history of pastoral drama had unfolded in the past half century — had already been annexed by Pope Clement VIII. Guarini himself had left that court ten years before, and his play was about to be

---

[31] On this structurally and technically crucial scene, see Clubb, *Italian Drama*, pp. 179-80; Riccò, 'Ben mille pastorali', pp. 219, 235.
[32] Tellingly, Marzia Pieri (*La scena boschereccia*, p. 151) calls her chapter on pastoral drama 'La breve stagione della drammaturgia' ('The brief season of dramaturgy').

staged elsewhere, in Mantua, for the first and last time in something approaching its full theatrical pomp.

The fact that after the 1580s only two out of a myriad plays came to be identified with the whole genre may also have contributed to the theatrical downfall of pastoral fables. In their different ways, neither *Aminta* nor *Il pastor fido* were ideal starting points for a durable stage tradition. Tasso's play was too thin in dramatic terms — almost an eclogue to be read in public.[33] Guarini, for his part, had opted for a kind of spectacle that, in its full potential, was too rich and complex for any simple company of actors to realize. One of the strengths of pastoral plays had been their adaptability, the fact that they could, on occasion, be presented in princely gardens with little or no expense in terms of scenography. This was hardly true of *Il pastor fido*, whose author probably made things more difficult for himself by insisting that the play had to be presented in its entirety, with great performative accuracy and all of its stage accoutrements.[34] As a result, in the decade after its first publication, and while it was being reprinted as often as twice a year, Guarini's work was performed only three or four times. Even in Mantua, where it was presented as part of the celebrations for an important European dynastic marriage, it was probably cut for a mixture of moral and practical reasons.[35]

Most of the seventeenth-century European translators, in their texts and paratexts, confirm the status of *Il pastor fido* as dramatic fiction or poetry, rather than stageable play.[36] The first translator in any language, Roland Brisset, explained 'aux Lecteurs' in 1593 that he had eliminated Guarini's prologues from his prose-and-verse rendition because his book was meant 'not for a theatrical performance, but only to be read'.[37] The first Spanish translator treated the source as an excuse to experiment with as many metrical forms as possible.[38] The German translator Hans Assmann von Abschatz prefaced his version with a single theoretical page on poetic translation.[39] In general, the people who

---

[33] See Riccò, 'Ben mille pastorali', p. 106.

[34] See Pieri, *La scena boschereccia*, p. 213; Sampson, *Pastoral Drama*, pp. 185–89.

[35] See Sampson, 'The Mantuan Performance', 72–73.

[36] Perella (*The Critical Fortune*, p. 50) acknowledges this trend, but points out that 'representation, though necessarily less frequent, was quite common' in the seventeenth century. However, the example he gives to illustrate this is of a reading rather than of a theatrical production.

[37] Battista Guarini, *Le Berger Fidelle. Pastorale*, trans. by Roland Brisset (Tours: Iamet Mettayer, 1593), sig. A5ʳ. The author of the third and most popular French version, Antoine de Torche, also declared that it was more a closet than a stage play ('aussi est-elle plus du Cabinet que du Theatre'); Battista Guarini, *Il pastor fido. Le Berger fidelle.* [...] *En vers*, trans. by Antoine de Torche (Paris: Gabriel Quinet, 1664), sig. A2ᵛ.

[38] This is at least true of the second version he published — but both editions are clearly conceived as courtly presentation copies. See Sánchez García, '"Salientes acquae"', p. 191.

[39] The page is itself a translation from Aulus Gellius. Battista Guarini, *Der Teutsch-Redende Treue Schaeffer des berühmten Welschen Guarini*, trans. by Hans Assmann von Abschatz ([n.p.]: 1672), sig. A3ʳ.

produced their own vernacular 'faithful shepherds' thought of them either as profitable publishing ventures or, more often, as mirrors for princes and presentation copies for influential lords and ladies.[40]

The adventures of Guarini's faithful shepherd in England confirm this general trend. As noted above, a London edition of *Il pastor fido* and *Aminta* was printed as early as 1591 by John Wolfe ('Giovanni Volfeo'), at the expense of Giacomo (here 'Giacopo') Castelvetro, an Italian Protestant exile. In his dedication to Sir Charles Blount, Castelvetro explains that he was impelled to publish the book by the difficulties in procuring anything but a few copies of Guarini's play from across the Channel. The fame of the work, the editor says, very quickly reached England, and aroused in many 'singular spirits' a desire to 'see' it.[41] Of course, since he prints Guarini's work in all its parts, Castelvetro is perfectly aware that he is presenting a piece of dramatic writing. Nevertheless, when he uses the verb 'see' in his dedication he always means 'read', and he calls Guarini a 'poet', never making any mention of the fact that he was also a man of the theatre.

The 1602 translation, it will be pointed out in the next section, can be seen to have some theatrical potential — but it was never staged. Sidnam's manuscript version was more poetical than dramatic, as witnessed by its author's closer attempt to reproduce the varying lengths of Italian lines.[42] As for the most famous English version of the play, Richard Fanshawe's *Faithfull Shepherd*, it was conceived of as a poetic enterprise and as a Royalist book. Fanshawe rendered Guarini's unrhymed or loosely rhyming seven- and eleven-syllable lines as very tight pentameter couplets. He followed his source very closely in terms of content, and tried to outdo Guarini in some of his pre-baroque figurative flights. Famously, John Denham wrote a laudatory poem for the 1647 edition in which he praised 'the Authour of this Translation' for spurning 'unhappy Rimes' and preserving Guarini's 'flame', rather than his 'Ashes'.[43] Though Denham overstated the extent of Fanshawe's creative freedom, the model he had in mind was clearly that of poetic translation as imitation, an activity which involves vying with one's foreign model. Arguably, Fanshawe's 'play' is even less stageable than Guarini's, with its somewhat artificial and occasionally stilted dialogue ('Learn women from me this housewifery | Make you conserve of Lovers to keep by')[44] — but then, the paratextual apparatuses of the editions published in the translator's lifetime show that this was never intended as an English play-text. The 1647 book, for instance, concludes with a poetic postscript informing readers that the play was presented to Prince Charles 'At his going into the West [...] Together with

---

[40] On the seventeenth-century characterization of pastoral literature as proper for women, see Caemmerer, 'Die Schäferliteratur und die Frauen'.
[41] S1591, sig. A2^r: 'onde ne petti di molti di questi singulari spiriti destò un non picciol desiderio di poterla vedere'.
[42] See Greg, *Pastoral Poetry*, p. 243.
[43] Battista Guarini, *Il pastor fido, The faithfull Shepherd*, trans. by Richard Fanshawe (London: R. Raworth, 1647), sig. A1^r.
[44] Guarini, *Il pastor fido*, trans. by Fanshawe, p. 27.

Cesar's Commentaries'.[45] Fanshawe admired Guarini's poetical qualities and wanted to emulate them; but he also saw the *Pastor fido* as an ideologically sound work of fiction that could be presented to a prince and interpreted in political and dynastic terms.

All in all, the direct impact of Guarini's play on the English theatrical tradition was limited. The 1604/1605 Cambridge *Fidus pastor* mentioned above may have had an influence on the debate on pastoral drama, but its performance was certainly not attended by vast audiences.[46] Around the same period, two English plays written under the influence of Guarini enjoyed either niche stage success or none at all. Samuel Daniel's *Queenes Arcadia*, seen by Queen Anne and Prince Henry in 1605 and published one year later, was again written for the academic stage.[47] In 1608, John Fletcher presented to a wider public his English revision of Guarini, *The Faithful Shepherdess*. In the quarto version of the play, probably published one year later, he blamed the audience's ignorance for the utter failure of the performance, and incidentally gave his own simplified definition of tragicomedy ('A tragicomedy is not so called in respect of mirth and killing but in respect it wants deaths').[48] The terms of Fletcher's brief apology hark back to Guarini's *Compendio*, but they also reflect what must have been the common London theatregoer's disappointment with a lack of 'mirth and killing'.

The only moderately successful theatrical run for a translation of *Il pastor fido* came much later, and provides further confirmation that Guarini's play, in itself, was not a perfect fit for English audiences. When Elkanah Settle produced his own *Faithful Shepherd* in 1676 (and published it in 1677), he admittedly worked on the most recent English translation rather than on the Italian source. But the adaptations Settle had to make demonstrate that *Il pastor fido* had become a

---

[45] Guarini, *Il pastor fido*, trans. by Fanshawe, p. 217. In the 1664 edition Fanshawe added more of his own poems and 'A Summary Discourse of the Civil Wars of Rome, extracted out of the best Latine Writers in Prose and Verse'.

[46] See Nicoletta Neri, *Il pastor fido in Inghilterra* (Torino: Giappichelli, 1963), p. 17; Christine Sukic, 'Samuel Daniel et les traductions anglaises du *Pastor Fido* au XVIIe siècle en Angleterre: du voyage d'Italie à la naturalisation', *Études Épistémè*, 4 (2003), 18–29 (p. 18); Sheila Frodella, 'La migrazione del *Pastor fido* in Inghilterra', in *Studi di Anglistica e Americanistica. Percorsi di ricerca*, ed. by Fiorenzo Fantaccini and Ornella De Zordo (Firenze: Firenze University Press, 2012), pp. 105–61 (p. 136).

[47] This time the university was Oxford. See Raphael Lyne, 'English Guarini: Recognition and Reception', *Yearbook of English Studies*, 36.1 (2006), 90–102 (p. 93); Jason Lawrence, '"The Whole Complection of Arcadia Chang'd": Samuel Daniel and Italian Lyrical Drama', *Medieval and Renaissance Drama in England*, 11 (1999), 143–71 (p. 153). Samuel Daniel, as shall be seen, was among those responsible for publishing the first English *Pastor fido*. However, he also translated the Act 1 chorus from *Aminta*, and his *Queenes Arcadia* is arguably as much indebted to Tasso as it is to Guarini.

[48] John Fletcher, *The Faithful Shepherdess* (London: R. Bonian and H. Walley, [n.d.]), sig. A2ᵛ. On the native influences behind Fletcher's play (particularly Sidney, Spenser and Marlowe) see Lee Bliss, 'Defending Fletcher's Shepherds', *Studies in English Literature*, 23 (1983), 295–310.

poetic rather than a theatrical phenomenon: he practically cut Fanshawe's version in half, skipped the choruses, developed certain characters at the expense of others, avoided most passages of sustained metaphor and simile, and eliminated the original prologue and composed a more performative one. Evidently, Guarini's play in its native garb was perceived as too sophisticated for a Restoration audience — but even with all the alterations, the play never enjoyed the popularity of Settle's previous hit, *The Empress of Morocco* (1673). Though this version was reprinted twice, there is no evidence that it was revived on stage after 1676.[49]

Before the English stage history of the *Pastor fido* is abandoned, it is worth repeating that if the direct impact of the play was not great, the influence of its tragicomic example, of Guarini's ideas and of pastoral drama in general, was immense. Clubb has argued convincingly that pastoral tragicomedy, if it was not imported as such, still provided Tudor and Stuart playwrights with a model for a closer, more realistic exploration of human emotion, particularly as regards the sphere of love and romantic feelings. If Shakespeare did not produce a full-fledged pastoral tragicomedy, he wrote tragicomedies with pastoral elements, used a pastoral or bucolic setting in many of his later works, and exploited some of the plotlines, topoi and spectacular elements of Italian pastoral drama.[50] Therefore, even though *Il pastor fido* itself was never fully assimilated into the theatrical tradition, no study of the play can ignore its repercussions.

The 1602 Translation: A Very English Play

The English translation presented here saw the light at a very important time in the publishing history of *Il pastor fido*. In 1602, as seen above, the Siena-born, Venice-based printer Giovanni Battista Ciotti produced the authoritative Italian edition which included Guarini's notes and his observations on tragicomic poetry. The same year, in London, a stationer whose name did not appear on the title page printed a translation of the play crafted by a semi-anonymous translator. Apart from a couple of dedicatory sonnets and a nine-line dedication in prose, this quarto edition was devoid of all paratextual additions and visual decoration. Unlike many seventeenth-century Italian and European books presenting the play, it did not feature a single illustration. It also offered no notes and no postscripts; in fact, it skipped Guarini's argument and prologue to cut straight to 'the persons who speak in it' and the dialogue of Act 1, Scene 1.

Il pastor fido: or The faithfull Shepheard. Translated out of Italian into English

---

[49] On Settle's version see F. C. Brown, *Elkanah Settle: His Life and Works* (Chicago: The University of Chicago Press, 1910), p. 19; Denis Lagae-Devoldère, 'L'Adaptation du *Pastor Fido* de Fanshawe par Elkannah Settle (1676)', *Études Épistémè*, 4 (2003), 50–60; Massimiliano Morini, 'Restoration Theatre, Indirect Translation and the Canon: Settle's Guarini', *Theatralia* 24.1 (2021), 34–42.
[50] Clubb, *Italian Drama*, pp. 157, 160, 163–64.

was printed for Simon Waterson,[51] who was also responsible for the prose dedication 'to the right worthy and learned Knight, Sir Edward Dymock, Champion to her Majesty'.[52] In the dedication, Waterson says that he knew of no one else who could have been fitter to 'patronize' the work than the dedicatee, both because of his 'knowledge of the great worth of the Italian author' and 'by reason of the nearness of kin to the deceased translator'.[53] Homage is also paid to Sir Edward in the two dedicatory writings preceding Waterson's — a sonnet penned by Samuel Daniel and one by the translator himself. The latter has been identified as Tailboys Dymock, Edward's younger brother and the only one in the family to have published at least one other poetical work. Since there is no evidence to disprove that identification, and since, on the contrary, some intertextual elements — however slight — can be brought forward to confirm it, the attribution is accepted in this edition.[54]

Though their rather distinctive rhyme structure is exactly the same (ABBA ABBA CDCD EE), the two dedicatory sonnets are different in emphasis and originality of approach. Dymock makes use of various available translation metaphors (fashioning new clothes for the original text/author, making the author an English denizen, re-bearing his brain-child) to produce a classic act

[51] Simon Waterson was a successful London publisher who worked with Samuel Daniel on a number of publications. See Martha Straznicky, 'Introduction: What is a Stationer?', in *Shakespeare's Stationers: Studies in Cultural Bibliography*, ed. by Marta Straznicky (Philadelphia: University of Pennsylvania Press, 2013), pp. 1–16 (p. 14); also, in the same volume, Alexandra Halasz, 'The Stationers' Shakespeare', pp. 17–27 (p. 26).

[52] Sir Edward's family had held the medieval office of King's/Queen's Champion since the fourteenth century. Curiously enough, at present the dignity is still attributed to a member of the family, which is now known by the name of Dymoke. The involvement of Champions in the coronation ceremony, however, ceased in 1831. See A. J. Musson's article on the 'Dymoke [Dymmok] family (per. c. 1340–c. 1580)', in *ODNB*.

[53] See p. 32 in the present edition. Henceforth, internal references are given parenthetically in the text.

[54] It was Donno (pp. xxii–xiv) who proposed Tailboys (c. 1561–c. 1602) as Guarini's first English translator. Tailboys, under the pseudonym of Thomas Cutwode (cut wood = French *taille bois*), was the author of *Caltha Poetarum*, a bizarre 1599 satire which was ordered to be burned by church authorities (but somehow survived the fire). This work has some minor stylistic similarities with *The faithfull Shepheard*, is printed by the same stationer, and mentions Samuel Daniel favourably in the introduction. As further (slight) evidence, Tailboys is also known to have authored (wholly or in part) a slanderous play, in the context of a family feud which led to him and Edward being summoned to court shortly before Tailboys' death in 1602. Among other things, these legal troubles could have motivated a wish to hide behind the generic, misleading denomination of 'kinsman'. See Tailboys Dymock (Thomas Cutwode), *Caltha Poetarum: Or the Bumble Bee* (London: Richard Olive, 1599); Eleri Larkum's article on 'Tailboys Dymoke' in *ODNB*; and Martin Wiggins and Catherine Richardson, *British Drama 1533–1642: A Catalogue. Volume IV: 1598–1602* (Oxford: Oxford University Press, 2014), p. 310. It is worth mentioning here that Greg identified the translator as 'John Dymocke', on the basis of a list of plays appended to a 1656 book (*Pastoral Poetry*, p. 242). On Donno's attribution, see also Sukic, 'Samuel Daniel et les traductions anglaises', 20.

of preventive apology (in case his own 'silly hand' is to be 'taxed of blame').[55] Daniel's poem is far more self-assured and combative. It starts out by addressing the dedicatee ('learnèd and worthy knight') and rejoicing because 'Thy dear esteemed Guarini' is now available in English (he also uses a typical Renaissance figure when he says that the source author can now 'Speak as good English as Italian'). In the third quatrain and the final couplet, however, it becomes apparent that the poet's aim is not only celebratory: Daniel also has an axe to grind. More than a decade before, he had travelled to Italy in Sir Edward's company[56] — and the two of them had met Guarini, apparently more than once. On those occasions, the Italian playwright had evidently been dismissive of the poetic possibilities of English, still widely thought of in continental Europe as a barbarous language ('Saying, our coasts were with no measures graced, | Nor barbarous tongues could any verse bring forth'). With great nationalistic pride, Daniel now counters that Dymock's *Faithfull Shepheard* amounts to a full vindication of English eloquence ('I would he saw his own, or knew our store'), which can not only equal, but exceed the *copia* of Italian ('Whose spirits can yield as much, and if not more').

Such nationalistic assurance is interesting in itself, as it is fairly typical of the late Elizabethan era. For around three quarters of the sixteenth century, most English translators had complained that their vernacular was too rough, 'rude' and 'common' to express the meanings and stylistic traits found in Latin, Greek or the more refined European languages.[57] Towards the end of the century the very attribute of 'roughness' had been slowly turned into something of a positive quality, and now patriotic-spirited writers could claim that English was as rich, or even richer, than Italian or French (Latin was still untouchable, and would remain so for a few more decades).[58] Other writings by Daniel demonstrate that

---

[55] The most famous English example of the brain-child metaphor appeared one year later, in Florio's version of Montaigne. On Renaissance figures of translation, see Theo Hermans, 'Images of Translation: Metaphor and Imagery in the Renaissance Discourse on Translation', in *The Manipulation of Literature: Studies in Literary Translation*, ed. by Theo Hermans (London: Croom Helm, 1985), pp. 103–35; Massimiliano Morini, *Tudor Translation in Theory and Practice* (Aldershot: Ashgate, 2006), pp. 35–61; A. E. B. Coldiron, 'Commonplaces and Metaphors', in *The Oxford History of Literary Translation*, pp. 109–17.

[56] See Mark Eccles, 'Samuel Daniel in France and Italy', *Studies in Philology*, 34.2 (1937), 148–67; and June Schlueter, 'Samuel Daniel in Italy: New Documentary Evidence', *Huntington Library Quarterly*, 75.2 (2012), 283–90. Schlueter makes a convincing case for two years' stay in Italy, between 1590 and 1591. Eccles (p. 161) hypothesizes one or more meetings with Guarini, either in Padua or in Guarini's villa between Padua and Venice.

[57] See J. L. Moore, *Tudor-Stuart Views on the Growth Status and Destiny of the English Language* (Halle a.S.: Max Niemeyer, 1910), p. 15; Richard Foster Jones, *The Triumph of the English Language: A Survey of Opinions Concerning the Vernacular from the Introduction of Printing to the Restoration* (Stanford: Stanford University Press, 1953), p. 211; Morini, *Tudor Translation*, p. 26.

[58] See Morini, *Tudor Translation*, p. 25.

his linguistic patriotism was of a rather special hue, deriving partly from Sidney but also from the ideas of the 'archaizers' of the previous century:[59] he did not believe that English had to become more 'classical', more like Latin or the Romance languages, to vie with them in eloquence. On the contrary, he thought that the 'virtues of the North', the Germanic qualities of the vernacular, were the main sources of its strength.

However, if it is true that the slight paratextual apparatus of the play has a certain patriotic flavour (all three prefatory writings being dedicated to Edward Dymock, who is called 'Champion to her Majesty' in the first and last), it has to be pointed out that there is very little in the translation itself which can be called overtly nationalistic. Unlike other translators of the late Elizabethan age — John Harington and his 1591 *Orlando Furioso in English Heroical Verse* spring to mind — Dymock does not, as a rule, substitute English for Italian or classical references.[60] As for Daniel's pride in the linguistic 'virtues of the north', there is no direct evidence of it in the English dialogue. This is normally written in average, moderately neologizing English — where Daniel manages to use the Anglo-Saxon 'tongue' with the meaning of 'language', for instance, Dymock uses 'language' to mean 'idiom' and 'tongue' to denote a part of the human body. Even more tellingly, he tends to err on the side of foreignization by coining such near-incomprehensible calques as 'stilled' for 'stillò' ('trickled'), or repeatedly using 'prove' for 'provare' ('try') and 'attend' for 'attendere' ('wait', rather than 'wait on'). It appears, therefore, that Daniel is grinding his own axe in the dedicatory sonnet, and building a common ground of Italian recollections with Sir Edward — rather than presenting the English play as the Anglo-Saxonist manifesto it most certainly is not.

But if Dymock's text is not meant as a demonstration of the superiority of English, neither is it intended as a mere homage to a revered Italian author. Translations, as Toury famously put it, are always 'facts of the culture which hosts them':[61] and this basic tenet of descriptive translation studies is particularly useful when one is working on early modern Britain.[62] In spite of its repeated

---

[59] Philip Sidney, *A Defence of Poetry*, ed. by Jan Van Dorsten (Oxford: Oxford University Press, 1988), p. 20. See Massimiliano Morini, 'Goths and Greeks: The Rise of Anglo-Saxon England and Germanic English in Early Modern Britain', *Filologia Germanica / Germanic Philology*, 12 (2020), 171–90.

[60] Though he occasionally simplifies a classical allusion by substituting it with a simpler one (see for instance note 25 in the text). On Harington's domesticating techniques, see Morini, *Tudor Translation*, pp. 115–18; Bryan Brazeau, 'London Calling: John Harington's Exegetical Domestication of Ariosto in Late Sixteenth-Century England', *History of European Ideas*, 42 (2016), 640–50.

[61] Gideon Toury, *Descriptive Translation Studies and Beyond* (Amsterdam: John Benjamins, 1995), p. 24.

[62] As early as 2000, Warren Boutcher pointed out that one should read Renaissance translations as '"original" works by authors who happen to be translating' ('The Renaissance', in *The Oxford Guide to Literature in English Translation*, ed. by Peter France (Oxford: Oxford

calques and occasional source-driven difficulties of syntax, in fact, *The faithfull Shepheard* is anything but a slavish imitation. Before going into detail on how Dymock transforms Guarini, it is necessary to point out that precisely this idea, of the 1602 translation as a mere plodding, unimaginative reproduction of *Il pastor fido*, has been a successful critical commonplace for centuries. The tone was set early on, when Denham praised Fanshawe's 'new and nobler' work of 1647 by contrasting it with that of former practitioners whose artistic narrowness 'poorly sticks at words'.[63] Later commentators happily followed suit, mostly giving the impression that they had not even bothered to read anything more than a few passages from the earlier version. In his history of the pastoral genre in England, Walter W. Greg quoted a number of previous damning judgments to conclude that Dymock's translation 'keeps pretty faithfully to its original, but does no more than emphasize the tedious artificiality of the Italian'.[64] As recently as 2003, Line Cottegnies has reiterated that 'the 1602 translation [...] is very faithful, sometimes very literal'.[65] Finally, in his contribution to the *Oxford History of Literary Translation in English*, G. W. Pigman III shows signs of closer reading by admitting that Dymock does condense his source, rather than follow it line by line — but then concludes that the Elizabethan translator only does so when he fails to understand Guarini ('When he understands his text, Dymocke translates literally').[66] All in all, the impression one gets out of the slight critical tradition on the 1602 version is that it is overly faithful and filled with blunders — an unimportant parenthesis between Guarini's original and its only valuable English translation, Fanshawe's 1647 Royalist effort.

Of course, such readings are not wholly unmotivated — in the literal sense that there are elements in the 1602 translation that might seem to motivate them,

---

University Press, 2000), p. 45). This idea has been reiterated in various guises by numerous scholars working in the field, including Fred Schurink ('Introduction', in *Tudor Translation*, ed. by Fred Schurink (New York: Palgrave Macmillan, 2011), p. 5), A. E. B. Coldiron (with reference to Itamar Even-Zohar; in *Printers Without Borders: Translation and Textuality in the Renaissance* (Cambridge: Cambridge University Press, 2015), p. 11), and Alessandra Petrina ('Introduction: The Definition of Cultural Identity through Translation', in *Acquisition through Translation: Towards a Definition of Renaissance Translation*, ed. by Alessandra Petrina and Federica Masiero (Turnhout: Brepols, 2020), p. 24).

[63] Guarini, *Il pastor fido*, trans. by Fanshawe, sig. A1ᵛ.
[64] Greg, *Pastoral Poetry*, p. 243.
[65] Line Cottegnies, 'La traduction anglaise du *Pastor Fido* de Guarini par Richard Fanshawe (1647): Quelques réflexions sur la naturalisation', *Études Épistémè*, 4 (2003), 30–49 (p. 31).
[66] Pigman III, 'Pastoral Drama', p. 296. He is following Staton and Simeone, who in their edition of Fanshawe wrote of the 1602 version that 'a more incompetent translation can hardly be imagined', and that Dymock has the habit of 'skipping the more difficult passages'. The two editors, however, recognize that Fanshawe was less libertine a translator than Denham makes him out to be (Guarini, *A Critical Edition*, ed. by Staton and Simeone, pp. xix, xx). It is again to be noted that in the general climate of disapprobation for the Dymock version, the only exception is provided by Donno.

at least if taken in isolation. Firstly, as seen above, Dymock makes frequent use of calques: and there is nothing like the tangible mark of a foreign word to leave the immediate impression of a lack of creativity, of a translation written in translatorese. Secondly, it is true that on a number of occasions Dymock misunderstands Guarini's quite intricate, quotation-filled Italian.[67] Thirdly, any close reading of more than a single scene will reveal that he tends to condense or skip long stretches of Guarini's dialogue. On the face of it, respectful literal-mindedness might seem to be at odds with a willingness to compress the source text; but as Pigman III's reading shows, linguistic incompetence can be added to the picture to explain away all the exchanges in which the target text becomes something other than mere line-by-line or word-by-word reproduction. Dymock, therefore, ends up being presented as a mere plodding journeyman of dramatic translation who cannot even be trusted to do his job from beginning to end.

It is not the purpose of this edition to dethrone Fanshawe, and elevate Dymock's as the one true translation of *Il pastor fido*. The position of the 1647 version in the canon is fully merited, if nothing else by virtue of its metrical, rhetorical and political interest. However, the problem with canonized texts — even the canonized texts of translation history — is that they tend to obscure all predecessors and successors: and it is arguable that the popularity of Fanshawe has so far impeded a full reading of Dymock. If the earlier translation is considered in all its parts, if its overall style is viewed in the context of the book in which it is presented, and the book is placed in the historical context in which it was produced, the findings amply repay the labour of analysis. What stands out almost immediately is that *The faithfull Shepheard* is a very rare, perhaps unique specimen in the history of early modern English writing: the translation of a successful foreign play presented in the form of a native play, at a time when the printing press was beginning to bear the mark of Elizabethan popular theatre. In other words, Dymock's translation, as packaged by its publisher(s), was an attempt at transforming *Il pastor fido* into something akin to Marlowe's, Shakespeare's or Jonson's works.

Extraordinary as such a claim might seem in the absence of any explicit paratextual statement, it is easy enough to substantiate it when Dymock's cuts and alterations are sifted in search of a pattern. First of all, if *Il pastor fido* was to be made to fit into the mould of a native theatrical tradition, the first problem its translator and editors would have to face would be its overall length. Even compared with previous Italian attempts in the same genre, Guarini's play was incredibly rich in incident and extremely long-winded in dialogue. The comparison with the much slighter *Aminta* is, again, particularly striking — 6862

---

[67] An example is the chorus of Act I, where the translator fails to recognize the alternative spelling 'spera' for 'sfera' (sphere), mistakes the word for a shortened version of 'speranza' (hope), and writes about 'hopes of fire' which shed something unspecified into mortal beings (p. 60).

lines of verse against a mere 1996[68] — but the total word count of the later play, at around 41,000 words if the argument and the prologue are included, made it a potential juggernaut of theatrical production. To give some idea of how much that is, it is sufficient to say that it is very rare for Shakespeare's plays to exceed 30,000 words, and that the great tragedies like *Othello* and *King Lear* have lengths between 26,000 and 27,000.[69] Considering that Fanshawe's later poetical version reaches the notable word count of 46,000, the fact that Dymock managed to keep his own at around 37,000 words is surely noteworthy.

The observation is merely quantitative: but sheer numbers become significant when the quality of single cuts is observed. First of all, as pointed out above, the Dymock translation skips the prose argument and the undramatic, dynastic verse prologue spoken by the Arcadian river Alfeo. Both of these would later be translated by the supposedly libertine Fanshawe, and both were included in the 1591 Italian edition published in London. This fact, together with Daniel's knowledge of Guarini and Italian culture, makes it close to impossible that the people responsible for the 1602 book did not know what the *Pastor fido* looked like in its printed form. The result of these excisions is that the text immediately resembles a native playbook rather than a poetic translation, as the brief dedicatory paratext is immediately followed by the list of dramatis personae and the dialogue of Act I, Scene 1.

More conclusive evidence is provided by the dialogue itself. Though there are signs of translator fatigue towards the end of the play, and particularly in Act IV (where whole passages or strings of repartees are skipped), Dymock begins to shorten and simplify Guarini's dramatic language from the very first scene. To understand how the Elizabethan translator works, it is sufficient to compare his version of any passage with Guarini's Italian and Fanshawe's closer rendition. Here, for instance, is Linco's commonplace rebuke of Silvio's heartlessness in the original and in the 1647 version:

> LIN.   O Silvio, Silvio, a che ti die' natura
> ne' più begli anni tuoi
> fior di beltà sì delicato e vago,
> se tu se' tanto a calpestarlo intento?
> Ché s'avess'io cotesta tua sì bella
> e sì fiorita guancia,
> — Addio, selve! — direi;
> e seguendo altre fère
> e la vita passando in festa e 'n gioco,
> farei la state a l'ombra e 'l verno al foco.

---

[68] Selmi, p. 16.
[69] For the purposes of this brief numerical excursus, all philological questions on textual sources and variants are of course ignored. Different sites give different numbers, but the difference is not so great as to be relevant to the present discussion. See for instance the list provided by *Open Source Shakespeare* <https://www.opensourceshakespeare.org>.

SIL.   Così fatti consigli
non mi desti mai più: come se' ora
tanto da te diverso?
LIN.   Altri tempi, altre cure.
Così certo farei, se Silvio fussi.
SILV.   E io, se fussi Linco.
Ma, perché Silvio sono,
oprar da Silvio e non da Linco i' voglio.[70]

[LIN. Oh, Silvio, Silvio, why did nature give you in your prime a flower of beauty so delicate and fair, if you are so intent on trampling it underfoot? If I myself had that fair and flowery cheek of yours — Farewell, woods — I would say; and following other beasts, and whiling away my life in partying and playing, I would spend my summers in the shade and my winters before the fire. SIL. You never gave me that kind of advice; why are you now so different from yourself? LIN. With changing times come changing cares. But certainly I would act that way, if I were Silvio. SIL. And so I would, if I were Linco. But since I am Silvio, I want to act like Silvio, not like Linco.]

LIN.   O Silvio, Silvio,
Why did frank Nature upon thee bestow
Blossoms of Beauty in thy prime, so sweet
And fair, for thee to trample under feet?
Had I thy fresh and blooming cheek, Adieu
I'd say to beasts, and nobler game pursue.
The Summer I would spend in feasts and mirth
In the cool shade, the Winter by the hearth.
SIL. How's this? Thou art not Linco sure; for he
Such counsell never us'd to give to me.
LIN. Counsell must change as the occasion doth:
If I were Silvio, so I'd do insooth.
SIL. And I, if I were Linco would do so,
But as I am, I'll do like Silvio.[71]

    Fanshawe demonstrates great ability in sticking both to his chosen metre and Guarini's discursive development, mostly finding elegant rhyme solutions (e.g. mirth/hearth) which do not alter the substance of the exchange. The fact that his version displays a slightly higher word-count than the source (113 words versus 106) is motivated by occasional padding ('frank', 'cool', 'insooth'). More interestingly for the present purposes, this English rendition does not miss a single beat either of Guarini's rhetorical structure or of his elocutionary flourishes.[72] The sustained floral metaphor in Linco's reproach, for instance, is

---

[70] Selmi, p. 86; I. 1. 36–53.
[71] Guarini, *Il pastor fido*, trans. by Fanshawe, sig. B4ᵛ.
[72] On occasion, Fanshawe develops Guarini's sustained metaphors even further. This, together with his double servitude to the source language and his chosen metre, explains why the 1647 version is so much longer than the Italian play. See Massimiliano Morini, '"To reforme a frame"': The 1602 Translation of *Il pastor fido* and Elizabethan Theatrical Publishing', *Cahiers Élisabéthains*, 104.1 (2021), 42–60 (pp. 50–51).

retained from beginning to end, Silvio's 'fior di beltà' ('Blossoms of Beauty') leading to his 'fiorita guancia' ('blooming cheek') — where even the repetition of the root is maintained ('fior' in Italian, the alliterating and probably cognate 'bloom' and 'blossom' in English). The final series of witty repartee is reproduced in its full complexity, with Silvio asking why Linco and his advice are so different from what they used to be; Linco replying that with changing times comes changing counsel, and that he would behave as he says, if he were Silvio; and Silvio countering that he would do as Linco says, if he were Linco, but as he is Silvio he must act like Silvio.

If Dymock's version is compared with Guarini's and Fanshawe's, the immediate impression is one of greater simplicity and directness:

LINCO
                              Oh Silvio,
Did nature on these youthful years of thine
Bestow such beauty to be cast away?
Had I but such a ruddy cheek, so fresh,
Farewell to woods, I'd follow other sports:
I'd wear my days in mirth: all summertide
In dainty shades, winter by the fireside.

SILVIO
Thy counsel, Linco, is like unto thyself.

LINCO
At other pleasures would I aim, were I Silvio

SILVIO
So would I, were I Linco, but I Silvio am,
Therefore I Silvio's deeds do like, not Linco's. (p. 36)

The passage is visibly shorter than Guarini's (or Fanshawe's: just 85 words), yet its development shows a perfect understanding of what is going on in the source. Dymock, in other words, is not abridging in order to get out of a tight spot. His condensing techniques, therefore, are to be considered a matter of choice, and must be interpreted stylistically. In this sense, what one immediately notices is a dislike for exactly those metaphorical and rhetorical complexities which rouse Fanshawe's imitative, competitive muse.[73] The floral metaphor is completely dropped, though the general sense of Linco's pointed compliment is retained ('such beauty [...] such a ruddy cheek, so fresh'). Analogously, some of the discursive complications in the exchange are edited out, presumably because the translator deems them unnecessary in the development of the action. Thus,

---

[73] This reticence is all the more striking, as well as indicative of Dymock's dramatic bent, in an age in which abundance, rhetorical *copia*, was so often identified with elegance. See F. A. Kretschmer, 'The "res/verba" Dichotomy and "copia" in Renaissance Translation', *Renaissance and Reformation / Renaissance et Reforme*, 11.1 (1975), 24–29; Brian Cummings, 'Encyclopaedic Erasmus', *Renaissance Studies*, 28.2 (2014), 183–204; and see Morini, *Tudor Translation*, pp. 65–95, for some analyses of 'copious' translations.

when the Italian Silvio wonders about Linco giving him different advice from what he used to give, the 1602 English Silvio just says that Linco's advice is just what one would expect from Linco — which eliminates the need for Linco's rejoinder ('Counsell must change as the occasion doth', in Fanshawe's phrasing). Nor are these cuts and simplifications the only relevant stylistic features of Dymock's rendition. The diction he employs is at least as significant: and here, one must note that though a number of dignified words keep the register relatively high, other lexical choices contribute to making the exchange more homely and English (the very Anglo-Saxon 'ruddy', for instance; or 'sports', turning Guarini's classicizing, Diana-hallowed hunt into a courtly entertainment for northern kings).

To ears attuned to late Tudor drama, these changes make the passage look more dramatic — and in this effect, of course, the adoption of unrhymed iambic pentameter also plays a decisive role. Dymock does not use blank verse uniformly: as this passage itself shows, he allows for the occasional rhyming couplet (again, so does late Tudor drama), whether there is one in the source (more often) or not (not uncommonly). Furthermore, some of his lines are longer, both in syllabic and accentual terms (e.g. 'At other pleasures would I aim, were I Silvio'); and the English translator attempts a closer metrical rendition of Guarini's choruses, which in the 1602 version are often confusing and rather pedestrian. But again, the dialogue is mostly in blank verse, and this creates a compression that may either sound matter-of-fact or, at moments of great dramatic tension, stately and dignified:

> TIRENIO
> And is this true?
>
> MONTANUS
>   Behold my witness here.
>
> CARINO
> That which he saith is true.
>
> TIRENIO
>   And who art thou?
>
> CARINO
> I am Carino, his father thought till now.
>
> TIRENIO
> Is this the child the flood so bare away?
>
> MONTANUS
> The very same. (p. 189)

It is at this juncture that Dymock's personal style and taste — of which it is almost impossible to know anything outside the translation itself, the sonnet, and some more slight textual and biographical evidence — become entangled with the style and taste of a whole era. For if many twenty-first-century ears are attuned to the dramatic jargon of late Tudor drama, so of course were the ears of late Tudor readers and theatregoers. The 1602 translator cannot have been unaware that the choice of blank verse as the metrical language mostly spoken by his characters would make his work sound like a contemporary English play.

What makes this observation particularly interesting is the fact that *The faithfull Shepheard* not only sounds like a late Elizabethan play — it also looks like one, in its paratextual organization and in its overall appearance as a material object. The fact that it skips Guarini's argument and dedicatory prologue to cut straight to the dramatic chase has been mentioned above, and the conciseness of its paratext has been noted. What remains to be said is that the first edition of the Dymock *Faithfull Shepheard* was printed in the quarto format, like the popular English plays of its time; and that for this translational enterprise, the publisher chose a stationer whose name (though it does not feature on the title page) was closely linked with the diffusion of play-texts on the London book market.

Before the identity of the stationer is revealed and a plausible reconstruction is proposed of the motives of all the persons involved, it may be useful to point out that, at this time, plays were still far from being considered prestigious cultural capital. Most of the canonizing work that endowed a few Tudor and Stuart playwrights with the aura of great authors would be done after the Restoration: and though Shakespeare was posthumously honoured with the stately folio of 1623, only seven years before that time, and fourteen after Dymock's translation, Ben Jonson was made the object of mockery for daring to present his *Workes* in the same format.[74] Clearly, in the late Tudor and early Stuart age, the more serviceable and unassuming quarto was seen as appropriate for a genre whose status was still relatively lowly. And in fact, if contemporary plays were seen as fit material for publication at all, at least some of the merit has to be given to the printers who decided to stake their money on their eventual success. Unsurprisingly, this happened in the 1590s, at a time of great flourishing for the London theatres: in this decade, while bigger investments continued to be made on histories and bulky romances, a small number of stationers began to associate their names with William Shakespeare and his peers. Of these select few, no one printed more plays during that period than Thomas Creede, who lived and worked in Thames Street, whose catalogue

---

[74] As Richard Dutton (*Ben Jonson: Authority, Criticism* (Houndmills, Basingstoke: Palgrave Macmillan, 1996), p. 57) has pointed out, it was the very idea of treating plays as works of literature that incurred ridicule. One rhyming jibe went: 'Pray tell me Ben, where doth the mystery lurk, | What others call a play, you call a work.' On the canonization of Shakespeare after the Restoration, see Massimiliano Morini, 'Shakespeare's Language and the Restoration', in *The Shakespeare Apocrypha*, ed. by Douglas A. Brooks (Lewinston: Edwin Mellen Press, 2007), pp. 339–88.

included Shakespearean titles such as *Romeo and Juliet* and *Richard III* — and who was also the unnamed printer of the 1602 *Faithfull Shepheard*.[75]

The fact that his name is not given on the title page (not even in the formula 'printed by [...] for [...]') does not mean that the stationer's identity is completely hidden from sight: Creede is in fact recognizable from his emblem — a figure of truth crowned and running, scourged with a rod by a hand reaching down from the clouds, and encircled by the motto 'virescit vulnere veritas' ('truth flourishes in wounds'). However, the partial erasure of Creede's identity must be seen as significant, because in the title pages of other plays published by the same stationer around this time, like the 1599 quarto edition of *Romeo and Juliet*, his name is included. Whatever the specific reasons for its absence here,[76] whatever the exact nature of the relationships between Creede, Daniel and Waterson, it is likely that the printer had no share in the financial investment required to bring the first English *Pastor fido* to light.

At this point, a partial, speculative reconstruction of the process leading to publication is possible. Tailboys Dymock completes his translation, either at his brother's instigation or, more probably, to gratify him with a reminder of his Italian travels. Shortly after finishing the work, he dies, leaving his *Faithfull Shepheard* in Waterson's hands. Waterson, who has been working on Italian projects with Daniel since the appearance of the latter's 1585 Paolo Giovio — and who would later publish Daniel's Guarinian *Queenes Arcadia* — has the idea of dedicating the whole to Edward Dymock, and implicates his friend the translator, historian and sonneteer, who had been to Italy with the Queen's Champion. Of course, this reconstruction leaves room for many different configurations of forces and initiatives. Daniel, for instance, might have been the prime mover of the whole enterprise: he might have wanted to pay homage

---

[75] See Holger Schott Syme, 'Thomas Creede, William Barkley, and the Venture of Printing Plays', in *Shakespeare's Stationers*, ed. by Straznicky, pp. 28–46 (p. 28). According to Schott Syme, Creede printed twenty-six play-texts between 1590 and 1604 — though most of his profits probably came from such publications as Munday's 'Palmerin' cycle. On Creede, see also Akihiro Yamada, *Thomas Creede: Printer to Shakespeare and His Contemporaries* (Tokyo: Meisei University Press, 1994); Robert A. H. Smith, 'Thomas Creede, *Henry V* Q1, and *The Famous Victories of Henrie the Fifth*', *The Review of English Studies*, 49.193 (1998), 60–64.

[76] If the person responsible for the text was indeed Tailboys Dymock, it is possible that the translator's legal troubles (see note 54) may have led not only himself but also the stationer to hide behind a thin veil of relative anonymity. Conversely, the anonymity of the translation might be seen as evidence that Tailboys was indeed its author, as it is difficult to envisage reasons other than prudence for an early modern translator keeping his name and identity hidden in the paratext. See A. E. B. Coldiron, 'Visibility Now: Historicizing Foreign Presences in Translation', *Translation Studies*, 5.2 (2012), 189–200; Marie-Alice Belle, 'Rhetorical *Ethos* and the Translating Self in Early Modern England', in *Trust and Proof: Translators in Renaissance Print Culture*, ed. by Andrea Rizzi (Leiden: Brill, 2018), pp. 62–84; Marie-Alice Belle and Brenda M. Hosington (eds), *Thresholds of Translation: Paratexts, Print, and Cultural Exchange in Early Modern Britain (1473–1660)* (Basingstoke: Palgrave Macmillan, 2018).

to his former travelling companion, involved Waterson and decided to task Tailboys Dymock with the translation. At any rate, though the pattern of agency cannot be defined with anything approaching certainty, what is evident is that the Dymock-Waterson-Daniel group chose to present the work not as a mere poetical translation, but in the garb of a native play. The translator cut various undramatic passages and used blank verse for most of the dialogue. The publisher (and/or Daniel) sought a London stationer whose name was strongly associated with the publication of English play-texts, and had the translation printed in very similar fashion to *Richard III* and *Romeo and Juliet*.

Did the Dymock-Waterson-Daniel group decide to do that because they hoped that someone would acquire the play and stage it? It is very unlikely, for two different but related reasons. On the one hand, anybody with an eye for a play (like Samuel Daniel) would have recognized immediately that Guarini's *Pastor fido*, even in Dymock's Englishing, was a completely different proposition from the fare on show in the London theatres, and would not have appealed to any company in its published form. On the other hand, even if some company had decided to use or adapt the play to fit their purposes, it would have been very hard for the publisher of *The faithfull Shepheard* to derive any profits from the transaction, given the fluid state of copyright at the beginning of the seventeenth century[77] and the predatory habits of contemporary playwrights. More probably, the agents behind the 1602 version simply hoped to align their book with a genre which was perceived as being on the rise, in commercial if not in cultural terms. It is unlikely that their strategy was successful: the only reprint of Dymock's translation was the duodecimo of 1633, which did not directly involve any of the people responsible for the publication of the 1602 quarto;[78] but if that means three decades of oblivion, it also testifies to some enduring interest — as does the fact that Denham's above-quoted poem in praise of Fanshawe appears to acknowledge Dymock's work (if only to disparage its quality).[79]

Whatever the aims of the people who brought it to the printing press, it can

---

[77] See W. S. Holdsworth, 'Press Control and Copyright in the 16th and 17th Centuries', *The Yale Law Journal*, 29.8 (1920), 841–58; Ian Gadd, 'The Stationers' Company in England before 1710', in *Research Handbook on the History of Copyright Law*, ed. by H. Tomás Gómez-Arostegui and Isabella Alexander (Cheltenham: Elgar, 2016), pp. 81–95.

[78] Dymock and Daniel were dead. So was probably Simon Waterson, who had ceded his rights in the book to William Sheares, as stated in the 6 September 1633 entry in the Stationers' Register. The book contained a dedication to 'Charles Dymock, Esquire, Champion to his Majestie', identified as the son of the original dedicatee by John Waterson (the son of the original publisher); T1633, sig. A3^r. Charles Dymock is also mistakenly identified as the translator in the Stationers' Register.

[79] See Guarini, *A Critical Edition*, ed. by Staton and Simeone, p. xix. Maristella Gatto, 'Sulla "scena" della storia: traduzione e riscrittura in *The Faithfull Shepherd* di Sir Richard Fanshawe', in *Forme del tragicomico nel teatro elisabettiano e giacomiano*, ed. by Vittoria Intonti (Napoli: Liguori, 2004), pp. 217–46 (p. 225).

be said in conclusion that the first English *Pastor fido* does in some way represent the 'virtues of the North' — though not, perhaps, in the strict linguistic terms envisaged by Daniel elsewhere. Dymock took an Italian courtly play and steered it, at least partially, in the direction of the popular London stage. Waterson and/or Daniel and/or Dymock himself decided to dress it up and market it much as if it were an original creation by Shakespeare, Marlowe or Jonson.[80] Had the Italian author, as Daniel fantasized, been able to read English or understand English eloquence, he would have found proof, in this by-product of his creation, that even a barbaric northern country could evolve a distinctive dramatic tradition.

Ultimately, this is the reason why Dymock's work repays the scrutiny of scholars investigating early modern translation and the early modern theatre. In the dearth of actual theatrical translations which made it both onto the public stage and into print, and in a publishing panorama in which translated plays were marketed as learning or reading material (and were almost exclusively of classical provenance),[81] the 1602 *Faithfull Shepheard* is an absolute rarity. If it is arguably inferior to Fanshawe's version in terms of poetic merit, it possesses dramatic qualities which the later translator could not infuse, and would not have been interested in infusing, in his own work. The Dymock-Waterson-Daniel group did not decide to turn Guarini's masterpiece into a popular theatrical product, but neither did they choose to ignore the claims of the popular theatre. They were aware of what Guarini's name stood for in the European literary world, but they were clearly also conscious of how dramatic works were written and presented in England. Their publication, therefore, is invaluable for the comparative information it provides on what was considered appropriate for an English play, both in stylistic and in editorial terms. If, as F. O. Matthiessen once wrote, studying the translations of the Tudor period means understanding the means whereby the Renaissance came to England,[82] then this edition of *Il pastor fido* is one of the very few documents we possess testifying at first hand to the English landing of European Renaissance theatre.

---

[80] Viewed holistically, as both text and object, *The faithfull Shepheard* is thus a perfect illustration of what A. E. B. Coldiron sees as the co-transformative powers of translation and the printing press in the Renaissance (see *Printers without Borders*).

[81] Translations from Seneca and Terence, for instance, though their theatrical repercussions are well known, were almost unfailingly presented as repositories of eloquence and appropriate reading material for classical students. Maurice Kyffin, the translator of *Andria* (1588), praised Terence's language as 'right requisite to be studied of all such as would attain to the knowledge of right speaking and readiness of well writing in the Latin tongue'. *English Renaissance Translation Theory*, ed. by Neil Rhodes, Gordon Kendal and Louise Wilson (London: The Modern Humanities Research Association, 2013), p. 434.

[82] F. O. Matthiessen, *Translation: An Elizabethan Art* (New York: Octagon Books, 1965 (1931)), p. 3.

IL PASTOR FIDO:

OR

The faithfull Shepheard.

Translated out of Italian into *English.*

∽

LONDON

Printed for Simon Waterson.

1602

To the right worthy and learnèd Knight, Sir Edward Dymock, Champion to her Majesty, concerning this translation of *Pastor Fido*.

    I do rejoice, learnèd and worthy knight,
    That by the hand of thy kind countryman
    (This painful[1] and industrious gentleman)
    Thy dear esteemed Guarini comes to light:
5 Who in thy love I know took great delight
    As thou in his, who now in England can
    Speak as good English as Italian,
    And here enjoys the grace of his own right.
    Though I remember he hath oft imbased[2]
10 Unto us both, the virtues of the north,
    Saying, our coasts were with no measures graced,
    Nor barbarous tongues could any verse bring forth.
    I would he saw his own, or knew our store,
    Whose spirits can yield as much, and if not more.
          Sam. Daniell.

---

[1] painful] painstaking, diligent.
[2] imbased] presented as base, worthless. The reference is to meetings in Italy between Samuel Daniel, Sir Edward Dymock and Guarini himself. See Introduction, p. 17.

A Sonnet of the Translator, dedicated to that honourable Knight his kinsman, Sir Edward Dymock.

A silly hand hath fashioned up a suit
Of English clothes unto a traveller,
A noble mind though shepherd's weeds he wear,
That might consort his tunes with Tasso's lute,[3]
5   Learnèd Guarini's first begotten fruit,
I have assumed the courage to rebear,
And him an English denizen made here,
Presenting him unto the sons of Brute.[4]
If I have failed t'express his native look,
10   And be in my translation taxed of blame,
I must appeal to that true censor's book[5]
That says, 'tis harder to reform a frame,
Than for to build from groundwork of one's wit,
A new creation of a noble fit.

---

[3] Torquato Tasso was the author of the 'woodland fable' *Aminta* (1573), which was the direct predecessor of Guarini's *Pastor fido*. The two Italian pastoral works had been published in a single volume by the English printer John Wolfe (1591). See Introduction, p. 3.

[4] A reference to the medieval myth of Brutus, a descendant of Aeneas and the founder of Britain. The sons of Brute are the British.

[5] true censor's book] Quintilian's *Institutio oratoria* (10, 2. 10): 'Adde quod plerumque facilius est plus facere quam idem' ('Consider, also, that it is easier to do more than to do exactly the same thing').

To the right worthy and learnèd Knight, Sir Edward Dymock,
Champion to her Majesty.

Sir, this work was committed to me to publish to the world, and by reason of the nearness of kin to the deceased translator, and the good knowledge of the great worth of the Italian author, I knew none fitter to patronize the same than your worthiness, to whom I wish all happiness, and a prosperous new year. London this last of December. 1601.

Your Worship's ever to be commanded.
Simon Waterson.

The persons which speak in it.

Silvio, the son of Montanus.
Linco, an old servant of Montanus.
Mirtillo, in love with Amarillis.
Ergasto, his companion.
Corisca, a nymph, in love with Mirtillo.
Montanus, high priest.
Titirus, a shepherd.
Dametas, an old servant of Montanus.
Satyr, an old lover of Corisca's.
Dorinda, enamoured of Silvio.
Lupino, a goatherd, her servant.
Amarillis, daughter of Titirus.
Nicander, chief minister of the Priest.
Coridon, a lover of Corisca's.
Carino, an old man, the putative father of Mirtillo.
Uranio, an old man, his companion.
Nuntio.[6]
Tirenio, a blind prophet.

---

[6] Nuntio] Messenger.

Pastor Fido, or *The faithful Shepherd*

Chorus of Shepherds, Huntsmen, Nymphs, Priests.
The Scene is in Arcadia.

Act 1, Scene 1[7]
SILVIO, LINCO

SILVIO
Go you that have enclosed the dreadful beast,
And give the sign that's usual to our hunting,
Go swell[8] your eyes and hearts with horns and shouts.
If there be any swain of Cynthia's troupe
5   In all Arcadia delighted in her sports,[9]
Whose generous affects are stung with care,
Or glory of these woods: let him come forth
And follow me, where in a circle small
(Though to our valour large) enclosèd is
10 The ugly boar, monster of nature and these woods,
That vast and fierce (by many harms well known)
Inhabitant of Erimanthus,[10] plague to the fields,
Terror to country clowns. Go then prevent
Not only, but provoke with horns' shrill sound
15 Blushing Aurora out.[11] Linco, we'll go
And worship first the Gods: for there 'tis best
We any work begin.

LINCO
                    Silvio, I praise
Thy worshipping the Gods, but yet to trouble them
That are their ministers I do not praise.
20 The keepers of the temple are asleep,
They cannot see the day break for the mountain's top.

---

[7] Guarini's prologue is omitted (see Introduction, p. 15).
[8] Go swell] A bizarre translation of 'ite svegliando' (1. 1. 3; go wake), probably motivated by phonetic similarity.
[9] Cynthia ('Cinthia' in Dymock's spelling) is the goddess Diana/Artemis (said to have been born on Mount Cynthus), who delights in hunting.
[10] Erimanthus] A mountain range in the Peloponnese. The allusion is to Hercules' labours, because Silvio is a descendant of the Graeco-Roman demigod.
[11] Aurora] The dawn, again in its Latin mythological garb.

SILVIO
To thee perhaps, that art not yet awake,
All things do seem asleep.

LINCO
                    Oh Silvio,
Did nature on these youthful years of thine
25 Bestow such beauty to be cast away?
Had I but such a ruddy cheek, so fresh,
Farewell to woods, I'd follow other sports:
I'd wear my days in mirth: all summertide
In dainty shades, winter by the fireside.

SILVIO
30 Thy counsel, Linco, is like unto thyself.[12]

LINCO
At other pleasures would I aim, were I Silvio.

SILVIO
So would I, were I Linco, but I Silvio am,
Therefore I Silvio's deeds do like, not Linco's.

LINCO
Oh fool, that seekst so far for hurtful beasts
35 And hast one lodged so near thy dwelling house.

SILVIO
Art thou in earnest? or dost thou but jest?

LINCO
Thou jests, not I.

SILVIO
                  And is he then so near?

LINCO
As near as 'tis to thee.

SILVIO
                  Where? in what wood?

---

[12] Here Dymock simplifies Silvio's statement. In the Italian he says, on the contrary, that Linco is contradicting his previously held opinions ('Così fatti consigli | non mi desti mai'; I. 1. 45–46). See Introduction, pp. 23–24.

LINCO
Silvio, thou art the wood:[13] the ugly beast
40 That's harboured there, is this thy beastliness.

SILVIO
Was't not well guessed of me thou didst but jest?[14]

LINCO
A nymph so fair, so delicate! But tush!
Why do I call her nymph? A goddess, rather,
More fresh, more dainty than the morning rose,
45 More soft, more purely white than swanny down[15]
(For whom there's not a shepherd 'mongst us all so brave,
But sighs, and sighs in vain), for thee alone
Reserves herself, ordained by heaven and men:
And yet thou neither thinkst of sighs or plaints.
50 Oh happy boy (though most unworthily),
Thou that mightst her enjoy, still fliest her, Silvio,
Still her despisest. Is not then thy heart
Made of a beast, or of hard iron rather?

SILVIO
If to relinquish love be cruelty,
55 Then is it virtue, and I not repent
That I have banisht love my heart:[16] but joy
That thereby I have overcome this love,
A beast more dangerous than th'other far.

LINCO
How hast thou overcome that which thou never proved?[17]

SILVIO
60 Not proving it, I have it overcome.

---

[13] wood] mad (you are the mad one).
[14] 'Come ben m'avisai che vaneggiavi!' ('I was right in thinking you were out of your mind'; I. 1. 65). Dymock's choice of 'guess' and 'jest' creates an internal rhyme that is particularly evident in the T1602 spelling ('Was't not well gest of me thou didst but iest?').
[15] swanny] Pertaining to swans: so rare that the OED gives this passage as one of very few examples. In the Italian, Linco says that the girl is whiter and softer than a swan ('e più molle e più candida del cigno'; I. 1. 71).
[16] my heart] from my heart.
[17] proved] Here and in the following lines, the verb has the very rare (according to the OED) meaning of 'feel', under the influence of Guarini's 'provare'. Note that this is a twelve-syllable line, condensing two of Guarini's settenari (I. 1. 88–89).

LINCO
Oh, if thou hadst but proved it, Silvio, once,
If thou but knewst what a high favour 'twere,
To be beloved, and loving to possess
A loving heart, I'm sure thou then wouldst say,
65 Sweet lovely life, why hast thou staid so long?
These woods and beasts leave, foolish child, and love.

SILVIO
Linco, I swear a thousand nymphs I'll give
For one poor beast that my Melampo kills:[18]
Let them that have a better taste than I
70 In these delights possess them. I will none.

LINCO
Dost thou taste ought, since love thou dost not taste,
The only cause that the world tasteth all?[19]
Believe me, boy, the time will one day come
Thou wilt it taste. For love once in our life
75 Will show what force he hath. Believe me, child,
No greater pain can any living prove
Than in old limbs the lively sting of love.[20]
Yet if in youth love wound, that love may heal:[21]
But come it once in that same frozen age,
80 Wherefore oftentimes the disability
More than the wound we plain,[22] oh mortal then,
And most intolerable are those pains.
If thou seekest pity, ill if thou findst it not,
But if thou findst it ten time worse. Do not
85 Protract it till thy better time be past,
For if love do assail thy hoary hairs,
Thy silly flesh a double torment tears

---

[18] Melampo] Silvio's dog — again, a name from Greek mythology. Dymock keeps it in its Italian form.

[19] This is a confusing line. What Linco says in the Italian play is that love is the only reason why the world feels anything (I. 1. 106–07; maybe Dymock meant to write 'at all': the line would then become hendecasyllabic; as iambic pentameter it is awkward in any case).

[20] Here Guarini has a rhyming couplet ('non è pena maggiore, | che 'n vecchie membra il pizzicor d'amore' (I. 1. 114–15; 'no pain is greater | than in old limbs the sting of love')). Dymock recreates it by different means, and again by using 'prove' with the meaning of 'feel'.

[21] Dymock condenses so much (five lines in one) that the result is barely comprehensible. What Linco means is that if a youth is wounded by love, there will be time for him to heal.

[22] plain] mourn. A calque of Guarini's 'piagne' (I. 1. 118).

Of this which when thou wouldst thou canst not.
These woods and beasts leave, foolish boy, and love.

SILVIO
90 As though there were no life but that which nursed
These amorous follies and fond ecstasies.

LINCO
Tell me, if in this pleasant time now flowers renew,[23]
And the world waxeth young again, thou shouldst
Instead of flowery valleys, fragrant fields,
95 And well clad woods, see but the oak, the ash, the pine,
Without their leafy hairs: grassless the ground,
The meadows want their flowers. Wouldst thou not say
The world doth languish? Nature did decay?
Now that same horror, that same miracle,
100 That monstrous novelty thou hast thyself.
As love in old men is ridiculous,
So youth without love is unnatural.
Look but about, Silvio, what the world hath
Worthy to be admired. Love only made
105 The heavens, the earth; the seas themselves do love.
And that same star that the daybreak foretells
Tasteth the flames of her thrice puissant son.
And at that hour, because perhaps she leaves
The stolen delights and bosom of her love,
110 She darteth down abroad her sparkling smiles.[24]
Beasts in the woods do love; and in the seas
The speedy dolphins and the mighty whales.
The bird that sweetly sings, and wantonly
Doth fly, now from the oak unto the ash,
115 Then from the ash unto the myrtle tree,
Says in her language, I in love do burn.
(Would I might hear my Silvio answer her the same!)
The bull amid the herd doth loudly low,
Yet are those lows but bidding to love's feasts.
120 The lion in the wood doth bray, and yet
Those brays are not the voice of rage, but love.
Well, to conclude, all things do love but thou,

---

[23] As often happens, Dymock's grammar is shaky: 'flowers', here a noun, is present as a verb in Guarini's traditional characterization of spring as the season that renews and covers the world with flowers ('stagion che 'nfiora e rinnovella il mondo'; I. 1. 143).

[24] And that same star […] smiles] Venus as the morning star (Lucifer). She too feels the power of her son, Cupid. The adulterous lover of her 'stolen delights' is Mars.

Thou only, Silvio, art in heaven, in earth,
In seas, a soul uncapable of love.
125 Leave, leave these woods, these beasts, and learn to love.

SILVIO
Was then my youth committed to thy charge
That in these soft effeminate desires
Of wanton love, thou shouldst it nurse and train?
Rememberest not what thou, and what I am?

LINCO
130 I am a man, and human me esteem.
With thee a man, or rather shouldst be so,
I speak of human things. Which if thou scornst
Take heed least in dishumaning thyself,
A beast thou prove not sooner than a God.

SILVIO
135 Neither so famous nor so valiant
Had been that monster-tamer, of whose blood
I do derive myself, had he not tamèd love.

LINCO
See blind child how thou errst: where hadst thou been
Had not that famous Hercules first loved?[25]
140 The greatest cause he monsters tamed was love.
Knowest thou not that fair Omphale to please[26]
He did not only change his lion's skin
Into a woman's gown, but also turned
His knotty club into a spindle and a rock?
145 So was he wont from trouble and from toil
To take his ease, and all alone retire
To her fair lap, the haven of happy love.
As rugged iron with purer metal mixed
Is made more fit (refined) for noble use:
150 So fierce and untamed strength that in his proper rage
Doth often break, yet with the sweets of love
Well tempered proveth truly generous.
Then if thou dost desire to imitate
Great Hercules, and to be worthy of his race,
155 Though that thou wilt not leave these savage woods,

---

[25] Dymock simplifies Guarini's classical allusions by using the Latin name of the Graeco-Roman hero — the Italian author refers to him by the patronymic 'Alcide' (I. 1. 216).
[26] Omphale] Queen of the kingdom of Lydia. Hercules agreed to perform menial feminine work for her.

Do follow them: but do not leave to love
A love so lawful as your Amarillis.
That you Dorinda fly I you excuse,
For 'twere unfit your mind on honour set
160 Should be made hot in these amorous thefts,
A mighty wrong unto your worthy spouse.

SILVIO
What sayst thou, Linco? She's not yet my spouse.

LINCO
Hast thou not solemnly received her faith?
Take heed, proud boy, do not provoke the gods.

SILVIO
165 The gift of heaven is human liberty.
May we not force repel, that force receive?[27]

LINCO
Nay, if thou wouldst but understand! The heavens
Hereto do tie thee that have promisèd
So many favours at thy nuptial feast.

SILVIO
170 I'm sure that gods have other things to do
Than trouble and molest them with these toys.[28]
Linco, nor this, nor that love pleaseth me.
I was a huntsman, not a lover born,
Thou that dost follow love, thy pleasure take. *Exit Silvio*

LINCO
175 Thou cruel boy, descended of the gods?
I scarce believe thou wert begot by man,
Which if thou wert, thou sooner wert begot
With venom of Meger and Ptisifo,[29]
Than Venus' pleasure which men so commend.

---

[27] Dymock slightly alters the sense of Silvio's words here, making him more defiant. The Italian character says that heaven does not force those on which it bestows force (I. 1. 253–54).
[28] The grammar is shaky. What Silvio appears to mean is that the Gods have other things to do, and therefore humans should not trouble them with such unimportant matters. In Italian, Silvio is sarcastic rather than literal (I. 1. 259–60).
[29] Megaera and Tisiphone, two of the three Greek furies, or goddesses of vengeance. Actually, Guarini has 'Tisifone' and 'Aletto' (Alecto; I. 1. 270) — but Dymock, either for prosodic reasons or because Megaera punishes oath-breakers, chooses a different pair.

Act 1, Scene 2
MIRTILLO, ERGASTO

MIRTILLO

180 Cruel Amarillis, that with thy bitter name
Most bitterly dost teach me to complain.[30]
Whiter than whitest lilies and more fair,
But deafer and more fierce than th'adder is.
Since with my words I do so much offend,
185 In silence will I die: but yet these plaints
These mountains and these woods shall cry for me,
Whom I so oft have learnèd to resound[31]
That lovèd name. For me my plaints shall tell
The plaining fountains and the murm'ring winds:
190 Pity and grief shall speak out of my face,
And in the end though all things else prove dumb,
My very death shall tell my martyrdom.

ERGASTO

Love (dear Mirtillo)'s like a fire enclosed,
Which straightly kept, more fiercely flames at last.
195 Thou shouldst not have so long concealed from me
The fire, since it thou couldst not hide.
How often have I said: Mirtillo burns,
But in a silent flame, and so consumes.[32]

MIRTILLO

Myself I harmèd her not to offend,
200 Courteous Ergasto, and should yet be dumb,
But strict necessity hath made me bold.
I hear a voice which through my scarèd ears
Woundeth alas my wretched heart with noise
Of Amarillis' nighing nuptial feast.[33]
205 Who speaks ought else to me he holds his peace,[34]
Nor dare I further search, as well for fear
To give suspicion of my love, as for to find
That which I would not. Well! I know, Ergasto,
It fits not with my poor and base estate
210 To hope at all a nymph so rarely qualified,

---

[30] bitterly] Because 'Amarillis' contains the Italian word 'amaro' (bitter).
[31] learned] taught.
[32] consumes] is consumed.
[33] nighing] nigh, getting close.
[34] A confusing line: he means that people who speak about this do not give any details.

Of blood and spright truly celestial,[35]
Should prove my wife. Oh no, I know too well
The lowliness of my poor humble star.
My destiny's to burn! Not to delight
215 Was I brought forth, but since my cruel fates
Have made me love my death more than my life,
I am content to die, so that my death
Might please her that's the cause thereof;
And that she would but grace my latest gasp
220 With her fair eyes, and once before she made
Another by her marriage fortunate
She would but hear me speak. Courteous Ergasto,
If thou lov'st me, help me with this favour.
Aid me herein, if thou tak'st pity of my case.

ERGASTO
225 A poor desire of love, and light reward
Of him that dies: but dang'rous enterprise.
Wretched were she, should but her father know
She had bowed down her ears to her lover's words,
Or should she be accusèd to the priest
230 Her father-in-law; for this perhaps she shuns
To speak with you, that else doth love you well,
Although she it conceals; for women though
They be more frail in their desires,
Yet are they craftier in hiding them.
235 If this be true, how can she show more love
Than thus in shunning you? She hears in vain,
And shuns with pity that can give no help.
It is sound counsel soon to cease desiring,
When we cannot attain to our aspiring.

MIRTILLO
240 Oh were this true, could I but this believe,
Thrice happy pain. Thrice fortunate distress.
But tell me sweet Ergasto, tell me true,
Which is the shepherd whom the stars so friend?[36]

---

[35] spright] Used by Dymock as a variant spelling of 'sprite' — 'spirit', 'soul', but elsewhere also 'living being'. The *OED* records a few instances of this graphemic form.
[36] friend] befriend.

ERGASTO
Knowst thou not Silvio, Montane's only son?[37]
245 Diana's priest:[38] that rich and famous shepherd,
That gallant youth? He is the very same.

MIRTILLO
Most happy youth, that hast in tender years
Found fate so ripe. I do not envy thee,
But plain myself.

ERGASTO
                Nor need you envy him
250 That pity more than envy doth deserve.

MIRTILLO
Pity! And why?

ERGASTO
              Because he loves her not.

MIRTILLO
And lives he? Hath a heart? And is not blind?
Or hath she on my wretched heart spent all her flames?
And her fair eyes blown all their loves on me?
255 Why should they give a gem so precious
To one that neither knows it, nor regards it?

ERGASTO
For that the heavens the health of Arcady
Do promise at these nuptials. Know you not
How we do still appease our goddess' wrath,
260 Each year with guiltless blood of some poor nymph?
A mortal and a miserable tribute.

MIRTILLO
'Tis news to me, that am a new inhabitant,[39]
As 't pleaseth love and my poor destiny:
That did before inhabit savage woods.
265 But what I pray you was that grievous fault
That kindled rage in a celestial breast?

---

[37] Here and elsewhere, whenever the metrical need arises, Montanus becomes Montane.

[38] It is Montanus who is 'Diana's priest'.

[39] Mirtillo's outsider status gives Ergasto an occasion to expatiate on the narrative background to Guarini's play. The story itself dates back to Pausanias, but the names are changed — and the choice of Amintas, of course, is a nod to Guarini's pastoral predecessor in Ferrara, Torquato Tasso.

ERGASTO

I will report the doleful tragedy
From the beginning of our misery,
That able are[40] pity and plaints to draw
From these hard rocks, much more from human breasts.
In that same golden age when holy priesthood and
The temple's charge was not prohibited
To youth, a noble swain, Amintas called,
Priest at that time, lovèd Lucrina bright:
A beauteous nymph, exceeding fair: but therewithal
Exceeding false, and light. Long time she lovèd him,
Or at the least she seemèd so, with feignèd face[41]
Nursing his pure affections with false hopes.
Whilst she no other suitors had. But see
Th'unconstant wretch! no sooner was she wooed
By a rude shepherd, but at first assault,
At his first sigh, she yielded up her love,
Before Amintas dreamed of jealousy.
At last Amintas was forlorn, despised,
So that the wicked woman would nor see, nor hear
Him speak; now if the wretch did sigh
Be thou the judge that knowst his pain by proof.

MIRTILLO

Ay me,[42] this grief all other griefs exceeds.

ERGASTO

After he had his heart recoverèd
From his complaints, he to his goddess turns,
And praying says: Great Cynthia, if I have
At any time kindled with guiltless hands
The holy flames, revenge thou then for me
This broken faith of my unconstant nymph.
Diana hears the prayers of her priest,
And straight out-breathing rage, she takes her bow

---

[40] are] There is no apparent reason why the verb should be in the plural here. It looks like a complete oversight, repeated in T1633.
[41] Appropriately for the translation of a play that is preoccupied with the falsity of courtly life, 'feignèd face' recalls a poem by Edmund Spenser, 'Prosopopoia; or Mother Hubbard's Tale', in which it is said of the good courtier that 'He will not creep, nor crouch with feigned face'; *Spenser, and His Poetry. Vol. III*, ed. by George L. Craik (London: Charles Knight, 1845), p. 161.
[42] Ay me] One of several occasions on which Dymock translates the Italian 'oimè' ('alas') phonetically.

And shoots shafts of inevitable death⁴³
Into the bowels of Arcadia.
People of every sex, of every age,
300 Soon perishèd; no succour could be found.
'Twas bootless art to search for remedies,
For often on the patient the physician died.
One only remedy did rest,⁴⁴ which was
Straight to the nearest oracle they went,
305 From whom they had an answer very clear,
But above measure deadly horrible.
Which was, our Cynthia was displeased, and to
Appease her ire, either Lucrina or some else for her⁴⁵
Must by Amintas' hands be sacrificed.
310 Who when she had long time in vain complained,
And looked for help from her new friend in vain,
Was to the sacred altars led with solemn pomp,
A woeful sacrifice. Where at those feet
Which had pursuèd her long time in vain,
315 At her betrayèd lovers feet, she bends⁴⁶
Her trembling knees, attending cruel death.⁴⁷
Amintas stretcheth out the holy sword,
Seeming to breath from his inflamèd lips
Rage and revenge; turning to her his face,
320 Speaks with a sigh, the messenger of death:
Lucrina, for thy further pains, behold
What lover thou hast left, and what pursued
Judge by this blow.⁴⁸ And with that very word
Striketh the blade into his woeful breast,
325 Falling a sacrifice upon the sacrifice.
At such a strange and cruel spectacle,
The nymph amazèd stands⁴⁹ twixt life and death,

⁴³ inevitable] T1602 has 'mennitable' here — evidently a misprint, which was corrected to 'inevitable' in T1633.
⁴⁴ rest] Another calque from the Italian (though similar uses are recorded in the *OED*, and are probably due to the interference of French); here with the meaning of 'remain'.
⁴⁵ At fourteen syllables, one of the longest and most irregular lines in the English play.
⁴⁶ Dymock's verse makes the pattern of agency in these lines near-incomprehensible: Lucrina is bending her knees in front of her lover's feet — the feet that had pursued her so long and in vain (I. 2. 443–45).
⁴⁷ attending] waiting. Another calque from the Italian, though of course the English verb 'attend' can be used with the meaning of 'wait on'.
⁴⁸ Again, the syntax is confusing: judge by this blow the nature of the lover that you left, and of the one you pursued.
⁴⁹ stands] 'stand' in T1602, sensibly corrected to 'stands' in T1633.

Scarce yet assured whether she wounded were
With grief, or with the sword. At last, as soon
330 As she recovered had her spright, and speech,
She plaining says: Oh faithful valiant love!
Oh too late known! That by thy death hast giv'n
Me life and death at once. If 'twere a fault
To leave thee so, behold, I'll mend it now,
335 Eternally uniting both our souls.
And therewithal she takes the sword, all warm,
With the blood of her too late lovèd friend,
And strikes it through her heart, falling upon
Amintas, that was scarcely dead as yet,
340 And felt perchance that fall. Such was their end,
To such a wretched end did too much love,
And too much treachery conduct them both.

MIRTILLO
Oh wretched Shepherd, and yet fortunate,
That hadst so large and famous scope to show
345 Thy troth, and waken lively pity of thy death
Within another's breast. But what did follow?
Was Cynthia pleased, found they a remedy?

ERGASTO
Somewhat it slaked, but yet not quite put out:
For after that a year was finishèd,
350 Her rage began afresh, so that of force
They driven were unto the oracle
To ask new counsel, but brought back again
An answer much more woeful than the first.
Which was to sacrifice then,[50] and each after year,
355 A maid, or woman, to our angry power,
Even till the third and past the fourth degree:[51]
So should one's blood for many satisfy.
Besides, she did upon th'unhappy sex
Impose a wretched and a cruel law,
360 And, if you mark their nature, inobservable.
A law recorded with vermilion blood:

[50] then] Both T1602 and T1633 have 'them' here, but it is clearly a misprint: 'Che si sacrasse allora' (1. 2. 488).
[51] This confusing line is probably due to a misunderstanding of the Italian word 'lustro', meaning a period of five years. What Ergasto says in the Italian play is merely that the virgins or women should be at least fifteen years old, but not older than twenty (between three and four *lustri*; 1. 2. 490).

Whatever maid or woman broken had
Their faith in love, and were contaminate,
If they should find none that would die for them
365 They were condemned without remission.
To these our grievous great calamities,
The fathers hoped to find a happy end,
By this desirèd marriage day. For afterward
Having demanded of the oracle
370 What end the heavens prescribèd had our ill,
Answer was giv'n in such like words as these:
No end there is to that which you offends,
Till two of heaven's issue love unite;
And for the ancient fault of that false wight
375 A faithful shepherd's pity make amends.
Now is there not in all Arcadia
Other boughs left of that celestial root
Save Amarillis and this Silvio,
Th'one of Pan's seed, th'other of Hercules'.
380 Nor to our mischief yet hath never hapt
That male and female met at any time
Till now. Therefore good reason Montane hath
To hope, though all things sort not to the oracle.[52]
Yet here's a good foundation laid: the rest
385 High fates have in their bosoms bred,
And will bring forth at this great marriage day.

MIRTILLO
Oh poor Mirtillo! wretched man!
So many cruel enemies? Such wars?
To work my death cannot great love suffice,
390 But that the fates their arms will exercise?[53]

ERGASTO
This cruel love, Mirtillo, feeds himself
With tears, and grief, but's never satisfied.
I promise thee to set my wits a work,
That the fair nymph shall hear thee speak. Let's go!
395 These burning sighs do not, as they do seem,
Bring any cooling to th'inflamèd heart,
But rather are huge and impetuous winds,
That blow the fire, and make it greater prove,

[52] Though things do not seem to turn out exactly as the oracle foretold.
[53] There is no rhyming couplet in the Italian play (1. 2. 529-30) — which makes this distich of iambic pentameters even more reminiscent of Elizabethan drama.

With swelling whirlwinds of tempestuous love,
400 Which unto wretched lovers always bears
Thick clouds of grief, and showers of dreary tears.

Act 1, Scene 3
CORISCA

Who ever saw or heard a stranger and
A fonder passion of[54] this foolish love?
Both love, and hate, in one self heart combined
405 With such a wondrous mixture: as I know not how,
Or which of them hath got the deeper root.
If I Mirtillo's beauty do behold,
His gracious countenance, good behaviour,
Actions, customs, words and manly looks,
410 Love me assails with such a puissant fire
That I burn altogether. And it seems
Other affections are quite vanquishèd with this.
But when I think upon th'obstinate love
He to another bears, and that for her
415 He doth despise (I will be bold to say)
My famous beauty of a thousand sought,
I hate him so, I so abhor the man,
That's impossible methinks at all
One spark of love for him should touch my heart.
420 Thus with myself sometime I say: oh, if I could
Enjoy my sweet Mirtillo! Were he mine,
And had not others interest in him,
Oh more than any other happy Corisca!
And then in me upflames such great good will,
425 And such a gentle love to him, that I resolve
Straight to discover all my heart to him,
To follow him, and humbly sue to him:[55]
Nay more, even to fall down and worship him.
On th'other side, I all reclaimèd say,[56]
430 A nice proud fool? One that disdaineth me?
One that can love another, and despise myself?
One that can look on me, and not adore me?
One that can so defend him from my look

---

[54] of] than.
[55] sue to him] beg him.
[56] reclaimèd] recalled to myself, or reclaiming against him. A strange usage, not justified by Corisca's resentment in Italian ('i' mi risento'; I. 3. 578).

That he dies not for love? And I that should
See him (as I have many more ere this)
An humble suppliant before my feet,
Am humble suppliant at his feet myself.
Then such a rage at him possesseth me
That I disdain my thoughts should think on him,[57]
Mine eyes should look on him. His very name,
And all my love, I worse than death do hate.
Then would I have him the woefulst wight alive,
And with these hands then could I kill the wretch.
Thus hate and love, spite and desire make war.
I that have been till now tormenting flame
To thousand hearts must languish now myself,
And in my ill know others' wretchedness.
I that so many years in cities, streets, courts
Have been invincible to worthy friends,
Mocking their many hopes, their great desires,
Now conquered am with silly rustic love
Of a base shepherd's brat.[58] Oh above all
Wretched Corisca now. What shall I do
To mitigate this amorous furious rage?
Whilst other women have a heap of loves
I have no other but Mirtillo only.
Am I not stoutly furnishèd? Oh thousand times
Ill-counselled fool![59] That now reducèd art
Into the poverty of one sole love:
Corisca was ne'er such a fool before.
What's faith? What's constancy? But fables feigned
By jealous men, and names of vanity
Simple women to deceive. Faith in a woman's heart
(If faith in any woman's heart there be)
Can neither virtue nor yet goodness be,
But hard necessity of love, a wretched law
Of beauty weak that pleaseth only one
Because she is not gracious in the eyes of more.
A beauteous nymph, sought too by multitudes
Of worthy lovers, if she be content
With only one, and all the rest despise,

---

[57] This personification of the lover's thoughts is wholly Dymock's.

[58] Corisca is presented as the experienced citizen and courtier, an outsider in the unsullied pastoral world of Arcadia.

[59] Ill-counselled] Again, a calque, though this time a comprehensible one: the Italian is 'malconsigliata' (1. 3. 616; 'Mal consigliata' in S1591).

Either she is no woman, or if so she be,
She is a fool. What's beauty worth unseen?
Or seen, unsought? Or sought too but of one?
475 The more our lovers be, the greater men,[60]
The surer pledge[61] have we in this wild world
That we are creatures glorious and rare.
The goodly splendour of a beauteous nymph
Is to have many friends. So in good towns
480 Wise women ever do.[62] It is a fault,
A foolish trick, all to refuse for one.
What one cannot, many can well perform:
Some serve, some give, some fit for other use.[63]
So in the city lovely ladies do,
485 Where I by wit, and by example too,
Of a great lady learned the art of love.
Corisca, would she say, let thy
Lovers and thy garments be alike.
Have many, use, wear but one, and change often.
490 Too much conversing breedeth noisomeness,
And noisomeness despite, which turns to hate.
We cannot worser do than fill our friends:
Let them go hungry rather from thee still.
So did I always, always loving store,
495 One for my hand, another for mine eye;
The best I ever for my bosom kept,
None for my heart, as near as e'er I could.
And now I know not how Mirtillo comes
Me to torment; now must I sigh, and worse,
500 Sigh for myself, deceiving no man else.[64]
Now must I rob my limbs of their repose,
Mine eyes of sleep, and watch the break of day.
Now do I wander through these shadowed woods,
Seeking the footsteps of my hated love.
505 What must Corisca do? Shall I entreat him?

---

[60] Here Donno eliminates the comma, thus obscuring the fact that Corisca prizes both number and rank ('E quanto sono | più frequenti gli amanti e di più pregi'; I. 3. 634-35).
[61] By translating 'pegno' literally as 'pledge', Dymock creates a confusing passage. What Corisca means is that having many lovers, and of great rank, reassures a woman that she is a rare creature.
[62] women] 'men' in T1602 and T1633 — evidently a misprint, not least because 'women' rounds off the iambic pentameter.
[63] Here Dymock skips three lines on the usefulness of jealousy (I. 3. 639-43).
[64] 500] I must sigh in earnest, not to deceive men.

No: my hate not gives me leave. I'll give him o'er?
Nor will my love consent.⁶⁵ What shall I do?
Prayers and subtleties I will attempt:
I will bewray my love,⁶⁶ but not as mine.
510 If this prevail not, then I'll make disdain
Find out a memorable huge revenge.
Mirtillo, if thou canst not like my love,
Then shalt thou try my hate. And Amarillis,
Thou shalt repent thou e'er my rival wert.
515 Well, to your costs you both shall quickly prove,
What rage in her can do that thus doth love.⁶⁷

Act 1, Scene 4

TITIRUS, MONTANUS, DAMETAS

TITIRUS
So help me Gods, I know I now do speak
To one that understands more than I do.
These oracles are still more doubtful than
520 We take them, for their words are like to knives,
Which taken by the hafts are fit for use,⁶⁸
But by the edges held, they may do harm.
That Amarillis, as you argue, is
By the high heavenly destinies elected for
525 Arcadia's universal health: who ought
More to desire, or to esteem the same
Than I that am her father? But when I regard
That which the oracle foretold, ill do the signs
Agree with our great hopes: since love should them
530 Unite, how falls it out he flies from her?
How can hate and despite bring forth love's fruit?
Ill could he contradict, had heavens ordained it.
But since he doth contrary it, 'tis clear
Heavens do not will: for if so they would
535 That Amarillis should be Silvio's wife,
A lover, not a huntsman, him they would have made.

---

⁶⁵ Nor will my love consent] Nor will my heart consent to give him up.
⁶⁶ bewray] divulge.
⁶⁷ There is no concluding couplet in the source ('e finalmente proverete entrambi | quell che può sdegno in cor di donna amante'; I. 3. 688-89).
⁶⁸ hafts] handles.

MONTANUS
Do you not see he is a child as yet?
He hath attained scarcely to eighteen years.
All in good time he may yet taste of love.

TITIRUS
540 Taste of a beast; he'll never woman like.[69]

MONTANUS
Many things alter in a young man's heart.

TITIRUS
But always love is natural to youth.

MONTANUS
It is unnatural where years do want.

TITIRUS
Love always flowers in our green time of age.

MONTANUS
545 It doth but flower, 'tis quite without all fruit.

TITIRUS
With timely flowers love ever brings forth fruit.
Hither I came not for to jest, Montane,
Nor to contend with you. But I the father am
Of a dear only child, and (if 't be lawful so to say)
550 A worthy child, and by your leave of many sought.

MONTANUS
Titirus, if the destinies have not ordained
This marriage, yet the faith they gave on earth
Binds them unto 't, which if they violate,
They violate their vow to Cynthia,
555 Who is enraged 'gainst us, how much thou knowst.
But for as much as I discover can
The secret counsels of th'eternal powers,
This knot was knit by th'hand of destiny.
All to good end will sort, be of good cheer.
560 I'll tell you now a dream I had last night.
I saw a thing which makes my ancient hope
Revive within my heart, more than before.

---

[69] This line is more obscure than its Italian source. In Guarini, Titiro merely asks how it can be possible for a young man to feel love for a beast, but not for a young woman ('E'l può sentir di fèra, e non di ninfa?'; I. 4. 717).

TITIRUS
Dreams in the end prove dreams, but what saw you?

MONTANUS
Do you remember that same woeful night
565 When swelling Ladon[70] overflowed his banks,
So that the fishes swam where birds did breed,
And in a moment did the ravenous flood
Take men and beasts by heaps and herds away?
Oh, sad remembrance. In that very night
570 I lost my child, more dear than was my heart:
Mine only child, in cradle warmly laid,
Living, and dead, dearly beloved of me.
The torrent took him hence ere we could prove[71]
To give him succour, being buried quite
575 In terror, sleep, and darkness of the night:
Nor could we ever find the cradle where he lay,
By which I guess some whirlpit swallowed both.[72]

TITIRUS
Who can guess otherwise? and I remember now
You told me of this your mishap before:
580 A memorable misadventure sure,
And you may say you have two sons begot,
One to the woods, the other to the waves.

MONTANUS
Perhaps the piteous heavens will restore
My first son's loss in him that liveth yet.
585 Still must we hope. Now listen to my tale.
The time when light and darkness strove together,
This one for night, that other for the day,
Having watched all the night before, with thought
To bring this marriage to a happy end,
590 At last, with length of weariness, mine eyes
A pleasing slumber closed, when I this vision saw.
Methought I sat on famous Alpheios' bank,
Under a leafy plane tree, with a baited hook
Tempting the fishes in the stream, in midst
595 Whereof there rose methought an agèd man,

---

[70] Ladon] A tributary of the Alpheios river. The narrative function of this inundation will become apparent in Act v, when Mirtillo's real ancestry is revealed. See also Montanus' dream below, prefiguring that anagnorisis.
[71] prove] Another Italian calque from 'provar', here with the meaning of 'try'.
[72] whirlpit] whirlpool.

His head and beard dropping down silver tears,
Who gently raught[73] to me with both his hands
A naked child, saying, behold thy son,
Take heed thou killst him not. And with that word
600 He divèd down again. When straight the skies
Waxed black with clouds, threatening a dismal shower,
And I, afraid, the child took in mine arms,
Crying, ah heavens, and will you in an instant then
Both give and take away my child again?
605 When on the sudden all the sky waxed clear
And in the river fell a thousand bows
And thousand arrows, broken all to shivers.
The body of the plane tree trembled there,
And out of it there came a subtle voice
610 Which said, Arcadia shall be fair again.
So is the image of this gentle dream
Fixed in my heart, that still methinks I see 't:
But above all the courteous agèd man.
For this when you me met I coming was[74]
615 Unto the temple for to sacrifice,
To give my dream's presage prosperous success.

TITIRUS
Our dreams are rather representments vain[75]
Of idle hopes than any things to come:
Only day's thoughts made fables for the night.

MONTANUS
620 The mind doth not sleep ever with the flesh,
But is more watchful then, because the eyes
Do not lead it a wandering where they go.

TITIRUS
Well, of our children what the heavens disposèd have
Is quite unknown to us; but sure it is
625 Yours 'gainst the law of nature feels not love,[76]
And mine hath but the bond of his faith giv'n

---

[73] raught] reached, gave. As shown by the citations in the *OED*, this apophonic form of the past tense was still in infrequent use at the beginning of the seventeenth century.
[74] Occasionally, the impulse to write a perfect iambic pentameter leads Dymock to these syntactic extremes.
[75] representments] presentiments. There is no record in the *OED* of the word being used with this meaning.
[76] Your son does not feel love (and that is against the laws of nature).

For her reward.⁷⁷ I cannot say she loves,
But well I wot she hath made many love:
And 'tis unlike⁷⁸ she tastes not that she makes
630 So many taste. Methinks she's altered much
From that she was: for full of sport and mirth
She's wont to be. But 'tis a grievous thing
To keep a woman married and unmarried thus.
For like a rose that in some garden grows,
635 How dainty 'tis against the sun doth rise,⁷⁹
Perfuming with sweet odours round about,
Bidding the humming bees to honey feast:
But if you then neglect to gather it,
And suffer Titan in his midday course⁸⁰
640 To scorch her sides, and burn her dainty seat,
Then ere sunset discolourèd she falls,
And nothing worth upon the shadowed hedge.
Even so a maid whom mother's care doth keep,
Shutting her heart from amorous desires.
645 But if the piercing looks of hungry lovers' eyes
Come but to view her, if she hear him sigh,
Her heart soon opes, her breast soon takes in love:
Which if for shame she hide, or fear contain,
The silent wretch in deep desire consumes.⁸¹
650 So fadeth beauty if that fire endure,
And losing time,⁸² good fortune's lost be sure.

MONTANUS
Be of good cheer, let not these human fears
Confound thy spright, let's put our trust i'th'Gods
And pray to them ('tis meet) for good success.
655 Our children are their offspring, and be sure
They will not see them lost that others' keep.⁸³
Go'w,⁸⁴ let us to the temple jointly go,

⁷⁷ Dymock probably failed to understand this passage. Titirus is saying that his daughter, so far, has only felt the obligation of the betrothal without its advantages ('e che la mia fin qui l'obbligo solo | ha de la data fé, non la mercede'; I. 4. 846–47).
⁷⁸ unlike] unlikely.
⁷⁹ The first hemistich of this line is unclear. In all this passage, Dymock is condensing Guarini's much longer natural simile (nine lines vs nineteen; I. 4. 858–76).
⁸⁰ This added mythological reference is to one particular Greek titan, Helios (the sun).
⁸¹ consumes] is consumed.
⁸² losing time] if time is lost.
⁸³ 656] The gods, who preserve the offspring of common humans, will certainly defend their own.
⁸⁴ Go'w] go we, let us go. This contraction appears to be Dymock's invention.

And sacrifice you a he-goat to Pan,
I a young bull to mighty Hercules.
660 He that the herd makes thrive can therewithal
Make him thrive that with the profits of his herd
Hallows the altars. Faithful Dametas,
Go thou and fetch a young and lovely bull
As any's in the herd, and bring it by the mountain's way,
665 I at the Temple will attend for thee.[85]

TITIRUS
A he-goat bring, Dametas, from my herd. *Exeunt Montanus and Titirus*

DAMETAS
Both one and other I will well perform.
I pray the Gods, Montane, thy dream do sort
Unto as good an end as thou dost hope.
670 I know remembrance of thy son thou lost
Inspires thee with a happy prophecy.

Act 1, Scene 5
SATYR alone

Like frost to grass, like drought to gentle flowers,
Like lightning unto corn, like worms to seeds,
Like nets to deer, like lime to silly birds,
675 So to mankind is Love a cruel foe.
He that Love likened unto fire knew well
His perfidous and wicked kind.[86] For look
But on this fire, how fine a thing it is!
But touch it, and 'tis then a cruel thing.
680 The world hath not a monster more to dread.
It ravens worse than beasts,[87] and strikes more deep
Than edgèd steel, and like the wind it flies:
And where it planteth his imperious feet,
Each force doth yield, all power giveth place.
685 Even so this love, if we it but behold
In two fair eyes and in a golden tress,
Oh how it pleaseth! oh how then it seems

---

[85] Again, 'attend' for 'attendo' ('I'll wait').
[86] perfidous] There are no other recorded occurrences of this variant spelling of the adjective in the *OED* — so that Donno feels she has to edit the word as 'perfid'ous'. However, 'perfidious' itself, as a borrowing from Latin, was probably young enough for Dymock to create an alternative version from Italian for metrical reasons. He uses 'perfidous' twice and 'perfidious' three times in the course of the play.
[87] ravens] eats ravenously.

To breathe out joy, and promise largely peace!
But if you it approach, and tempt it once,
690 So that it creep and gather force in you,
Hircane no tigers, Liby no lions hath,[88]
Nor poisonous worms, with teeth or stings so fierce
That can surpass or equal love's disease,
More dreadful than is hell, than death itself,
695 Sweet pity's foe, the minister of rage:
And to conclude, Love void of any love.
Why speak I thus of Love? Why blame him thus?
Is he the cause that the whole world in love,
Or rather love-dissembling, sinneth so?
700 Oh, woman's treachery! That is the cause
That hath begotten love this infamy.
However Love be in his nature good,
With them his goodness suddenly he loseth.
They never suffer him to touch their hearts,
705 But in their faces only build his bower.
Their care, their pomp, and all their whole delight
Is in the bark of a bepainted face.[89]
'Tis not in them now faith with faith to grace,
And to contend in love with him that loves,
710 Into two breasts dividing but one will:
Now all their labour is, with burnished gold
To dye their hair, and tie it up in curls,
Therein to snare unwary lovers in.
Oh what a stinking thing it is to see them take
715 A pencil up and paint their bloodless cheeks,
Hiding the faults of nature and of time,
Making the pale to blush, the wrinkled plain,[90]
The black seem white, faults mending with far worse.
Then with a pair of pincers do they pull
720 Their eyebrows till they smart again.
But this is nothing, though it be too much,
For all their customs are alike to these.
What is it that they use, which is not counterfeit?
Ope they their mouths? They lie. Move they their eyes?
725 They counterfeit their looks. If so they sigh,

[88] Hircane [...] Liby no lions hath] Hyrcania is a region of ancient Persia. 'Liby' stands for Libya, or, metonymically, northern Africa.
[89] bark] This very strange metaphor originates in Guarini's 'scorza' — meaning the outer rind, i.e., the outer appearance of a woman's face (I. 5. 967).
[90] plain] smooth. Guarini has the similar-sounding verb 'appiani' here (I. 5. 982).

Their sighs dissembled are. In sum, each act,
Each look, each gesture, is a very lie.
Nor is this yet the worst. 'Tis their delight
Them to deceive even most, that trust them most;
730 And love them least, that are most worthy love;
True faith to hate worser than death itself.
These be the tricks that make love so perverse.
Then is the fault, faithless Corisca, thine?
Or rather mine, that have believed thee so?
735 How many troubles have I for thy sake sustained?[91]
I now repent, nay more I am ashamed.
Lovers, believe me: women, once adored,
Are worser than the grisly powers of hell.
Straight by their valour[92] vaunt they that they are
740 The same you by your folly fashion them.
Let go these base sighs, prayers and plaints,
Fit weapons for women and children only.
Once did I think that prayers, plaints and sighs
Might in a woman's heart have stirrèd up
745 The flames of love, but tush! I was deceived.
Then if thou wouldst thy mistress conquer, leave
These silly toys, and close thou up all love.
Do that which love and nature teacheth thee,
For modesty is but the outward virtue of
750 A woman's face. Wherefore to handle her with modesty
Is a mere fault; she, though she use it, loves it not.
A tender-hearted lover shalt thou not,
Corisca, ever find me more, but like a man
I will assail and pierce thee through and through.
755 Twice have I taken thee, and twice again
Thou hast escaped (I know not how) my hands:
But if thou com'st the third time in my reach,
I'll fetter thee for running then away.[93]

---

[91] These occasional twelve-syllable lines work better, on the metrical plane, when they are iambic and split along the middle like a French alexandrine (see, a few lines above, 'O what a stinking thing it is to see them take').

[92] Straight by their valour] This expression is unclear, and one suspects that Dymock did not quite catch Guarini's meaning. In the source the satyr complains that women boast they are as valuable in themselves as you yourself esteem them to be ('ché d'esser tal per suo valor si vanta, | qual tu per tua viltà la figni ed orni'; I. 5. 1027–28). Clearly, Dymock wanted to insert the word 'valour' there, but did not understand its co-text.

[93] I will fetter you so that you will be unable to flee from me.

Th'art wont to pass these woods;⁹⁴ I like a hound
760 Will hunt thee out. Oh what a sweet revenge
I mean to take: I mean to make thee prove⁹⁵
What 'tis unjustly to betray thy love.   *Exit.*

CHORUS

Oh high and puissant law writ, rather born
Within Jove's mighty breast,⁹⁶
765 Whose ever sweet and lovely loving force
Towards that good which we unseen suborn⁹⁷
Our hearts doth pull and wills doth wrest,
And even nature's self to it doth force;
Not only our frail corpse
770 Whose sense scarce sees, is born and dies again
As daily hours wax and wain;
But even inward causes, hidden seeds
That moves and governs our eternal deeds.
If great with child the world do wondrous frame
775 So many beauties still,⁹⁸
And if within as far as sun doth see
To the mighty moon and stars' titanian fame⁹⁹
A living spright doth fill
With his male value this same vast degree,
780 If thence man's offspring be,
The plants have life, and beasts both good and bad,
Whether the earth be clad
With flowers, or nipped have her ill-featherèd wing,¹⁰⁰
It still comes from thine everlasting spring.
785 Nor this alone, but that which hopes of fire¹⁰¹

---

⁹⁴ Th'art] Thou art. T1602 has 'T' hart', evidently a misprint occasioned by the mention of a hound in the same line ('The hart'). The misprint is corrected in T1633.
⁹⁵ prove] Again, meaning 'feel' — but this time without 'provare' in the Italian.
⁹⁶ In the chorus, Dymock attempts to follow Guarini's versification more closely, with dubious results. In particular, he renders the Italian *settenari* as shorter lines, normally of six or eight syllables.
⁹⁷ suborn] The meaning of this verb in the context is unclear. It is clearly introduced to follow Guarini's rhyme pattern.
⁹⁸ 774–75] If the world still gives birth to so many beautiful things.
⁹⁹ While much in Guarini's chorus is hard to follow, a lot in Dymock's is obscure and ungrammatical. The meaning of this allusion to Book VI of the *Aeneid* (lines 724–26) is simply that a (masculine) spirit inhabits all celestial and sublunar bodies (I. Chorus. 1086–89).
¹⁰⁰ or nipped [...] wing] Again, Dymock seems to have misunderstood Guarini's metaphorical description of the snow covering the earth ('o se canuta ha la rugosa fronte'; I. Ch. 1093).
¹⁰¹ hopes of fire] Here Dymock misreads Guarini's 'spera' (I. Ch. 1095; meaning *sfera*, celestial

    Sheds into mortal wights:
    From whence stars gentle, now straight fierce are found,
    Clad in good fortune's or mishap's attire,
    From whence life's frailest lights
790 The hour of birth have, or of death the bound;[102]
    That which makes rise or else pull down
    In their disturbed affects all human will,
    And giving seems, or taking still[103]
    Fortune, to whom the world would this were given,[104]
795 All from thy sovereign bounty is deriven.
    Oh word inevitably true and sure,[105]
    If it thy meaning is[106]
    Arcadia shall after so many woes
    Find out new rest and peace, new life procure;
800 If the foretold bliss[107]
    Which the great oracle did erst expose
    Of the fair fatal marriage rose
    Proceed from thee and in thy heavenly mind
    Her fixèd place doth find;
805 If that same voice do not dissemble still,
    Who hinders then the working of thy will?
    See love's and pity's foe, a wayward swain,
    A proud and cruel youth
    That comes from heaven, and yet with heaven contends.[108]
810 See then another lover, faithful in vain,[109]
    Battering a heart's chaste truth,[110]
    Who with his flames perhaps thy will offends;

body) for 'speranza' ('hope'). Hence the strange idea that 'hopes of fire' shed things into mortal beings. See Introduction, p. 20.

[102] From whence [...] bound] Again, it is doubtful whether Guarini understood this passage, not least because of those 'hopes of fire' above. What is meant is that even the destiny of mortals, commonly attributed to the influence of stars, stands within the compass of divine volition (I. Ch. 1095–105).

[103] Another difficult line, though this time for reasons having to do with the rhyme pattern. Guarini's line is 'e par che doni e toglia' (I. Ch. 1103), in the sense that the initial 'spera' appears to give humans good fortune, and then to take it away.

[104] to whom the world would this were given] Guarini's verb is the subjunctive 'ascriva' — humans (the world) attribute their fortunes to the motions of the stars (I. Ch. 1104).

[105] word] Fate, as proceeding from Jove's will.

[106] meaning] Guarini's word is 'concetto' (I. Ch. 1108; intention; if it be thy will).

[107] foretold] Both in T1602 and T1633 this is printed as 'fore-told-on'. The meaning or function of that additional 'on', however, is unclear (again, it is probably there for metrical reasons).

[108] Silvio.

[109] Mirtillo.

[110] In Italian, 'combatte un cor pudico' (i.e., he fights against a chaste heart; I. Ch. 1120).

The less that he attends[111]
   Pity to's plaints, reward to his desert,
815 More strongly flames in faith his heart.[112]
   Fatal this beauty is to him that it high prizeth,
   Being destinèd to him that it despiseth.
   Thus in itself, alas, divided stands
   This heavenly power,
820 And thus one fate another jostles still,
   Yet neither conquered is, neither commands.
   False human hopes that tower
   And plant a siege to th'elemental hill,
   Rebellious unto heaven's will,
825 Arming poor thoughts like giant fools again,
   Lovers and no lovers vain.[113]
   Who would have thought love and disdain, blind things,
   Should mount above the sovereign starry wings?
   But thou that standst above both stars and fate,
830 And with thy wit divine,
   Great mover of the skies, dost them restrain,
   Behold: we thee beseech our doubtful state
   With destiny combine,
   And father's loving zeal love and disdain
835 Mix flame and frozen vain.[114]
   Let them that shunned to love, now learn to love,
   Let not that other moan.
   Ah, let not others' blindest folly thus
   Thy gently promised pity take from us.
840 But who doth know? Perhaps this same that seems
   An unavoidable mischievous estate
   May prove right fortunate.
   How fond a thing it is for mortal sight
   To search into the eternal sun's high light!

---

[111] attends] Another calque, this time with the meaning of 'expects'. The less Mirtillo expects to see his complaints pitied and his deserts rewarded, the more he feels love burning in his heart.

[112] strongly] T1602 has 'straungely', but in this case T1633 appears to be correct.

[113] False [...] vain] Guarini is comparing these lovers to the earth-born giants who, in Greek mythology, tried to defeat the gods (I. Ch. 1135; see Dymock's 'giant fools').

[114] And father's [...] vain] Again, these two lines are hardly comprehensible. The chorus is asking Jove/Fate to reconcile love and disdain with destiny, and to temper flame and ice with fatherly zeal (I. Ch. 1143–45). Maybe 'vain' is to be read as 'vein' ('frozen vein'; the *OED* includes 'vain' in the list of variant spellings), but it is mostly the syntax that makes the passage so hard to read.

Act II, Scene 1
ERGASTO, MIRTILLO

ERGASTO
How I have searched along the riverside,
About the meadows, fountains, and the hills,
To find thee out: which now I have, the gods be praised.

MIRTILLO
Ah that thy news, Ergasto, may deserve
5 This haste. But bringst thou life or death?

ERGASTO
This though I had I would not give it thee.
That do I hope to give thee, though I have it not
As yet. But fie, thou must not suffer grief
To overthrow thy senses thus. Live, man, and hope.
10 But to the purpose of my coming now:
Ormino hath a sister, knowst her not?
A tall big wench, a merry-countenanced nymph[115]
With yellow hair, somewhat high-colourèd.

MIRTILLO
What is her name?

ERGASTO
           Corisca.

MIRTILLO
                      I know her well,
15 And heretofore have spoke with her.

ERGASTO
Then know that she (and see withal your luck)
Is now become, I know not by what privilege,
Companion to your beauteous Amarillis.
I have discovered all your love to her,
20 And this which you desire, and readily
She me hath giv'n her faith to bring't about.

MIRTILLO
Oh happy Mirtillo if this same prove true:
But said she nothing of the means whereby?

---

[115] countenanced] 'countnaun'st' in T1602: it should be read as a disyllable.

ERGASTO
Nothing as yet, nor would she that conclude
25 Until she knew the manner of your love.
How it began, and what hath hapt therein,
That she might easilier spy into the heart
Of your beloved nymph, and better know
How to dispose by prayers or by fraud
30 Of her request. For this I came to you,
And make me now acquainted from the head[116]
With all the history of your dear love.

MIRTILLO
So will I do, but yet, Ergasto, know
This memory (a bitter hopeless thing)
35 Is like a firebrand tossèd in the wind,
By which how much the fire increaseth still
So much the brand with blazing flame consumes.[117]
Oh piercing shaft made by some power divine,
The which the more we seek to draw it out,
40 The faster hold it takes, the deeper root.
Well can I tell you, that these lover's hopes
Are full of vanities and falsehoods still;
Love's fruit is bitter, though the root be sweet.
In that sweet time when days advantage get
45 Above the nights, then when the year begins,
This dainty pilgrim, beauty's bright new sun,
Came with her countenance like another spring
T'illuminate my then thrice happy soil
Of Pisa and Eglidis fair.[118] Brought by her mother
50 To see the sacrifices and the sports
That celebrated in those solemn days
Were unto Jove.[119] Where while she meant to make
Her eyesight blessed with that same spectacle,
She blessed the spectacle with her fair eyes,
55 Being love's greatest miracle beneath the skies.
No sooner had I seen that face, but straight

---

[116] from the head] from the beginning. Another calque ('da capo'; II. 1. 41).
[117] consumes] burns itself.
[118] Pisa and Eglidis] Pisa and Elis, ancient towns of the Peloponnese, both in the proximity of Olympia. Elis is always 'Elide' in Guarini, but Dymock calls it alternately 'Eglidis', 'Elidis' and 'Elide'.
[119] The Olympic Games, held in honour of Zeus.

I burnt, defending not the foremost look[120]
Which through mine eyes into my breast directed
Such an imperious beauty, as methought did say:
60 Mirtillo, yield thy heart, for it is mine.

ERGASTO
Oh in our breasts what mighty power hath love?
There's none can tell, save they the same which prove.[121]

MIRTILLO
See how industrious love can work even in
The simplest breasts. A sister which I had
65 I made acquainted with my thoughts, who was
By chance companion to my cruel nymph,
The time she staid in Pisa and Elide.
She faithful counsel and good aid me gave.
She dressed me finely in one of her gowns,
70 Circling my temples with a periwig
Which gracefully she trimmèd up with flowers.
A quiver and a bow hung at my side;
She taught me furthermore to feign my voice
And looks, for in my face as then there grew no hair.
75 This done, she me conducted where the nymph
Was wont to sport herself, and where we found
A noble troupe of maidens of Megara,[122]
By blood or love allièd to my goddess.
'Mongst them she stood like to a princely rose
80 Among a heap of humble violets.
We had not long been there before uprose
One of the maidens of Megara, and thus bespake:
Why stand we idly still in such a time,
When palms and famous trophies are so rife?
85 Have not we arms counterfeit fights to make
As well as men? Sisters, be ruled by me:
Let's prove among ourselves our arms in jest,[123]
That when we come to earnest them with men,
We may them better use. Let's kiss, and strive
90 Who can kiss sweetliest among ourselves:
And let this garland be the victor's gain.
All at the proposition laughed, and all

[120] defending not] having no defence against ('e, senza far difesa'; II. 1. 81).
[121] save they the same which prove] save those who ('which') feel it.
[122] Megara] Another Attic town.
[123] prove] try.

Unto it straight agreed. Straightway began
A fight confusèd, no signal we attended.
95 Which by her seen that first ordained the sport,
She says again: let's make her worthy judge
That hath the fairest mouth. All soon agreed
And Amarillis chose. Who sweetly bowing down
Her beauteous eyes, in modest blushing stained,[124]
100 Did show they were as fair within as th'were without.
Or that her face her rich-clad mouth envièd,
And would be clothed in pompous purple too,
As who should say, I am as fair as it.

ERGASTO
In good time did you change into a nymph,
105 A happy token of good luck to come.

MIRTILLO
Now did the beauteous judge sit in her place,
According as the Megarence prescribed.[125]
Each went by lot to make due proof of her
Rare mouth, that heavenly paragon of sweetness,
110 That blessed mouth that may be likened to
A perfumed Indian shell of oriental pearl,
Op'ning the dainty treasure, mixed with honey sweet
And purple blush. I cannot, my Ergasto, tell
Th'inexplicable sweetness which I felt
115 Out of that kiss. But look, what Cypre's canes[126]
Or hives of Hybla have, are nothing all
Compared with that which then I tasted there.

ERGASTO
Oh happy theft, sweet kiss.

MIRTILLO
                        Yea sweet,
But yet not gracious, for it wanted still
120 The better part: love gave it, but love not
Returned it back.

---

[124] stained] reddened (II. 1. 153; 'di modesto rossor tutta si tinse').
[125] Megarence] Megarian.
[126] canes] Both T1602 and T1633 have 'caves' here, but it is clearly a misprint, as Dymock, given the context, could not have confused 'canne' with 'cave'. The sugarcanes of Cyprus and the honey of Megara Hyblaea were proverbial in Hellenistic writing (II. 1. 185).

ERGASTO

                But then how did you
When it was your lot to kiss?

MIRTILLO

                     Unto those lips
My soul did wholly fly, and all my life
So shut therein, as in a little space
125 It waxèd nothing but a kiss.[127] And all
My other limbs stood strengthless trembling still
When I approachèd to her lightning looks.
Knowing my deed was theft and deceit[128]
I feared the majesty of her fair face,
130 But she assures me with a pleasing smile,
And puts me forward more,[129] love sitting like
A bee upon two fresh and dainty roses close.[130]
Kissing, I tasted there the honey sweet,
But having kissed, I felt the lovely bee
135 Strike through my heart with his sharp piercing sting.
And being wounded thus, half desperate,
I thought t'have bitten those manslaughtering lips,
But that her odoriferous breath, like air divine,
Wakened my modesty, and still my rage.[131]

ERGASTO

140 This modesty molesteth lovers still.

MIRTILLO

Now were the lots fulfilled, and every one
With heedful minds the sentence did attend,[132]
When Amarillis, judging mine the best,
With her own hands she crowns my tresses with
145 The gentle garland kept for victory.
But never was shadeless meadow drier parched
Under the baleful fury of the heavenly dog[133]

---

[127] 123–25] Mirtillo's life was wholly encompassed within the kiss.
[128] T1633 adds the filler 'eake' to this line to round it off as an iambic pentameter, and Donno follows suit ('Knowing my deed was theft and eake deceit').
[129] The agency is confusing here. In the Italian Mirtillo, reassured by Amarillis's smile, dares to go further (II. 1. 207–09).
[130] close] One of Dymock's sound-driven translations. The Italian adjective is 'ascoso', hidden (II. 1. 212).
[131] still] Probably with the meaning of 'stilled', 'quelled' ('e quel furore estinse'; II. 1. 238).
[132] attend] await ('attendea'; II. 1. 243).
[133] heavenly dog] The constellation of the dog (Canis Major), whose brightest star, Sirius, is associated with summer.

Than was my heart in sunshine of that sweet,
Never so vanquished as in victory.
150 Yet had I power to take the garland off,
And reach it her, saying: to you belongs
Alone the same. 'Tis due to you, that made
Mine good by virtue of your mouth.
She gently took't and crowned herself therewith,
155 And with another that she wore crowned mine.[134]
'Tis this I wear thus drièd as you see.
It will I carry to my grave with me,
In dear remembrance of that happy day,
But more for sign[135] of my dead hopes' decay.

ERGASTO

160 Thou pity more than envy dost deserve,
That wert another Tantalus in love's delights,
That of a sport a torment true didst make.
Thou payest too dear for thy stolen delicates.[136]
But did she e'er perceive thy policies?

MIRTILLO

165 That know I not, Ergasto, yet thus much I know,
That in the time she made Elidis blessed
With her sweet countenance, she liberal was
Of pleasing looks to me. But thereof did
My cruel fates rob me so suddenly,
170 That I perceived it not till they were gone.
When I, drawn by the power of her beauteous look,
Leaving my home came hither, where thou knowst
My father had this poor habitacle.[137]
But now the day that with so fair a spring began,
175 Come to his western bound, thunders and lightens out:[138]
Ah, then I saw these were true signs of death.
Now had, alas, my tender father felt
My not-foreseen departure, and o'ercome

---

[134] mine] my head — but the cohesive link presupposed by the possessive is not present in the text.

[135] for sign] as a token ('per segno'; II. 1. 270).

[136] delicates] delicacies.

[137] habitacle] dwelling-place.

[138] This is clearer in the source text, partly because Dymock compresses a lot of lines in a short space. Taking advantage of an old Arcadian dwelling still belonging to his father, Mirtillo followed Amarillis there, but when he found her he discovered that her kindness had turned to hostility (II. 1. 286–98).

With grief, fell sick nigh hand to death,
180 Whereby I was constrainèd to return.
Ah, that return provèd the father's health
But deadly sickness to the son: for in short time
I languishèd and pinèd quite away.
Which held me from the time the sun had left
185 The Bull, until his entry into Capricorn.[139]
And so had still, had not my piteous father sought
For counsel to the oracle, which said
Only Arcadia could restore my health.
So I returned to see her that can heal
190 My body's grief (O oracle's false lie)
But makes my soul sick everlastingly.

ERGASTO
Strange tale thou tellst, Mirtillo, though't be true.
The only health to one that's desperate
Is to despair of health.[140] And now 'tis time
195 I go communicate with our Corisca.
Go to the fountain, you; there stay for me,
I'll make what haste I can.

MIRTILLO
                    Go happily.
The heavens, Ergasto, quit thy courtesy.

Act II, Scene 2
DORINDA, LUPINO, SILVIO

DORINDA
Oh fortunate delight, and care of my
200 Fair spiteful Silvio. Ah that I were
As dear unto thy cruel master as thou art.
Happy Melampo, he with that white hand
That nips my heart, thee softly stroking feeds.
With thee all day and all the night he is,
205 Whilst I that love him so, sigh still in vain.
And that which grieves me worst, he gives thee still
Kisses so sweet, that had I one of them
I should go blessed away. I cannot choose
But kiss Melampo. Now if the happy stars[141]

---

[139] 185] From April to December.
[140] *Aeneid* II. 354: 'Una salus victis, nullam sperare salutem'.
[141] the happy] These words should be read as two syllables ('th'appy' in both T1602 and T1633).

210 Of love sent thee to me because thou shouldst
     Find out his steps, go'w whither me great love,
     Thee nature teacheth.¹⁴² But I hear a horn
     Sound in these woods.

SILVIO
                    Uo ho ho, Melampo, ho!

DORINDA
     If my desire deceive me not, that is the voice
215 Of my beloved Silvio that calls his dog.
     He hath our labour saved.

SILVIO
                    Uo ho ho, Melampo, ho!

DORINDA
     Doubtless 'tis he: happy Dorinda, heavens
     Have sent him whom thou soughtst; 'tis best I put
     The dog aside, so may I win his love.
220 Lupino!

LUPINO
          What's your will?

DORINDA
                              Go hide thyself
     In that same thick,¹⁴³ and take the dog with thee.

LUPINO
     I go.

DORINDA
          And stir not till I call.

LUPINO
                              No more I will.

DORINDA
     Go soon.

LUPINO
               And call you soon, lest hunger make
     The dog believe I am a shoulder of mutton, and so fall to.

---

¹⁴² go'w [...] teacheth] let's go ('go'w') where I am taught to go by love, you by instinct.
¹⁴³ thick] thicket.

DORINDA

225 Go, get you hence, hen-hearted wretch.

SILVIO
Oh wretched me, whither shall I go
To follow thee, my dear, my faithful dog?
The dales, the mountains, I have sought with care,
All weary now I am. Cursed be the beast
230 Thou didst pursue. But see, a nymph: perhaps
She can tell news of him. Out upon her,
'Tis she that's still so troublesome to me.
I must dissemble. Fair and gracious nymph,
Did you my good Melampo see today?

DORINDA
235 I fair, good Silvio? Can you call me fair
That am not fair a whit unto your eyes?

SILVIO
Or fair or foul, did you not see my dog?
Answer to this, or I am quickly gone.

DORINDA
Still thou art forward unto her that thee adores.
240 Who would believe that in that smooth aspect[144]
Were harbourèd such ruggèd thoughts? Thou through
These savage woods and rocky hills pursu'st
A beast that flies thee, and consum'st thyself
In tracing out thy greyhound's steps: and me
245 Thou shunst and dost disdain that loves thee so.
Ah, leave these does that run so fast away,
Take hold of me, thy preordainèd prey.[145]

SILVIO
Nymph, I Melampo came to seek, not to lose time.
Farewell.

DORINDA
                    Do not so shun me, cruel Silvio,
250 I'll tell thee news of thy Melampo, man.

---

[144] aspect] appearance. Another calque ('aspetto'; II. 2. 387), though this time the usage finds analogous examples in Marlowe and Shakespeare (see *OED*).
[145] Dymock makes Dorinda more explicit here. In the source, she invites Silvio to give up the hunt for the kind of doe that flies away from him, and to follow a more loving, tamer doe ('segui amorosa e mansüeta damma'; II. 2. 394–95).

SILVIO
Thou jests, Dorinda.

DORINDA
                    Silvio, I protest
By that dear love that me thy handmaid makes,
I know where thy Melampo is that coursed the doe.

SILVIO
How did he lose her?[146]

DORINDA
                    Both dog and doe are in my power.

SILVIO
255 Both in your power?

DORINDA
                    Why, doth it grieve you then
That I them hold that do adore you so?

SILVIO
Dear Dorinda, quickly give me him.[147]

DORINDA
See, wavering child,[148] am I not fortunate
When a beast and a dog can make me dear to thee?[149]

SILVIO
260 Good reason too, but yet her I'll deceive.

DORINDA
What will you give me?

SILVIO
                    Two gilded apples
Which my mother gave me yesterday.

---

[146] The question sounds strange, and seems to arise from a misunderstanding of the source. In Guarini, Silvio says that he lost track of the dog ('e ne perdei tosto la traccia'; II. 2. 406). Dymock might have mistaken 'perdei' for 'perdè' (he lost).

[147] Another slight misreading on Dymock's part. Not understanding that by the mention of the 'doe' she means herself, Silvio is asking Dorinda to give him both beasts (II. 2. 410).

[148] wavering] inconstant ('mobile'; II. 2. 411).

[149] Here Dymock skips two lines in which Dorinda tells Silvio that he is not going to have the two beasts without paying a price ('Ma vedi, core mio, tu non gli avrai | senza mercede'; II. 2. 413–14). This omission makes Silvio's reply ('[And with] good reason') less than clear.

DORINDA
I want no apples, and perhaps I could
Thee better-tasted give,[150] didst thou not thus
265 Disdain my gifts.

SILVIO
                    What wouldst thou have, a kid,
A lamb? Ah, but my father gives me no such leave.[151]

DORINDA
Nor kids, nor lambs do I desire; it is thy love,
My Silvio, which I seek.

SILVIO
                    Wilt thou nought but my love?

DORINDA
Nought else.

SILVIO
                    I give it thee. Now, my dear nymph,
270 Give me my dog and doe.

DORINDA
                    Ah, that thou knewst
That treasure's worth whereof thou seemst so liberal,
Or that thy heart did answer to thy tongue.

SILVIO
Hear me, fair nymph, thou ever tellst me of
A certain love: I know not what it is.
275 Thou dost desire I should thee love, and so I do,
As far forth as I can, or understand.
Thou callst me cruel, and I know not cruelty.[152]

DORINDA
Wretched Dorinda, how hast thou placed thy hopes
In beauty feeling ne'er a spark of love?
280 Thou, lovely boy, art such a fire to me,
And yet burns not thyself. Thee under human shape,
Oh dainty mother, did the Cyprian dame

---

[150] better-tasted] better-tasting apples. The ellipsis somewhat obscures this bit of sexual innuendo.
[151] To give his animals away.
[152] Here Dymock skips 'né so che farti' (II. 2. 437; 'nor do I know what to do to you'), thus making Dorinda's despair less understandable.

Bring forth; thou hast his arrows and his fire.[153]
Well, know my breast both burnt and wounded too.
285 Get but his wings unto thy shoulders, and
New Cupid shall thou be; wer't not thy heart
Is made of rocky frozen icy shelf,
Thou wantest naught of love, but love itself.

SILVIO
Tell me, what kind of thing is this same love?

DORINDA
290 If in thy face I look, oh lovely boy,
Then is this love a paradise of joy.
But if I turn and view my spirit well,
Then 'tis a flame of deep infernal hell.[154]

SILVIO
Nymph, no more words. Give me my dog and doe.

DORINDA
295 Nay, give me first the love you promisèd.

SILVIO
Have I not giv'n it? What a stir is here[155]
Her to content. Take it, do what thou wilt;
Who doth forbid thee? What wouldst thou have more?

DORINDA
Thou sowst thy seed in sand, wretched Dorinda.

SILVIO
300 What would you have? Why do you linger thus?

DORINDA
As soon as you have got what you desire,
Perfidious Silvio, you are gone from me.

SILVIO
No, trust me, nymph.

DORINDA
              Give me a pledge.

SILVIO
                              What pledge?

---

[153] 281–83] Venus bore thee. 'His' arrows and fire are Cupid's weapons.
[154] Here Guarini has two rhyming couplets of seven-syllable lines (II. 2. 455–58). Dymock follows suit with his rhyming pentameters.
[155] What a stir is here] How hard it is.

ACT II

DORINDA
I dare not tell.

SILVIO
    And why?

DORINDA
       I am ashamed.

SILVIO
305 Are you ashamed to speak, and not ashamed
It to receive?

DORINDA
      If you will promise me
To give it, I will tell.

SILVIO
       I promise you.

DORINDA
Silvio, my dear, do you not understand me yet?
I should have understood you but with half of this.

SILVIO
310 Thou are more subtle much than I.

DORINDA
I am more earnest, and less cruel much than thou.

SILVIO
To say the truth, I am no prophet, I;
You must speak if you'll have me understand.

DORINDA
Oh wretch, one of those which thy mother gave to thee.

SILVIO
315 A blow on th'ear?

DORINDA
      A blow on th'ear to one that loves thee?

SILVIO
Sometime she maketh much of me with one of them.[156]

DORINDA
Doth she not kiss you then?

---

[156] Dymock seems not to have caught the ironic meaning of 'careggiar' here (II. 2. 487–88; 'she often caresses me with such blows').

SILVIO
                          Nor she nor any else
Doth kiss me.¹⁵⁷ But perhaps you'd have a kiss.
You answer not, your blushing you accuseth.
320 I am content, but give me first my dog.

DORINDA
Y'have promised me?

SILVIO
                    'Tis true, I have promised thee.

DORINDA
And will you stay?¹⁵⁸

SILVIO
                    Tush, what a stir is here! I will.

DORINDA
Come forth, Lupino, dost not hear?

LUPINO
Who calls? I come, I come; it was not I,
325 It was the dog that slept.

DORINDA
                              Behold thy dog,
More courteous than thyself.

SILVIO
                    Oh happy me.

DORINDA
He in these arms that thou despisest so
Did put himself.

SILVIO
                    Oh my most dear Melampo.

DORINDA
Esteeming dear my kisses and my sighs.

---

¹⁵⁷ In the source, Silvio says that his mother does not kiss him, and does not want other people to kiss him.
¹⁵⁸ stay] Another possible misunderstanding. Here Guarini's 'attenderai' means 'manterrai' (II. 2. 496; 'and will you keep the promise?'). Dymock seems to have read it literally as 'will you wait for me?'.

SILVIO

330 I'll kiss thee thousand times, poor cur.
Hast thou no harm in running, poor Melampo?

DORINDA

Oh happy dog, might I change lots with thee:
Am I not brought unto an excellent pass,
That of a dog I should be jealous thus?
335 Lupino, go unto the hunting straight,
I'll follow thee.

LUPINO

    Mistress, I go.   *Exit*

Act II, Scene 3
SILVIO, DORINDA

SILVIO

Is ought behind?[159] Where is the doe you promised me?

DORINDA

Will you her have alive or dead?

SILVIO

I understand you not.
340 How's she alive? Hath not my dog her killed?

DORINDA

But say the dog hath not.

SILVIO

      Is she alive?

DORINDA

Alive.

SILVIO

   So much more welcome she is.

DORINDA

Only she's wounded in the heart.

SILVIO

        Thou mockst:
How can she live, and wounded in the heart?

---

[159] Is ought behind?] Are you not forgetting something?

DORINDA

345　My cruel Silvio, I am that same doe,
　　Without pursuit or conquest taken so.
　　Quick, if thou pleasest to accept of me,
　　Dead, if thou dost despise my company.[160]

SILVIO

　　Is this the doe, the game you told me of?

DORINDA

350　This is the same. Ay me, why look you so?
　　Hold you a nymph no dearer than a doe?[161]

SILVIO

　　I neither hold thee dear nor like of thee,
　　But hate thee, brute, wild, lying filth.　　*Exit*

DORINDA

　　Is this my guerdon, cruel Silvio?
355　Ungrateful boy, is this all my reward?
　　I gave Melampo and myself with him to thee,
　　Hoping that thus thou wouldst not have denied
　　The sunshine of thine eyes to me. I would
　　Have kept thee and thy dog most faithful company.
360　I would have wiped thy brows from toilful sweat.
　　Upon this lap that never taketh rest[162]
　　Thou mightst have ta'en thy rest. I would
　　Have carried all thy tew and proved thy prey:[163]
　　When beasts had wanted in the woods thou mightst
365　Have shot at me for one, and in this breast
　　Have usèd still thy tough, well-sinewed bow[164]
　　So as thou wouldst. I like thy servant might
　　Thy weapons carried have, or proved thy prey,[165]
　　Making my breast both quiver and the mark
370　For those thy shafts. But unto whom speak I?
　　To him that hears me not, but's fled from me.

---

[160] Again, three couplets of rhyming seven-syllable lines (II. 3. 524–29) are turned into a pentameter quatrain.
[161] This time, the rhyme is added by Dymock.
[162] Because of the love she bears him ('che per te mai non posa'; II. 3. 547). It is to be noted, however, that all this passage is in the indicative mood and in the future tense in Guarini.
[163] tew] gear.
[164] The added 'well-sinewed' makes the double entendre even clearer than it is in the source.
[165] proved thy prey] Guarini's subtly varied iterations of the same concept become mere repetition here.

Fly where thou wilt, thee will I still pursue,
Even into hell, if any hell can be
More painful than my grief, than thy great cruelty. *Exit*

Act II, Scene 4
CORISCA

375 Oh, how fortune favours my designs
More than I looked for. She good reason hath,
For I ne'er asked her favour shamefastly.[166]
Great power she hath, and with good cause the world
Calls her a puissant goddess: yet must we not sit still,
380 For seldom idle folks prove fortunate.
Had not my industry made me companion unto her,
What would this fit occasion have availèd me
To bring my purpose unto pass? Some fool
Would have her rival shunned, and showed signs of
385 Her jealousy, bearing an evil eye
About, but that had been ill done, for easilier
May one keep her from an open than a hidden foe.[167]
The covered rocks are those which do deceive
The wisest mariners. Who cannot friendship feign
390 Cannot truly hate. Now see what I can do;
I am not such an ass to think she doth not love,
It might she make some other fool believe.[168]
But tush, I am the mistress of this art. A tender wench,
Scarce from the cradle crept, in whom love hath
395 Stilled[169] but the first drops of his sweet, so long
Pursued and wooèd by a worthy friend,
And worse, kissed, and rekissed, and yet not love:
She is an ass that it believes. I'll not believ't.
But see how fortune favours me:[170] behold
400 Where Amarillis is herself. I'll make
As though I saw her not, and stand aside.

---

[166] 377] Because I was never reluctant to ask.
[167] for easilier [...] foe] it is easier (for Amarillis, in this case) to defend oneself against an open foe.
[168] The word-order makes this line incomprehensible: she may try to fool someone else — not me.
[169] Stilled] Another calque. 'Stillò' (II. 4. 592) means 'oozed', 'trickled'.
[170] This near-repetition of the initial line of the scene has no parallel in the source.

Act II, Scene 5
AMARILLIS, CORISCA

AMARILLIS
Dear blessèd woods, and you the silent groves,
Of rest and peace the harbour-houses true:
How willingly I turn to visit you.[171]
405 And if my stars had so been pleased t'have let
Me live unto myself, I with th'Elysian fields,[172]
The happy gardens of the demigods,
Would not have changed your gentle shadow spots.
If I judge right, these worldly goods are nought
410 But mischiefs: still the richest have least goods,
And he possesseth most that is most poor.
Riches are ever snares of liberty.
What's fame of beauty worth in tender years?[173]
Or heavenly nobleness in mortal blood?
415 So many favours, both of heaven and earth,
Fields large, and happy, goodly meadow plains,
Fat pastures that do fatter flocks present,
If in the same the heart be not content?
Happy that shepherdess whose scarcely knees
420 A poor, but yet a cleanly gown doth reach:[174]
Rich in herself, only in nature's gifts,
Who in sweet poverty no poorness knows,
Nor feels no tortures which this riches brings.
Desire to have much ne'er doth her torment:
425 If she be poor, yet is she well content.
She nature's gifts doth nurse with nature's gifts,
Making milk spring with milk, saucing her native sweet
With honey of the bee; one fountain serveth her
To drink, to wash, and for her looking-glass.
430 If she be well, then all the world is well.
Let the clouds rise, and thunder threat amain,
Her poverty doth all the fear prevent:
If she be poor, yet is she well content.
Finely the flock committed to her charge

---

[171] turn] return.
[172] Elysian fields] Here seen as the dwellings of the heroic demigods.
[173] Again, the word-order makes this line confusing: what is the worth, Amarillis is asking rhetorically, of being considered beautiful when young?
[174] Possibly: happy the shepherdess whose poor gown barely (scarcely) reaches to her knees, as long as the gown is 'cleanly'.

435 Feeds on the grass, the whilst her shepherd friend
Feeds on her eyes, not whom the stars, or men,
Her destinies, but whom affection chooseth.
Then in the shadow of a myrtle tree,
Cherished, she cherisheth again; nor doth
440 She feel that heat which she discovers not:[175]
Nor ever heat discover which she doth not feel.
Always declaring troth of her intent,
If she be poor, yet is she well content.
True life that knows not death before they die.
445 Ah, that I might my fortune change with theirs.
But see, Corisca. Gods save you, good Corisca.

CORISCA
Who calleth me? Dear Amarillis, dearer than
Mine eyes, my life, whither go you alone?

AMARILLIS
No further than you see; glad I have found you out.

CORISCA
450 You have her found that will not part from you.
And even now, thus was I thinking with myself:
Were I her soul,[176] how could she stay away so long?
And therewithal you came, my dear; and yet
You do not love your poor Corisca.

AMARILLIS
                    Why so?

CORISCA
455 Ask you why so? And you a bride today?

AMARILLIS
A bride?

CORISCA
              A bride, and yet from me you keep it.

AMARILLIS
How should I utter that I do not know?

CORISCA
Yet will you feign?

---

[175] nor doth [...] not] she never feels love but she shows it openly to her lover ('né per lui | sente foco d'amor che non gli scopra'; II. 5. 661–62).
[176] Were I] If I really were.

AMARILLIS
>   You jest.

CORISCA
>   'Tis you that jest.

AMARILLIS
And can it then be true?

CORISCA
>   Most certain true.
460 Do not you know thereof?

AMARILLIS
>   I know I promised was,
But know not that the marriage is so near.

CORISCA
I heard it of my brother Ormin:[177] and to say the truth,
There is no other talk.[178] But you look pale.
This news perhaps doth trouble you.

AMARILLIS
>   It is
465 Long since the promise passed, and still my mother said
This day it should revive.[179]

CORISCA
>   Unto a better life
You shall revive; for this you should be merry.
Why do you sigh? let that poor wretch go sigh.

AMARILLIS
What wretch?

CORISCA
>   Mirtillo, whom even now I found
470 Ready to die: and surely he had died
Had I not promised him this marriage to disturb,
Which though I only for his comfort said,
Yet were I fit to do it.

---

[177] Ormin] Elsewhere (e.g. II. 1) 'Ormino' — again, Dymock modifies first names for his metrical convenience.

[178] There is no other talk] It is the talk of the town.

[179] Here Dymock either misunderstands or modifies the source. In the Italian, Amarillis says that her mother told her that a woman is reborn when she marries ('che quel dì si rinasce'; II. 5. 697).

AMARILLIS
               And did he give consent?[180]

CORISCA
Aye,[181] and the means.

AMARILLIS
               I pray you how?

CORISCA
                        Easily:
475 So you thereto disposèd be to yield.

AMARILLIS
That could I hope, and would you give your faith
Not to disclose it, I discover would
A thought which in my heart I long have hid.

CORISCA
I it disclose! Ground, open first thy jaws
480 And swallow me up by a miracle.

AMARILLIS
Know then, Corisca: when I think I must
Be subject to a child that hates, that flies from me,
And hath no other sport but woods and beasts,
And loves a dog better than thousand nymphs,
485 I malcontented live, half desperate,
But dare not say so for respect I bear
Unto mine honesty, unto my faith
Which to my father, and what worser is,
Which to our puissant goddess I have giv'n:
490 If by thy help, my faith, my life both saved,[182]
I might divide me from this heavy knot,
Then shouldst thou be my health, my very life.

CORISCA
If so for this thou sighst, good reason thou,
Dear Amarillis, hast. How oft he said,
495 A thing so fair to one that can despise it?

---

[180] Here Dymock misreads Amarillis's question. In the source, she asks Corisca if she would be so daring as to disturb ('sturbare') the marriage. However, the verb in the third person ('e ti darebbe | l'animo di sturbarle?'; II. 5. 708) leads the translator to think that the grammatical subject is Mirtillo.
[181] Aye] I, in both T1602 and T1633. Using 'I' for 'aye' was common at the time.
[182] my faith, my life both saved] without losing my life or my faith.

So rich a gem to one that knows it not?
But you too crafty are to tell the truth.
What lets you now to speak?[183]

AMARILLIS

                                  The shame I have.

CORISCA

Sister, you have a mischievous disease.
500 I'd rather have the pox, the fever, or the fistula,
But trust to me, you'll quickly leave the same:
Once do but master it, and then 'tis gone.

AMARILLIS

This shamefastness that nature stamps in us
Cannot be masterèd, for if you seek
505 To hunt it from your heart, it flies into your face.[184]

CORISCA

Oh Amarillis, who too wise conceals
Her ill, at last great folly she reveals.
Hadst thou but at the first discoverèd
This thought to me, thou hadst been loose ere this.
510 Now try Corisca's art; you could not have
Entrusted you into more subtle faithful hands.
But when you shall be freèd by my help
From this same captive husband, will you not
Provide you of another lover then?

AMARILLIS

515 At better leisure we will think of that.

CORISCA

Trust me, you cannot faithful Mirtillo.[185]
You know there is not at this day a swain
For value, honest truth and beauty, worthier
Of your affection. And you will let him die,
520 Without so much as saying so. Yet hear him once.

AMARILLIS

How better 'twere to give him peace, and stub
The root of such desire as hath no hope.

---

[183] lets you now to speak] hinders you now from speaking.
[184] it flies into your face] it causes blushing.
[185] The verb is missing. Corisca is telling Amarillis that it would be wrong for her to abandon faithful Mirtillo ('non puoi mancare al tuo fedel Mirtillo'; II. 5. 759).

ACT II

CORISCA
Give him this comfort yet before he die.

AMARILLIS
It rather double will his misery.

CORISCA
525 Leave that to him.

AMARILLIS
                      But what becomes of me
If ever it be known?

CORISCA
                      Small hurt thou hast.

AMARILLIS
And small 'tshall be before my name it do endanger.

CORISCA
If you may fail in this, then in the rest
I you may fail. Adieu.

AMARILLIS
                      Nay stay, Corisca,
530 Hear me but speak.

CORISCA
                      No, not a word, unless
You promise me.

AMARILLIS
                      I promise you, so you
Do tie me to nought else.

CORISCA
                      To nothing else.

AMARILLIS
And you shall make him think I knew not of it.

CORISCA
I'll make him think it was by chance.

AMARILLIS
                      And that I may
535 Depart as soon as I think good.

CORISCA
          As soon
As you have heard him speak.

AMARILLIS
            And that he shall
Quickly dispatch.

CORISCA
         So shall he do.

AMARILLIS
             And that
He come not near me by my dart's length, never.

CORISCA
Oh what a toil 'tis to reform your simpleness:
540 All parts saving his tongue we'll surely tie.
Will you ought else?

AMARILLIS
        No, nothing else.

CORISCA
            When will you do't?

AMARILLIS
When you think good; give me but so much time
I may go home and hear more of this marriage.

CORISCA
Go. But take heed you do it warily.
545 But hear what I am thinking on. Today
About noon-time among these shadow trees
Come you without your nymphs; here shall you find
Me to that end, with me shall be Nerine,
Aglaure, Elisa, Phillis and Licoris, all mine own,
550 As wise as faithful good companions.
Here may you now (as often you have done)
Play at blind buff.[186] Mirtill will easily think[187]
That for your sport and not for him you came.

AMARILLIS
This pleaseth me, but yet I would not have
555 Your nymphs to hear the words Mirtillo speaks.

---

[186] blind buff] blind man's buff.
[187] Mirtill] As usual, Dymock shortens a name whenever the metrical need arises.

CORISCA
I understand, and well advised; let me alone,[188]
I'll make them vanish when I see my time.
Go, and forget not now to love your poor Corisca.

AMARILLIS
How can I choose but love her in whose hands
560 I have reposed my life?   *Exit*

CORISCA
                So she is gone.
Small force will serve to batter down this rock.
Though she have made defence to my assault,
Yet will she never his abide. I know too well
How hearty prayers of a gracious love
565 Can tempt a tender wench's heart. Yet with this sport
I'll tie her so she'll scarcely think it sport.
I'll by her words, will she or nill she, spy
And pierce into the bowels of her heart;
I'll make me mistress of her secrets all.
570 Then I'll conduct her so that she shall think
Her most unbridled love, and not my art,
Hath brought her in to play this wretched part.[189]

Act II, Scene 6
CORISCA, SATYR

CORISCA
Oh, I am dead.

SATYR
          And I alive.[190]

CORISCA
                Ah, turn,
My Amarillis, turn again, I taken am.

SATYR
575 Tush. Amarillis hears thee not, be quiet now.

---

[188] let me alone] leave it to me ('fie mia cura'; II. 5. 813).
[189] The source text does not have a closing couplet.
[190] alive] In T1602, this is followed by a question mark which is rightly corrected in T1633 to a full stop, because the tone is triumphant.

CORISCA
Oh me,[191] my hair.

SATYR
                    I have hunted thee so long
That at the last th'art fall'n into my snare.
This is the robe, sister, this is the hair.[192]

CORISCA
Speak you to me, Satyr?

SATYR
                    Aye, even to thee.
580 Are you not that same famous Corisca, that
Excellent mistress of lies, that at so dear a rate
False hopes, feigned looks, and lying words dost sell,
That hast betrayèd me so many ways, perfidious Corisca?

CORISCA
I am Corisca, gentle Satyr, but not now
585 So pleasing to thine eyes as I have been.

SATYR
Aye, gentle, wicked wretch. I was not so[193]
When me thou left to follow Coridon.

CORISCA
I left thee for another.[194]

SATYR
                    See, see, a wonder,
This is news indeed. But when I stole
590 Fair Lilla's bow, Clori's scarf, Daphne's rich robe
And Silvia's buskins, then thou promised me
Thy love thou gav'st another should be my reward.[195]
The dainty garland which I gave to thee
Thou gav'st to Nisus. And when me thou mad'st
595 To watch so many frosty nights both in

---

[191] Oh me] Alas.

[192] This line sounds strange because Dymock has missed a 'non' in the source. Satyr says that this time he has not merely taken hold of Corisca's robe, but of her hair (II. 6. 846); he is deluding himself, as will be seen.

[193] I was not so] You did not think or call me gentle.

[194] This is a question in the source text ('te per altrui?'; II. 6. 859). Corisca is protesting her innocent surprise — which explains Satyr's ensuing sarcasm.

[195] This very compressed line actually joins two of Guarini's hendecasyllables together ('fosse di quell'amor poscia mercede, | ch'a me promesso, fu donato altrui'; II. 6. 864–65).

The cave, the woods, and by the riverside,
And ever mockedst me, was I not gentle then?
Believe me, now thou shalt me pay for all.

CORISCA
Thou stranglest me as if I were a dog.[196]

SATYR
600 Now see if thou canst run away again.
Thy policies shall not avail thee now.
If but thy head hold on, 'tis vain to strive.[197]

CORISCA
Good Satyr, give me leave to speak to thee.

SATYR
Speak, then.

CORISCA
               How can I speak? let me go:
605 Upon my faith, I will not run away.[198]

SATYR
What faith, oh faithless woman, hast? Dar'st thou
Yet speak of faith to me? I'll carry thee
Into the darkest cave this mountain hath:
Where never sun nor human step approached,
610 I'll hide the rest there;[199] thou with my delight
And with thy scorn shalt feel what I will do with thee.

CORISCA
And canst thou be so cruel to that hair
For which thou oft hast sworn 'twere sweet to die,
And that thou couldst not suffer too much ill for me?
615 Oh heavens, oh fates, whom shall a woman trust?

SATYR
Ah wicked, thinkst thou to deceive me yet?
Canst thou yet tempt me with thy subtleties?

---

[196] dog] A heifer in the source ('una giovenca'; II. 6. 874).
[197] Another compressed passage: seven lines (II. 6. 874–79) summed up in two iambic pentameters.
[198] Here two exchanges are shortened to one (II. 6. 880–84).
[199] I'll hide the rest there] This mystifying hemistich seems to have arisen from Dymock's misunderstanding of 'non che vestigio umano' (II. 6. 890; 'in that cave there is no sun, no human step, no "sign of humanity"').

CORISCA
Oh gentle Satyr, do not make a scorn
Of her that thee adores. If so thy heart
620 Be not of marble made, behold me at
Thy feet. If ever I offended thee, oh idol of
My soul, I pardon crave. By these same strong
And more than manlike knees which I embrace,
By that same love thou sometime bar'st to me,
625 By that same sweetness which thou wont'st to draw,[200]
Thou saidst, out of mine eyes, calling them stars,
Now wretched fountains of these bitter tears,
I pray thee pity me, let me but go.

SATYR
The wretch hath almost moved me. Should I but trust
630 Affection only I were overcome.[201]
But to be short, I will not trust thee, strive no more.
For all this humbleness thou art Corisca still.

CORISCA
Oh me,[202] my head, stay yet, do not deny
Me one poor favour yet.

SATYR
                              What favour's that?

CORISCA
635 Hear me but once.

SATYR
                    Thou thinkst with feignèd words
And forgèd tears to mollify my heart.

CORISCA
Ah courteous Satyr, what wilt thou make of me?

SATYR
We'll try.[203]

CORISCA
            No pity then?

---

[200] wont'st] were wont.
[201] The wretch [...] overcome] These lines are spoken as an aside.
[202] Oh me] Again: 'Oimè' ('alas').
[203] This reply seems absurd because Dymock translates the preceding question as an open one. In the Italian, Corisca asks Satyr if he will tear her to pieces ('far di me strazio'; II. 6. 932).

ACT II

SATYR
No pity, ay.

CORISCA
Art thou resolved of this?

SATYR
I am resolved.
640 Hast thou now made an end of all thy charms?

CORISCA
Oh villain indiscreet, unseasonable,
Half a man, half a goat, and all a beast:
Dried carogne,[204] defect of wicked nature.
Dost thou believe Corisca loves not thee?
645 It is most true. What should I love in thee:
This goodly bunch of that beslavered beard,[205]
These goatlike ears, that stinking toothless cave?

SATYR
Oh witch, are these to me?

CORISCA
These are to thee.

SATYR
Ribald,[206] to me?

CORISCA
Half goat to thee.

SATYR
And do
650 Not I with these my hands thrust out thy bitch's tongue?

CORISCA
Aye, if thou durst.

SATYR
A silly woman in my hands
Dares brave me? Dares despise me thus? Well I'll —

---

[204] carogne] Here Dymock translates the Italian 'carogna' ('carrion', and metaphorically 'bastard'; II. 6. 938) with the French (or Middle English) term (see *OED*). Strangely, he also uses italics and a capital initial (here the spelling has been normalized), as if he thought that this 'carogna' was a character. In S1591, 'Carogna' has a capital initial because it is placed at the beginning of its line.
[205] beslavered] slobbered over.
[206] Ribald] You ribald.

CORISCA
Villain, what wilt thou do?

SATYR
      I'll eat thee quick.

CORISCA
Where be thy teeth?

SATYR
      Oh heavens, who can endure?[207]
655 I'll pay you home, come on.

CORISCA
      I will not come.

SATYR
That will I see.

CORISCA
      Spite of thy heart, I will not.

SATYR
Come on, we'll see who hath the stronger, thou
The neck or I the arms. Nay, soft and fair.

CORISCA
Well, let us see.

SATYR
      Go to.

CORISCA
      Satyr, hold fast.
660 Farewell, I would thy neck were broke. *Exit*

SATYR
Oh me, my head, my back, my side! Oh what
A fall is this! I scarce can turn myself.
And is she gone and left her head behind?
Unusual wonder! Nymphs and shepherds, come,
665 Behold a witchcraft trick of one that's fled
And lives without a head! How light it is!
It hath no brains; there cometh out no blood.
Why look I so?[208] Oh, fool, she gone without a head!
Thou art without a head that seèst not

---

[207] In the source: 'O Ciel, come il comporti?' (II. 6. 954; 'Oh, Heavens, how can you allow this?').

[208] Why look I so?] In Italian: 'Ma che miro?' (i.e., 'but what do I see here?'; II. 6. 976).

670 How thou are mocked. Treacherous, perfidious witch,
Is't not enough th'ast made thy heart to lie,
Thy face, thy words, thy laughter and thy looks
But that thy hair must lie?[209] Poets, behold
Your native gold, your amber pure, that you
675 So fondly praise; for shame, your subject change.
Instead whereof, sing me a witch's subtlety,
That robbeth sepulchres and rotten heads
To dress her own. As well you may go praise
Megera's viperous monstrous hairs.[210] Lovers,
680 Behold, and be ashamèd wretches now;
Make this the means your senses to recover
That are ensnared in such without more plaints.
But why stay I to publish out her shame?[211]
This hair my tongue so famous made erewhile,
685 I will go prove to make again as vile.[212]

CHORUS

Great was her fault and error sure[213]
That did occasion all our teen,[214]
Who love's great laws holy and pure,
Breaking her faith, did violate
690 And thereby did illuminate[215]
The mortal rage of our immortal queen,
That neither tears nor blood[216]
Of many harmless souls have done us good.
So faith, to every virtue root,
695 The ornament of every soul well born,
In heaven hath surely set his foot,
That worthily are faithless held in scorn.[217]
So nature truth would ever happy make
Even for the true almighty maker's sake.[218]
700 Blind mortals, you that have so deep desire

---

[209] thy hair must lie] She was wearing a wig.
[210] Megaera had snakes for hair. Dymock refers to her as 'Meger' (for metrical reasons) in I. 1.
[211] 683] But why do I wait before I make her shame known?
[212] Again, ending the scene with a rhyming couplet is Dymock's decision.
[213] The reference is to Lucrina, the nymph who betrayed Amintas (see I. 2).
[214] teen] vexation.
[215] illuminate] Guarini's word is 'accese' (II. Ch. 1012), with the meaning of 'enflamed'.
[216] That] So much so that.
[217] 697] That faithless people are rightly held in scorn.
[218] Another obscure couplet. Guarini's three lines are about God's desire to turn everybody into lovers, because that is the state in which human nature is happy (II. Ch. 1019–21).

To get and to possess
A gilded carcass of a painted tire,[219]
That like a naked shadow walks on still,
Seeking her sepulchre by guess:
705 What love, or rather fond will,
Hath witched your heart, dead beauty to pursue?
Rich treasures are love's follies found. The true
And lively love is of the soul:
All other want what love requires,
710 Therefore they not deserve these amorous desires.
The soul because it only loves again,
Is only worthy of this loving pain.[220]
It is a pretty thing to kiss
The delicate vermilion rose
715 Of some fair cheek; they have proved that bliss[221]
(Right happy lovers) so will say. Yet those
Will say again, kisses are dead and vain
Where beauty kissed restores it not again.[222]
The strokes of two enamoured lips are those
720 Where mouth on mouth love's sweetest vengeance shows.
Those are true kisses where with equal wills
We ever give and take again our fills.
Kiss but a curious mouth, a dainty hand,
A breast, a brow, or what you can demand,
725 You will confess no part in woman is,
Save for sweet mouth, that doth deserve a kiss,
By which two souls with lively spirits meet,
Making live rubies kindly intergreet.
So 'mongst themselves those souly,[223] sprightful kisses
730 Do inter-speak, and in a little sound[224]

---

[219] tire] A dress, or a covering for a woman's head. Guarini's metaphorical description is difficult here, and Dymock seems to have misunderstood it. The Italian chorus introduces a moral tirade against the stupidity of mortals, who love gold and other 'dead things' instead of their fellow creatures (II. Ch. 1022-31). Dymock, however, seems to have taken Guarini's 'golden corpse' ('cadavero d'òr') for a metaphorical description of women's assumed, painted beauty.
[220] 711-12] Only the soul is worthy of love, because it is capable of it.
[221] they] those who.
[222] Where beauty [...] again] When they are not reciprocated.
[223] souly] endowed with a soul. In T1633, this was corrected to 'slowly' — but the fact that the word is followed by 'sprightful' (meaning much the same thing) makes the earlier reading preferable.
[224] sound] 'sowne' both in T1602 and T1633, to create an eye-rhyme with 'knowne'.

Great things bewray,²²⁵ and sweetest secret blisses,
To others hidden, to themselves well-known.
Such joy, nay, such sweet life doth loving prove,
Soul knit to soul by th'earthly knot of love,
735 Kisses that kisses meet do paint unmoved
Th'encounters of two hearts, loving beloved.

---

²²⁵ bewray] reveal.

Act III, Scene 1
MIRTILLO

Oh spring, the gentle childhood of the year,
Mother of flowers, fresh herbs and fresh desires,
Thou turnst again, but with thee do not turn[226]
The happy days of my delightful joys;
5 Thou turnst, thou turnst, but with thee turnst nought else
Save of the loss of my dear treasures lorn[227]
The miserable wretched memory.
Thou art the same thou wert, so fresh, so fair,
But I am not as I was wont to be,
10 So dear to other eyes. Oh bitter sweets of love,
Much worser 'tis to lose you once possessed,
Than never to have you enjoyed at all.[228]
Much like the grief to change a happy state,
The memory of any good that wastes
15 Consumes itself as th'other is consumed.[229]
But if my hopes be not as is their use,
Of brittle glass, or that my deep desire
Make not my hope much greater than the truth,
Here shall I see the sunbeams of mine eyes.[230]
20 Here if I be not mocked I shall her see
Stay her quick feet at sound of my lament.
Here shall my greedy eyes after long fast
Receive sweet food from her divinest look.
Here will she turn her sovereign lights on me:
25 If not gentle, yet cruel will they be,

---

[226] turn] Another calque for 'tornare' ('come back').

[227] lorn] forlorn, to be attributed to the 'loss', to the 'treasures' or to the 'memory' (but really a metrical filler).

[228] 11–12] It is much worse to lose what you once possessed than never to have possessed it at all.

[229] Much like [...] consumed] These three lines are obscure. Dymock did not manage to successfully translate Guarini's five lines to the effect that loving would be a happy state if it was never lost, or if at least the memory of love could be lost when love ends ('Come saria l'amar felice stato, | se 'l già goduto ben non si perdesse; | o, quando egli si perde, | ogni memoria ancora | del dileguato ben si dileguasse'; III. 1. 18–22). In Dymock's version it appears, on the contrary, that Mirtillo is lamenting the fact that even good memories turn to bad as love sours.

[230] the sunbeams of my eyes] Amarillis. In the source, more simply, my eyes' sun ('ch'è 'l sol degli occhi miei'; III. 1. 28).

ACT III

    If not the means to breed mine inward joy,
    So fierce yet as I die to mine annoy.[231]
    Oh happy day sighed for long time in vain,
    If after times so clouded with complaints,
30 Love, thou dost grant me sight of her fair eyes,
    I mean made bright as is the morning sun.
    Hither Ergasto sent me, where he said
    Corisca and my beauteous Amarillis
    Would be together playing at blind man's buff:
35 Yet here see I none blind, save my blind will
    That wandering seeks her sight by other means
    But finds it not. Oh poison to my food,
    This long delay blindeth my heart with fear.
    My cruel destiny will never change.
40 Each hour, each moment that a lover stays
    Expecting his contentment, seems a world.
    But who doth know? Perhaps I stayed too long,
    And here Corisca hath attended me.[232]
    Ay me! If this be true, then welcome death.

Act III, Scene 2
AMARILLIS, MIRTILLO, CHORUS OF NYMPHS, CORISCA

AMARILLIS
45 Behold the buff![233]

MIRTILLO
                Behold indeed! Ah, sight.

AMARILLIS
Why stay ye now?

MIRTILLO
                Ah voice that hast at once
Both wounded me and healèd me again!

AMARILLIS
Where be ye? What do ye? Lisetta, you
That so desired this sport, where are you now?
50 Where is Corisca? And where be the rest?

---

[231] So fierce yet as I die] At least those eyes will be so fierce that I will die: 'to mine annoy' is included merely as a filler and to reproduce Guarini's rhyme (gioia/moia; III. 1. 38–39).
[232] attended] awaited.
[233] buff] blind man's buff.

MIRTILLO
Now may't be truly said that love is blind,
And hath a scarf that bindeth up his eyes.

AMARILLIS
Come list to me! Guide me clear of these trees,
There set me in the plain: you round about
55 A circle make and so begin the play.

MIRTILLO
What shall I do? I see not how this sport
Can do me good, nor I Corisca see that is
The lodestar of my hopes. Heavens aid me.

AMARILLIS
Why are ye come? Think ye nought else to do
60 But blind mine eyes? Where are ye? Let's begin!

CHORUS OF NYMPHS[234]
Blind love, I do not trust to thee,
That makes desires full of obscurity.[235]
Thou hast small sight and lesser troth,
Unhappy they that trust thine oath.
65 Blind or not blind, thou temptst in vain,
For I can shift me in this plain.[236]
Blind, thou dost see through Argos' eyes,[237]
Blind thou best-sighted safely ties.[238]
Now that I am at liberty,
70 I were a fool to trust to thee.
In test nor earnest I'll not stay,[239]
Because thou killst when thou dost play.

---

[234] This lyrical interlude in four parts was composed by Guarini on a pre-existent musical score by Luzzasco Luzzaschi, a composer at the Estense court of Ferrara. As a consequence, as the Italian playwright points out in his 'Annotationi' (p. 149 in the 1602 Ciotti edition), the lines are of varying lengths (from five to eleven syllables). Dymock mostly reproduces Guarini's couplets, but writes iambic tetrameters (with two isolated exceptions). The nymphs dance to the music, representing in their movements (inspired by the game of blind man's buff) the inner freedom of the heart that does not yield itself to love. See Introduction, p. 11.
[235] Because they are blind.
[236] 66] I can flee from you when you are about to catch me (like those pursued by the blind man in blind man's buff).
[237] Argos' eyes] Argos, or Argus 'Panoptes' (all-seeing), the many-eyed giant in Greek mythology.
[238] Presumably: though you are blind, you are able to bind those who have good sight.
[239] 71] I will not stop, either as a test or in earnest.

AMARILLIS
But ye play too far off, ye should touch me.

MIRTILLO
Oh mighty gods! What do I see? Am I
75 In heaven or earth? Y'have no such harmony.

CHORUS OF NYMPHS
But you that blind and faithless prove,
That calleth me to play this hour,
Behold, I play, and with my hand
Hit your back and by you stand.
80 I play and round about you run,
And for I trust not you I shun.[240]
Here am I now, and there again,
Whilst you to take me strive in vain.[241]
The reason is, my heart is free,
85 Therefore you cannot handle me.

AMARILLIS
I thought I had Licoris caught, and I
Have got a tree. I hear you laugh full well.

MIRTILLO
Oh would I were that tree. Methinks I see Corisca
Hidden in yonder shrubs; she nods to me.
90 Tis even she, she beckons still to me.

CHORUS OF NYMPHS
Free hearts have ever feet to fly,
And so (enticing power) have I,
Yet will you tempt me in to train?[242]
In sooth, sweet, no: 'tis all in vain.
95 The reason is, my heart is free,
Therefore you cannot handle me.

AMARILLIS
I would this tree were burned; now had I thought
I had Elisa ta'en.

---

[240] 81] And I avoid you, because I do not trust you.
[241] This line reads 'Whilst you take me strive in vaine' in T1602. T1633 corrects this to 'Whilst you take mee you strive in vaine', and Donno follows suit. But the most likely explanation is that either Dymock or his printer forgot to insert a 'to' before 'take'.
[242] to train] so as to lead me astray.

MIRTILLO
       Yet doth Corisca point,
She threatens me,[243] sh'would have me put myself
100 Among these nymphs.

AMARILLIS
       Belike thus I all day
Must play with trees.

CORISCA
       I must spite of my heart
Go out and speak. Why stayst thou, fearful wretch?
Until she come into thy arms? Let her take thee.
Give me thy dart, fool: go and meet with her.

MIRTILLO
105 How ill agree my heart with my desire!
Th'one dares so little, th'other seeks so much.

AMARILLIS
'Tis time I turn again unto the sport,[244]
I almost weary am. Fie, fie: you make
Me run too much; in faith, you are to blame.

CHORUS OF NYMPHS
110 Now look about, triumphant power,
That the world's tribute dost devour.
Now bearst thou mocks and many a bat,[245]
And like an owl th'art wondered at
About whom birds flock thick and round,
115 Whilst them she strives in vain to wound.
So art thou, love, this instant, tied,
Laughed at and mocked on every side.
Some hit thy back and some thy face,
Sparing thee neither time nor place.
120 It will not boot thee spread thy wings,
Nor that thy pinions whistling flings.
Catch how thou wilt, thou getst not me:
The reason is, my heart is free.

     Amarilli takes Mirtillo now

---

[243] She threatens me] In the source, Corisca's threats are generic, not directed towards Mirtillo ('che sembra minacciar'; III. 2. 54).

[244] A slight misreading. In the source text, she says 'let's go back to our game, for this once' ('Per questa volta ancor tornisi al gioco'; III. 2. 167).

[245] bat] blow.

Him thou hast caught, it is no wonder,
125 For love holds all his senses under. *Exeunt chorus of nymphs*

Act III, Scene 3
AMARILLIS, MIRTILLO, CORISCA

AMARILLIS
In faith, Aglaura, I have caught you now.
Will you be gone? Nay, I'll hold you fast.

CORISCA
Trust me, had I not unawares to him
Thrust him on her,[246] this labour had been lost.

AMARILLIS
130 What, not a word? Are you she or not she?

CORISCA
Here do I take this dart, and in this grove
I turn me to observe what followeth.

AMARILLIS
So now I know; Corisca, are you not?[247]
'Tis so: you are so great and have no hair.
135 I could have wished no better match than this.
And since you tied me, do untie me too,
Quickly, my heart, and I will pay thee with
The sweetest kiss thou ever hadst. Why stayst?
Methinks your hands do shake. Put to your teeth,[248]
140 If with your nails you cannot do the deed.
How tedious y'are! Let me alone,
Myself will rid me of this trouble soon:
But see how many knots have made me sure.
Ah, that I may but make you play this part.
145 So now I see. Ay me, what do I see?
Let me alone, traitor! Ay wretched me.

MIRTILLO
Stand still, my soul.

AMARILLIS
                Let me alone, I say.

---

[246] 128–29] Had I not thrust him on her, catching him unawares.
[247] The grammar here is slightly confusing. Amarillis thinks she recognizes Corisca because of her size and lack of hair, because her wig was taken by Satyr in II. 6.
[248] Put to your teeth] Use your teeth, put your teeth to use.

Dare you thus offer force to nymphs? Aglaure,[249]
Elisa, treachors, where are you become?
150 Let me alone!

MIRTILLO
               Behold, I let you go.

AMARILLIS
This is Corisca's craft; well, keep you that
Which you have not deserved.

MIRTILLO
                     Why fly you hence?
Cruel, behold my death, behold this dart
Shall pierce my woeful breast.

AMARILLIS
                     What will you do?

MIRTILLO
155 That which perhaps grieves you, most cruel nymph,
That any else beside yourself should do.

AMARILLIS
Oh me, methinks I am half dead.

MIRTILLO
But if this work belong alone to you,
Behold my breast. Here, take this fatal dart.

AMARILLIS
160 Death you have merited. But tell me, who
Hath made you boldly thus presume?

MIRTILLO
                     My love.

AMARILLIS
Love is no cause of any villain act.[250]

MIRTILLO
Love, trust me, 'twas in me. I made me respective:[251]
And since you first laid hold on me, less cause
165 You have to call my action villainy.
Yea, even when I by so commodious means

---

[249] 'Aglaura' has become a disyllable for metrical reasons.
[250] One of Dymock's most literal lines: 'Amor non è cagion d'atto villano' (III. 3. 236).
[251] respective] respectful; i.e., I acted respectfully, I restrained myself.

Might be made bold to use the laws of love,
Yet did I quake a lover to be found.

AMARILLIS
Cast not my blind deeds in my teeth, I pray.

MIRTILLO
170 My much more love makes me more blind than you.

AMARILLIS
Prayers and fine conceits, not snares and thefts,
Discreetest lovers use.

MIRTILLO
                As savage beast
With hunger hunted, from the woods breaks forth
And doth assail the stranger on his way,
175 So I, that only by your beauteous eyes
Do live, since that sweet food me have forbad
Either your cruelty or else my fate,
A starvèd lover issuing from those woods
Where I have suffered long and wretched fast,
180 Have for my health assayed this stratagem
Which love's necessity upon me thrust.
Now blame not me, nymph cruel, blame yourself,
For prayers and conceits, true love's discretion,
As you them call, you not attend from me.[252]
185 You have bereaved with shunning me the means
To love discreetly.

AMARILLIS
                Discreetly might you to do[253]
To leave to follow that which flies you so.
In vain you know you do pursue me still.
What is't you seek of me?

MIRTILLO
                Only one time
190 Deign but to hear me, ere I wretched die.

---

[252] 183–84] You cannot expect (prayers and conceits) from me, a starved savage beast.
[253] A very awkward half-line. T1633 corrects this to 'Discreetly might you do', and Donno follows suit: but it is much more likely that Dymock aimed at a total of twelve syllables between Mirtillo's conclusion ('To love discreetly') and the reply.

AMARILLIS

'Tis well for you the favour that you ask
You have already had: now get you hence.

MIRTILLO

Ah, nymph, that which I have already said
Is but a drop of that huge ample sea
195 Of my complaints; if not for pity's sake,
Yet for your pleasure now hear, cruel, but
The latest accents of a dying voice.

AMARILLIS

To ease your mind, and me this cumber rid,[254]
I grant to hear you, but with this condition:
200 Speak small, part soon, and never turn again.

MIRTILLO

In too, too small a bundle, cruel nymph,
You do command me bind my huge desires,
Which measure,[255] but by thought, nought could contain:
That I you love, and love more than life,
205 If you deny to know, ask but these woods
And they will tell, and tell you with them will
Their beasts, their trees and stones of these great rocks
Which I so oft have tender made to melt[256]
At sound of my complaints. But what make I
210 Such proof of love where such rare beauty is?
See but how many beauteous things the skies contain,
How many dress the earth in brave attire:
Thence shall you see the force of my desire.
For as the waters fall, the fire doth rise,
215 The air doth fly, the earth lies firmly still,
And all these same the skies do compass round,
Even so to you as to their chiefest good
My soul doth fly, and my poor thoughts do run,
With all affection to your lovely beauties.
220 He that from their dear object would them turn
Might fast turn from their usual course the sky,
The earth, the air, the water, and the fire,
And quite remove the earth from off his seat.

---

[254] cumber] burden. To ease myself of this weight.
[255] Which measure] The measure of which. T1633 and Donno turn the comma after 'measure' into an s ('measures').
[256] rocks [...] to melt] I have made the rocks tender to the point of melting.

But why command you me to speak but small?
225 Small shall I tell, if I but tell you shall
That I must die, and less shall dying do,
If I but see what is my ruin too.[257]
Ay me, what shall I do which may outlast
My miserable love? When I am dead,
230 Yet, cruel soul, have pity on my pains.
Ah fair! Ah dear! Sometime so sweet a cause
Why I did live whilst my good fates were pleased,
Turn hitherward those starry lights of love,
Let me them see once meek and full of pity
235 Before I die. So may my death be sweet.
As they have been good guides unto my life,
So let them be unto my death, and that
Sweet look which first begat my love, beget
My death. Let my love's Hesperus become[258]
240 The evening star of my decaying day.
But you, obdurate, never pity feel:
Whilst I more humble, you more haughty are.
And can you hear me, and not speak a word?
Whom do I speak to, wretch? A marble stone?
245 If you will say nought else, yet bid me die,
And you shall see what force your words will have.
Ah, wicked love, this is a misery extreme:
A nymph so cruel, so desirous of my death,
Because I ask it as a favour, scorns to give it,
250 Arming her cruel voice in silence so,
Lest it might favour mine exceeding woe.[259]

AMARILLIS
If I as well to answer as to hear
You promised had,[260] just cause you might have found
To have condemned my silence for unjust.
255 You call me cruel, imagining perhaps
By that reproof more easily to draw
Me to the contrary. No, know, Mirtillo,
I am no more delighted with the sound

---

[257] This line is obscure. Dymock may have failed to understand the meaning of the Italian lines 'e men farò morendo, | s'io miro a quel che del mio strazio brami' (III. 3. 326–27; 'And I'll suffer less by dying | if I see how much you want me to suffer').
[258] Hesperus] The evening star — the planet Venus as seen in the evening.
[259] 250–51] She is so cruel that she will not even give him the death he craves.
[260] If I [...] promised had] if I had promised to answer, and not only to listen.

      Of that desertless and dislikèd praise
260 You to my beauty give, than discontent
      To hear you call me cruel and unjust.
      I grant this cruelty to any else a fault,
      But to a lover virtue 'tis, and honesty,
      Which in a woman you call cruelty.
265 But be it, as you would, blameworthy fault
      To be unkind to one that loves, tell me:
      When was Amarillis cruel unto you?
      Perhaps when reason would not give me leave
      To use this pity: yet how I it used
270 Yourself can judge, when you from death I saved.
      I mean when you among a noble sort of maids,
      A lustful lover, in a woman's clothes
      Banded yourself,[261] and durst contaminate
      Their purest sports, mingling 'mong kisses innocent
275 Kisses lascivious and impure; which to remember
      I am ashamed.[262] But heavens my witness are,
      I knew you not, and after I you knew,
      I scorned your deed, and kept my soul untouched
      From your lasciviousness, not suffering at all
280 The venom there to run to my chaste heart.
      You violated nothing save th'outside
      Of these my lips. A mouth kissed but by force
      Spits out the kiss, and kills the shame withal.[263]
      But tell me you, what fruit had you received
285 Of your rash theft, had I discovered you
      Unto those nymphs? The Thracian Orpheus had not been
      So lamentably torn on Eber's banks[264]
      Of Bacchus' dames as you had been of them,[265]
      Had not you helped her pity whom you cruel call.[266]
290 That pity which was fit for me to give, I ever gave:
      For other, 'tis in vain you either ask or hope:
      If you me love, then love mine honesty,
      My safety love, and love my life withal.

[261] Banded] Dressed.
[262] She is referring to the episode related by Mirtillo himself in II. 1.
[263] A mouth [...] withal] These words are between inverted commas and form a rhyming couplet in Guarini — which means that Amarillis is repeating a proverb ('Bocca baciata a forza, | se 'l bacio sputa, ogni vergogna ammorza'; III. 3. 407–08).
[264] Eber] Evros, a river in Thrace.
[265] Orpheus was ripped to shreds by Maenads (female followers of Dionysus).
[266] 289] If you had not been helped by the pity of her you call cruel.

Thou art too far from that which thou desir'st.
295 The heavens forbid, the earth contraries it,
Death is the punishment thereof. And above all
Mine honesty defies forbidden acts:
Than which a safer keeper of her honour's flower
A soul well-born will ever scorn to have.[267]
300 Then rest in peace, Mirtillo, give o'er this suit,
Get thee far hence to live, if thou be wise.
T'abandon life for peevish grief or smart
Is not the action of a valiant heart.
From that which pleaseth virtue 'tis t'abstain,
305 If that which pleaseth breeds offence again.[268]

MIRTILLO
To save one's life is not within his power
That hath his soul forsaken and giv'n o'er.

AMARILLIS
One armed in virtue conquereth all desire.

MIRTILLO
Virtue small conquest gets where love triumphs.

AMARILLIS
310 Who cannot what he would will what he can.[269]

MIRTILLO
Oh, love's necessity no laws endures.

AMARILLIS
Distance of place may heal your wound again.

MIRTILLO
In vain one flies from that his heart doth harbour.

AMARILLIS
A new desire an old will quite displace.

---

[267] 297–99] A well-born soul will always scorn to have a safer keeper of its honour than its own honesty. The line as printed in all the existing editions appears to contain a misprint ('Then *with* a safer keeper'; italics mine; Dymock spells both 'then' and 'than' with an 'e' throughout).

[268] The two concluding couplets are not in Guarini (III. 3. 447–48; and note 'again' used as a rhyme-word and a filler).

[269] In T1602 there is an additional 'he' ('will he what he can') that is almost certainly a mistake, as it makes no sense either in metrical or grammatical terms. It was cancelled out in T1633 and Donno.

MIRTILLO
315 Had I another heart, another soul.

AMARILLIS
Time will at last clearly this love consume.

MIRTILLO
Aye, after love hath quite consumed my life.

AMARILLIS
Why then, your wounds will not be cured at all?

MIRTILLO
Never till death.

AMARILLIS
         Till death? Well, hear me now,
320 And look my words be laws unto your deeds.
Albeit I know to die is more the usual voice[270]
Of an enamoured tongue than a desire
Or firm conceit his soul hath entertained,
Yet if by chance such a strange folly hath
325 Possessed thy mind, know then thy death will be
Death to mine honour as unto thy life.
Now if thou lov'st me, live and let it be
A token of thy wit henceforth thou shun
To see me, or to seek my company.

MIRTILLO
330 Oh cruel sentence! Can I without life
Live, think you then? Or can I without death
Find end unto my torment and my grief?

AMARILLIS
Well now 'tis time you go, Mirtillo, hence!
You'll stay too long. Go, comfort yourself
335 That infinite the troupe of wretched lovers is.
All wounds do bring with them their several pain,
Nor can you only of this love complain.

MIRTILLO
Among these wretches I am not alone; but yet
A miserable spectacle am only I
340 Of dead and living, nor can live nor die.

[270] more the usual voice] T1602 has 'the more usual voice' — probably a misprint. It makes more sense (also in comparison with the source text) to shift the definite article and read the subsequent 'then' in the next line as comparative — as T1633 does.

AMARILLIS
Well go your ways.

MIRTILLO
                  Ah, sad departure,
End of my life, go I from you, and do not die?
And yet I feel the very pangs of death
That do give life unto mine ecstasy,[271]
345 To make my heart immortally to die.

Act III, Scene 4
AMARILLIS

Oh Mirtillo! Oh, my dearest soul,
Couldst thou but see into her heart whom thou
Callst cruel Amarillis, then wouldst thou say
Thou hadst that pity which thy heart desires.
350 Oh minds too much unfortunate in love!
What boots it thee,[272] my heart, to be beloved?
What boots it me to have so dear a love?
Why should the cruel fates so disunite
Whom love conjoins? and why should traitorous love
355 Conjoin them whom the destinies do part?
Oh, happy savage beasts whom nature gives
No laws in love, save very love itself.
Inhuman human law, that punish'st
This love with death, if't be so sweet to sin,
360 And not to sin so necessary be,
Imperfect nature that repugneth law,[273]
Or law too hard that nature doth offend.
But tush, she loves too little that fears death!
Would God's death were the worst that's due to sin.
365 Dear chastity, th'inviolable power
Of souls well-born that hast my amorous will
Retained in chains of holy rigour still:
To thee I consecrate my harmless sacrifice.
And thou my soul, Mirtillo, pardon me
370 That cruel am where I should piteous be.
Pardon her that in looks and only words

---

[271] ecstasy] The term is slightly out of place in its sexual innuendo. The Italian Mirtillo, in parting, feels 'a lively dying | that gives life to the pain | to make the heart die immortally' ('un vivace morire, | che dà vita al dolore | per far che moia immortalmente il core'; III. 3. 503–05).
[272] What boots it thee] What good is it to you.
[273] repugneth] 'Repugni' in the source (III. 4. 527).

Doth seem thy foe, but in my heart thy friend.
If thou wouldst be revenged, what greater pain
Wouldst thou inflict than this my cruel grief?
375 Thou art my heart, and shalt be spite of heaven
And earth; when thou dost plain and sigh, and weep,
Thy tears become my blood, thy sighs my breath:
And all thy pains they are not only thine,
For I them feel, and they are turnèd mine.

Act III, Scene 5
CORISCA, AMARILLIS

CORISCA
380 Hide you no more, my Amarillis, now.

AMARILLIS
Wretch, I discovered am.

CORISCA
                    I all have heard.
Be not afraid; did I not say I loved you,
And yet you are afraid? And hides yourself
From her that loves you so. Why do you blush?
385 This blushing is a common fault.

AMARILLIS
Corisca, I am conquered, I confess.

CORISCA
That which you cannot hide you will confess.

AMARILLIS
And now I see too weak a thing doth prove
A woman's heart to encounter mighty love.[274]

CORISCA
390 Cruel unto Mirtillo, but more cruel to yourself.

AMARILLIS
It is no cruelty that springs of pity.

CORISCA
Cicute and Aconite[275] do grow from wholesome roots.
I see no difference twixt this cruelty
That doth offend, and pity helping not.

---

[274] encounter] strive against.
[275] Hemlock and monkshood, plants notorious for their toxic properties.

AMARILLIS
395 Ah me, Corisca!

CORISCA
                    These sighs, good sister,
Are but weakness of your heart. Th'are fit[276]
For women of small worth.

AMARILLIS
                    I could not be
Thus cruel, but I should love, cherish hopelessly.[277]
Therefore to shun him shows I have compassion
400 Of his ill and mine.

CORISCA
                    Why hopelessly?

AMARILLIS
Do you not know I am espoused to Silvio,
And that the law each woman dooms to death
That violates her faith?

CORISCA
                    Oh simple fool,
Is this the let?[278] Which is more ancient among us,
405 Diana's law or love's? This in our breasts
Is bred and grows with us, Nature herself
With her own hands imprints in our hearts' breasts:
And where this law commands, both heaven and earth obey.

AMARILLIS
But if the other law do take my life,
410 How can love's law restore it me again?

CORISCA
You are too nice; were every woman so,
Had all such straight respects, good times farewell!
Small practisers are subject to this pain.[279]

---

[276] Th'are] They are.
[277] The translation here is rather obscure — so much so that T1633 adds the commas to make the line more meaningful. What Amarillis says in Italian is 'Would I not be crueller if I nourished his love where there is no hope?' ('Non sarei più crudele, | se 'n lui nudrissi amor senza speranza?'; III. 5. 581–82).
[278] let] hindrance.
[279] Small practisers] A rather obscure calque of Guarini's 'le poche pratiche' ('those who are not cunning enough'; III. 5. 609).

The law doth never stretch unto the wise.
415 Believe me, should blameworthy all be slain,[280]
The country then would soon prove womanless.
It needful was, theft should forbidden be
To them that closely could not cover theft.
This honesty is but an art to seem so;
420 Let others as they list believe, I'll think so still.

AMARILLIS
These are but vanities, Corisca; 'twere best
Quickly to leave that which we cannot hold.

CORISCA
And who forbids thee, fool? This life's too short
To pass it over with one only love:
425 Men are too sparing of their favours now
(Whether't be for want, or else for forwardness).[281]
The fresher that we are, the dearer still:
Beauty and youth once gone w'are like beehives
That hath no honey, no, nor yet no wax.
430 Let men prate on; they do not feel our woes,
For their condition differs much from ours:
The elder that they grow, they grow the perfecter.
If they lose beauty, yet they wisdom gain:
But when our beauty fades that oftentimes
435 Conquers their greatest wits, straight fadeth all our good;
There cannot be a wilder thing to see
Than an old woman. Therefore ere thou age attain,
Know me thyself,[282] and use it as thou shouldst.[283]
What were a lion worth did he not use his strength?
440 What's a man's wit worth that lies idly by?
Even so our beauty, proper strength to us,
As force to lions, wisdom unto men:
We ought to use whilst it we have. Time flies
Away and years come on; our youth once lost
445 We, like cut flowers, never grow fresh again.
And to our hoary hairs love well may run,
But lovers will our wrinkled skins still shun.

---

[280] should blameworthy all be slain] if all blameworthy women were slain.
[281] forwardness] A rather misleading translation of 'fierezza' ('pride'; III. 5. 629).
[282] Very obscure translation of Guarini's 'conosci i pregi tuoi' (III. 5. 654; 'Know your worth').
[283] Here Dymock skips two proverbial-sounding lines on taking life (and a good chance) as it comes ('Se t'è la vita destra, | non l'usar a sinistra'; III. 5. 655–56).

AMARILLIS
Thou speakest this, Corisca, me to try,
Not as thou thinkst,[284] I am sure. But be assured
450 Except thou showst some means how I may shun
This marriage bond,[285] my thought's irrevocable,
And I resolvèd am rather to die
That any way to spot my chastity.

CORISCA
I have not seen so obstinate a fool;[286]
455 But since you are resolved I am agreed.
But tell me, do you think your Silvio is
As true a friend to faith as you to chastity?

AMARILLIS
Thou mak'st me smile. Silvio a friend to faith?
How can that be? He's enemy to love.

CORISCA
460 Silvio an enemy to love? Oh fool,
These that are nice, put thou no trust in them:
Love's theft is never so securely done
As hidden under a veil of honesty.
Thy Silvio loves, good sister, but not thee.

AMARILLIS
465 What goddess is she? For she cannot be
A mortal wight that lighted hath his love.

CORISCA
Nor goddess, nor a nymph.

AMARILLIS
                          What do you tell?

CORISCA
Know you Lisetta?

AMARILLIS
                 She that your cattle keeps?

CORISCA
Even she.

---

[284] Not as thou think'st] Not because you really hold these convictions.
[285] Dymock condenses a lot here, thus missing Amarillis's insistence that the means must be honest ('e sopra tutto onesto'; III. 5. 680).
[286] Spoken as an aside in the source.

AMARILLIS
Can it be true?

CORISCA
The same's his heart.[287]

AMARILLIS
470 Sure he's provided of a dainty love.[288]

CORISCA
Each day he feigns that he on hunting goes.

AMARILLIS
I every morning hear his cursèd horn.

CORISCA
About noon-time when others busy are,
He his companions shuns, and comes alone
475 By a back way unto my garden; there,
Where a shadow hedge doth close it in,[289]
There doth she hear his burning sighs, his vows,
And then she tells me all, and laughs at him.
Now hear what I think good to do. Nay, I
480 Have done't for you already. You know the law
That ties us to our faith doth give us leave,
Finding our spouses in the act of perfidy,
Spite of our friends the marriage to deny,[290]
And to provide us of another if we list.

AMARILLIS
485 That know I well. I have examples two:
Leucipp to Ligurine, Armilla to Turingo.[291]
Their faith once broke, they took their own again.

---

[287] same's] Either 'is' or 'has'. If the former, 'heart' might stand for 'sweetheart'. In that case, the clause is a morphologically close translation of Guarini's 'questa è l'anima sua' (III. 5. 713).

[288] In Italian, Amarillis calls Silvio 'lo schifo' (III. 5. 713), with the meaning of 'the one who loathes (love)'.

[289] shadow] shadowed, shadowy ('ombrosa'; III. 5. 725).

[290] Spite of our friends] In the source, 'malgrado de' parenti suoi' (III. 5. 735; 'in spite of his/her parents'; without a care for what the old people think).

[291] Here Guarini seems to be using a mixture of invented and literary names: 'Leucippe' is from Achilles Tatius's Greek romance *Leucippe and Clitophon*; one 'Ligurino' can be found in Niccolò degli Angeli's 1574 pastoral fable *Ligurino*. Dymock skips a third couple formed by 'Egle' (an allusion to another important pastoral precedent, Giraldi Cinthio's 1545 *Egle*) and 'Licota' (a male name used by Propertius). 'Armilla' and 'Turingo' appear to be Guarini's inventions, though the female name occurs in later madrigals and pastoral plays and may have been in circulation at the time. It is also to be noted that Leucippe was Corisca's original name in Guarini's working notes.

CORISCA
Now hear! Lisetta by my appointment hath
Promised to meet th'unwary lover here
490 In this same cave, and now he is the best
Contented youth that lives, attending but the hour.
There would I have you take him. I'll be there
To bear you witness of't, for else we work
In vain; so you are free from this same noisome knot
495 Both with your honour, and your father's too.

AMARILLIS
Oh brave invention, good Corisca. What's to do?

CORISCA
Observe my words. In midst of this same cave
Upon the right hand is a hollow stone,
I know not if by art or nature made,
500 A little cave all lined with ivy leaves,
To which a little hole aloft gives light,
A fit and thankful receptacle for love's theft.[292]
Prevent their coming and attend them there:[293]
I'll haste Lisetta forward, and as soon
505 As I perceive your Silvio enter, so will I:
Step you to her, and as the custom is,
We'll carry both unto the priest, and there dissolve
This marriage knot.

AMARILLIS
              What, to his father?

CORISCA
What matters that? Think you Montanus dare
510 His private to a public good compare?

AMARILLIS
Then, closing up mine eyes, I let myself
Be led by thee, my dear, my faithful guide.

CORISCA
But do not stay now, enter me betime.[294]

---

[292] thankful] Guarini's 'grato' here means 'welcome' ('gradito'), rather than 'thankful' (III. 5. 764).
[293] Prevent] Anticipate ('prevenendo'; III. 5. 766).
[294] me] This pronoun seems completely superfluous, except for metrical purposes — yet it is repeated in T1602 and T1633.

AMARILLIS
I'll to the temple first, and to the gods
515 My prayers make, without whose aid no happy end
Can ever sort to mortal enterprise.

CORISCA
All places, Amarillis, temples are
To hearts devout; you'll slack your time too much.

AMARILLIS
Time's never lost in praying unto them
520 That do command the time.

CORISCA
                Go then, dispatch.   *Exit Amarillis*
Now if I err not, am I at good pass.
Only this staying troubles me; yet may it help,
I must go make new snares to train in Coridon.[295]
I'll make him think that I will meet him there,
525 And after Amarillis send him soon,
Then by a secret way I'll bring Diana's priests:
Her shall they find, and guilty doom to death.
My rival gone, Mirtillo sure is mine.
See where he comes. Whilst Amarillis stays
530 I'll somewhat try him. Love now once inspire
My tongue with words, my face with heavenly fire.[296]

Act III, Scene 6
MIRTILLO, CORISCA

MIRTILLO
Here, weeping sprights of hell,[297] new torments hear,
New sorts of pain, a cruel mind behold
Included in a look most merciful,
535 My love more fierce than the infernal pit.
Because my death cannot suffice to glut
Her greedy will, and that my life is but
A multitude of deaths, command me live,
That to them all my life might living give.

CORISCA
540 I'll make as though I heard him not; I hear

---
[295] to train in Coridon] to take him in.
[296] Guarini does not end the scene with a distich.
[297] hell] Dymock de-classicizes 'Averno' (III. 6. 815).

A lamentable voice plain hereabouts.
I wonder who it is: oh, my Mirtillo.

MIRTILLO
So would I were a naked shade or dust.

CORISCA
How feel you now yourself after your long
545 Discourse with your so dearly lovèd nymph?

MIRTILLO
Like a weak sick man that hath long desired
Forbidden drink, at last gets it unto his mouth
And drinks his death, ending at once both life and thirst.
So I, long sick, burnt and consumèd in
550 This amorous drought, from two fair fountains that
Ice do distil from out a rocky brain
Of an indurate heart,[298]
Have drunk the poison that my life will kill,
Sooner than half of my desire fulfil.

CORISCA
555 So much more mighty waxeth love as from
Our hearts the force is he receives, dear Mirtillo,
For as the bear is wont with licking to give shape
To her mishapen brood, that else were helpless born,
Even so a lover to his bare desire,
560 That in the birth was shapeless, weak and frail,
Giving but form and strength begetteth love,
Which whilst 'tis young and tender, then 'tis sweet,
But waxing to more years, more cruel grows,
That in the end (Mirtillo) an inveterate affect
565 Is ever full of anguish and defect.
For whilst the mind on one thought only beats,
It waxeth thick by being too much fixed.
So love, that should be pleasure and delight,
Is turned to melancholy, and what worser is,
570 It proves at last, or death, or madness at the least:
Wherefore wise is that heart that often changeth love.

MIRTILLO
Ere I change will or thought,[299] changed must my life
Be into death, for though the beauteous Amarillis

---

[298] A rare isolated three-beat line, rendering one of Guarini's heptasyllables.
[299] It is here that Mirtillo proves he is a 'faithful shepherd'.

Be most cruel, yet is she all my life:
575 Nor can this body's bulk at once contain
More than one heart, more than one soul retain.

CORISCA

Oh wretched shepherd, ill thou knowst to use
Love in his kind. Love one that hates thee, one
That flies from thee; fie, man, I had rather die.

MIRTILLO

580 As gold in fire, so faith in grief's refined,
Nor can, Corisca, amorous constancy
Show his great power but through cruelty.
This only rests amongst my many griefs,[300]
My sole content: doth my heart burn or die,
585 Or languish ne'er so much, light are the pains,
Plaints, torments, sighs, exile, and death itself,
For such a cause, for such a sweet respect.
That life before my faith shall broken be,
So worse than death I hold inconstancy.[301]

CORISCA

590 Oh brave exploit, lover magnanimous,
Like an enragèd beast or senseless rock.
There cannot be a greater damnèd plague,
More mortal poison to a soul in love,
Than is this faith. Unhappy is that heart
595 That let itself be gulled with vain phantasms
Of this erroneous and unseasonable
Disturber of these amorous delights.
Tell me, poor man, with this thy foolish virtue of constancy,[302]
What lov'st thou in her that doth thee despise?
600 Lov'st thou the beauty that is none of thine?
The joy thou hast not? the pity thou wantst?
The reward thou dost not hope for? If thou deemst right,
Thou lov'st thine ill, thy grief, thy very death,
Th'art mad to hunt thus that thou canst not have.
605 Lift up thyself, Mirtillo; happily thou wantst
Some choice of friends, thou finds none to thy mind.[303]

---

[300] This only rests] A calque of 'Questo solo mi resta' (III. 6. 892; 'Only this is left to me').
[301] So worse] So much worse.
[302] At fifteen syllables, one of the longest lines in the play.
[303] happily […] mind] In the source, Corisca asks two rhetorical questions (Do you think you are going to have no lovers? Or no one who likes and prizes you? III. 6. 928–29). Dymock's

ACT III

MIRTILLO
More dear to me is pain for Amarillis
Than any joy a thousand else can give:
If me my fates forbid her to enjoy,
610 For me then die all other kinds of joy.
I fortunate in any other kind of love?
No, though I would I could not:
Nor though I could I would not.[304]
And if I thought in any time henceforth
615 My will would wish, or power obtain the same,
I would desire of heaven and love at once
Both will and power might quite be ta'en away.[305]

CORISCA
Wilt thou then die for her that thee disdains?

MIRTILLO
Who pity not expects doth fear no pains.

CORISCA
620 Do not deceive thyself; perhaps thou thinkst
She doth dissemble in this deep despite,
And that she loves thee well for all this show.
Oh that thou knewst what unto me she ever says.

MIRTILLO
All these are trophies of my truest faith,
625 With which I will triumph over her cruel will,
Over my pains, and my distressèd chance,
Over world's fortune, and over death itself.

CORISCA
(What would he do, did he but know her love?)
How I bewail thee, wretched frenzied man:
630 Tell me, didst thou e'er any love besides?[306]

MIRTILLO
She was my first, and she my last shall be.

---

rendering would only make sense if 'happily' were substituted with 'haply' (maybe you only need a new set of friends).
[304] Here Dymock reproduces Guarini's seven-syllable lines, as well as the grammatical rhyme of the source (potrei/vorrei; III. 6. 937–38).
[305] 614–17] If I were willing and in a position to obtain someone else's love, I would desire to have both will and power (to do so) taken away from me.
[306] 630] Did you ever love anyone else? ('amasti tu mai | altra donna che questa?' III. 6. 966–67).

CORISCA
For ought that I can see you never tried
Love but in cruel moods, but in disdain.
Oh if you had but prov'd him one time kind.[307]
635 Prove him but so, and you shall see how sweet a thing
It is t'enjoy a grateful nymph; she'll you adore,
She'll make your Amarillis bitter to your taste.
How dear a thing it is wholly to have
What you desire, and be nought barred thereof.
640 Hear your nymph sigh to cool your scalding sighs,
And after say: my dear, all that you see is yours.
If I be fair, I am only fair for you:
Only for you I cherish these my cheeks,
My locks, my breast, your dear heart's only lodge.
645 But this, alas, is but a brook to that
Great sea of sweets which we in love might taste,[308]
Which none can utter save by proof.

MIRTILLO
Thousand times blessed that under such a star is born.

CORISCA
Hear me, Mirtillo (how like I was t'have said
650 My heart!): a nymph as gentle as the wind
Doth blow upon with hair of glistering gold,[309]
As worthy of your love as you of hers,
Praise of these woods, love of a thousand hearts,
By worthy youths in vain solicited,
655 You only loves more than her heart, her life.
If you be wise, do not despise her then.
She like a shadow to thyself will be,
A faithful follower of thy footsteps ever,
One at thy word obedient, at thy beck,[310]
660 All hours of day and night at thy command.
Do not forsake this rare adventure then:
No pleasure in this earth so sweet as this.
It will not cost a tear, no, not a sigh.

[307] prov'd] Again, with the meaning of 'tried'.
[308] we] Here Corisca appears to betray herself by using the plural (her construction is impersonal in the source; III. 6. 999).
[309] blow [...] gold] Dymock's translation is obscure in its compactness. In the source, Corisca is describing someone as graceful as nymphs leaving their golden hair free to blow in the wind ('fra quante o spieghi al vento [...] chioma d'or leggiadra'; III. 6. 1005–06).
[310] at thy beck] at your beck and call.

A joy accommodated to thy will,
665 A sweetness tempered sweetly to thy taste.
Is't not a treasure worth the having, man?
Leave then the feet of flying hopeless trace,³¹¹
And her that follows thee, scorn not t'embrace.
I feed you not with hopes of vanity.³¹²
670 If you desire to see her, you shall see her straight.

MIRTILLO
My heart's no subject for these love's delights.

CORISCA
Prove it but once, and then return again
Unto thy solitary grief, so mayst thou see
What are those joys that in love's pleasures be.

MIRTILLO
675 A taste corrupted pleasant things abhors.

CORISCA
Be not you cruel yet to rob her life
That on your eye depends; you know what 'tis
To beg with poverty.³¹³ If you desire
Pity yourself, do it not her deny.

MIRTILLO
680 What pity can he give that none can get?
In sum, I am resolv'd, whilst here I live,
To keep my faith to her howe'er she prove,
Cruel or pitiful, or how she will.

CORISCA
Oh truly blind, unhappy senseless man!
685 To whom preserv'st thou faith? Trust me, I am loth
T'augment thy grief, but for the love I bear thee
I cannot choose. Thinkst Amarillis is unkind
For zeal she to religion bears?
Or unto chastity? Thou art a fool,
690 The room is occupied and thou must weep
Whilst others laugh. What? Now th'art dumb?

---

³¹¹ 667] Leave off tracing the footsteps of a hopeless love that flies away from you.
³¹² hopes of vanity] vain hopes ('speranze vane'; III. 6. 1037–38).
³¹³ To beg with poverty] To beg, being poor.

MIRTILLO
Now stands my life in midst twixt life and death,
Whilst I in doubt do stand, if to believe,
Or not believe; this makes me so amazed.

CORISCA
695 You'll not believe me then?

MIRTILLO
                    Oh, if I do,
Straight shall you see my miserable end.

CORISCA
Live, wretched man, live and revengèd be.

MIRTILLO
Oh no, it is not true, it cannot be.

CORISCA
Well, there's no remedy, I must rehearse
700 That which will vex thy heart. Seest thou that cave?
That is the true custodian of her faith
And her religion. There thee to scorn she laughs,
There with thy torments doth she sauce the joys
Of thy thrice happy rival. There, to be plain,
705 Thy faithful Amarillis oft is wont
To dally in the arms of a base shepherd slave.[314]
Go sigh, preserve thy faith, there's thy reward.

MIRTILLO
Dost thou tell true, Corisca? May I believe thee?

CORISCA
The more thou seekst, the worse thou findest still.

MIRTILLO
710 But hast thou seen this thing, Corisca?

CORISCA
I have not seen't,[315] yet mayst thou if thou wilt,
For even this day is order ta'en this hour,

---

[314] shepherd slave] A 'coarse little shepherd' in Guarini ('rozzo pastorel', with clear social overtones; III. 6. 1101).

[315] Here Dymock misunderstands Guarini's 'pur' (meaning 'only') in 'Non l'ho pur vedut'io' ('Not only did I see it'; III. 6. 1110) for 'yet', 'although' (*eppure*). Psychologically, the fact that Corisca presents herself as an eyewitness is crucial. All the weight of her evidence is based on 'seeing', just like in Shakespeare's *Much Ado About Nothing*.

That they may meet. Hide thee but somewhere here,
And thou shalt see her first go in, then he.

MIRTILLO
715 Then comes my death.

CORISCA
                        See where she comes,
Softly descending by the temple's way. Seest thou her?
Do not her stealing feet bewray her stealing heart?
Attend thou here and thou shalt see th'effect.

MIRTILLO
Since I am here, the truth I now will see.
720 Till then, my life and death suspended be.

Act III, Scene 7
AMARILLIS

Let never mortal enterprise be ta'en in hand
Without this heavenly counsel; half confused
And doubtful was my heart when I went hence
Unto the temple, whence, thanks be to heaven,
725 I do well comforted, and well-disposed return.
Methought to my pure prayers and devout
I felt a spright celestial move within me
Heartening my thoughts, that as it were did say,
What fearst thou, Amarillis? Be assured.
730 So will I go assured, heavens be my guide.
Favour, fair mother of love, her pure designs
That on thy succour only doth depend.
Queen of the triple sky,[316] if e'er thou prov'dst[317]
Thy son's hot fire, take pity then of mine.[318]
735 Guide hither, courteous goddess, that same swain
With swift and subtle feet that hath my faith.
And thou, dear cave, into thy bosom take
Me, love's handmaid, and give me leave there to
Accomplish my desires. Why do I stay?
740 Here's none doth see or hear. Enter secure.
Oh, Mirtillo, couldst thou but dream to find me here!

---

[316] triple sky] In the Ptolemaic system, Venus inhabits the third sphere of heaven ('triple' is arguably employed instead of 'third' for metrical reasons).
[317] prov'dst] felt.
[318] of mine] of my fire.

Act III, Scene 8
MIRTILLO

What, am I blind, or do I too much see?
Ah, had I but been born without these eyes,
Or rather not at all had I been born.
745 Did spiteful fates reserve me thus alive[319]
To let me see so bad, so sad a sight?
Mirtill, thy torments pass the pains of hell.
No, doubt no more: suspend not thy belief:
Thine eyes, thine ears, have seen, have heard it true.
750 Thy love another owns not by the law
Of earth, that binds her unto anyone,
But by love's law that ties her sole to thee.[320]
Oh cruel Amarillis, was't not enough
To kill me, wretch, but thou must scorn me too?[321]
755 That faithless mouth that sometime graced my joys,
Did vomit out my hateful name because
She would not have it in her heart to be
A poor partaker of her pleasures sweet.
Why stayst thou now? She that did give me life
760 Hath ta'en't away, and giv'n't another man:
Yet wretch thou liv'st, thou dost not die. Oh, die
Mirtillo, die to thy tormenting grief,
As to thy joy thou art already dead.
Die dead Mirtillo, finished is thy life.
765 Finish thy torment too: fleet, wretched soul,
Through this sour, constrained and wayward death:[322]
'Tis for thy greater ill that thus thou livst.
But what? And must I die without revenge?
First will I make him die that gives me death:
770 Desire to live so long I will retain
Till justly I have that usurper slain.
Yield, grief, unto revenge: pity to rage,
Death unto life, till with my life I have

---

[319] reserve] preserve.
[320] The whole passage is confusing. In the source, Mirtillo tells himself that Amarillis belongs to someone else not because of 'the law of the world | that takes her away from anyone else; | but for the law of love | that takes her away from you alone' ('non per legge del mondo, | che la toglie ad ogni altro; | ma per legge d'Amore, | che la toglie a te solo'; III. 8. 1172–75).
[321] scorn] Another calque (Guarini's 'schernivi' means '[you] mocked'; III. 8. 1179).
[322] fleet [...] death] Maybe what is meant here is 'go through this death quickly'. In the source, Mirtillo is exhorting himself to die in order to escape this death-in-life (III. 8. 1200–01).

ACT III

Revenged the death another guiltless gave.[323]
775 This steel shall not drink mine unvengèd blood,
My hand shall rage ere it shall piteous be.
Whate'er thou art that joyst my comforts all,[324]
I'll make thee feel thy ruin in my fall.
I'll place me here, even in this very grove,
780 And as I see him but approach the cave,
This dart shall sudden wound him in his side.
It shall be coward-like to strike him thus,
I'll challenge him to single combat; ay.
Not so: for to this place so known and used
785 Shepherds may come to hinder us, and worse,
May search the cause that moved me to this fight,
Which to deny were wickedness; to feign
Will make me faithless held; and to discover
Will blot her name with endless infamy
790 In whom albeit I like not what I see,
Yet what I loved I do, and ever shall.
But what hope I to see th'adulterer die
That robbed her of her honour, me my life?
But if I kill him, shall not then his blood
795 Be to the world a token of this deed?
Why fear I death, since I desire to die?
But then this murder, once made plain, makes plain
The cause whereby she shall incur that infamy.
I'll enter then this cave, and so assail him.
800 Ay so, that pleaseth me: I'll steal in softly,
So that she shall not hear me. I believe
That in the secretst and the closest part,
I gather by her words,[325] I shall her find,
Therefore I will not enter in too far.
805 A hollow hole there is made in a rock,
The left side covered all with ivy leaves:
Beneath th'other ascent there will I stand,
And time attend t'effect what I desire.[326]
I'll bear my dead foe to my living foe:[327]
810 Thus of them both I shall be well revenged.

[323] In the source, the guiltlessness is attributed to Mirtillo, not to his (imagined) rival (III. 8. 1208).
[324] joyst] enjoy.
[325] by her words] by what she told him earlier.
[326] time attend] bide my time.
[327] 809] I'll show Amarillis her dead lover.

Then with this selfsame dart I'll pierce this breast,
So shall there be three pierced without relief,
First two with steel, the third with deadly grief.
Fierce,[328] she shall see the miserable end
815 Of her belovèd and her betrayèd friend.
This cave, that should be harbour of her joys,
Of both her loves, and, that which more I crave,
Of her great shame, may prove the happy grave.
And you the steps that I in vain have followed,
820 Could you me speed of such a faithful way?[329]
Could you direct me to so dear a bower?
Behold, I follow you. Oh Corisca, Corisca,
Now hast thou told too true, now I believe thee.

Act III, Scene 9
SATYR[330]

Doth this man then believe Corisca, following her steps
825 Into the cave of Ericina?[331] Well, he's mad,
He knows her not; believe me, he had need
Have better hold of her engagèd faith
Than I had of her hair: but knots more strangèd[332]
Than gaudy gifts[333] on her he cannot tie.
830 This damnèd whore[334] hath sold herself to him,
And here she'll pay the shameful market price.
She is within, her steps bewray the same.
This falls out for her punishment, and thy revenge:
With this great overstanding stone close thou the cave,
835 Go then about, and fetch the priest with thee,
By the hill way which few or none do know.
Let her be executed as the law commands,
For breach of marriage troth, which she to Coridon

---

[328] Fierce] The fierce Amarillis.
[329] He is addressing Amarillis's footsteps.
[330] All the editions have 'Satyre' as the speaking persona here. Elsewhere in the text, Dymock wavers between 'Satir' and 'Satyr' (the latter spelling has been used throughout in this edition).
[331] Satyr has misinterpreted Mirtillo's conclusion, and thinks the shepherd has a tryst with Corisca. 'Erycina' (from mount Erice, in Sicily) was one of the aspects of the goddess Venus, and there had been a temple dedicated to Venus Erycina in ancient Rome.
[332] stranged] A rather odd choice, repeated in all editions. Either 'strung' or '[made] strong' (in Italian 'possenti'; III. 9. 1292), rather than 'strange' or 'estranged'.
[333] In Italian, 'nodi' ('knots') is the anagram of 'doni' ('gifts'; III. 9. 1292).
[334] whore] In the source she is just wicked, and honesty's enemy ('malvagia, | nemica d'onestate'; III. 9. 1293–94).

Hath plighted, though she ever it concealed
840 For fear of me; so shall I be revenged
Of both at once. I'll lose no farther time:
From off this elm I'll cut a bough, with which
I may more speedily remove this stone! Oh, how great it is!
How fast it sticks. I'll dig it round about.
845 This is a work indeed: Where are my wonted forces?
Oh, perverse stars! In spite of you I'll mov't.
Oh Pan Liceus,[335] help me now, thou wert a lover once:
Revenge thy love disdained upon Corisca.
So, in the name of thy great power, it moves.
850 So, in the power of thy great name, it falls.
Now is the wicked fox ta'en in the trap.
Oh, that all wicked women were with thee within,
That with one fire they might be all destroyed.

CHORUS

How puissant art thou, Love,
855 Nature's miracle, and the world's wonder?
What savage nation, or what rustic heart
Is it that of thy power feels no part?
But what wit's so profound can pull asunder[336]
That power's strength?
860 Who feels[337] those flames thy fire lights at length,[338]
Immoderate and vain,
Will say, a mortal spright, thou sole dost reign
And live in the corporal and fleshly breast.
But who feels after how a lover is[339]
865 Wakened to virtue, and how all those flames
Do tremble out at sight of honest shames
(Unbridled blustering lusts brought down to rest),
Will call thee spright of high immortal bliss,
Having thy holy receptacle in the soul.
870 Rare miracle of human and divine aspects,

---

[335] Pan Liceus] Because of Mount Lykaion, in Arcadia, the seat of a wood and temple sacred to Pan. Dymock skips the other, more etymological attribute given to Pan in the source: 'che tutto se', che tutto puoi' (III. 9. 1332; 'that are everything, and can do everything').
[336] pull asunder] In the source, the profound wit is able to understand, or feel, the strength of love ('intende'; III. Ch. 1348).
[337] Who feels] Anyone who feels.
[338] at length] at a distance.
[339] But who feels after] But anyone who, after this first impression, considers.

That blind dost see, and wisdom mad corrects,[340]
Of sense and understanding intellects,
Of reason and desire confused affects.[341]
Such empery hast thou on earth,[342]
875 And so the heavens above dost thou control.
Yet, by your leave, a wonder much more rare,
And more stupendous hath the world than you,
For how you make all wonders yield and bow[343]
Is easily known. Your powers do berth
880 And being take from virtue of a woman fair.[344]
Oh woman, gift of the high heavenly sky,
Or rather his, who did their spangled gown
So gorgeous make unto our mortal eye:
What hath it which a woman's beauty push not down?[345]
885 In his vast brow, a monstrous Cyclops like,
It only one eye hath,[346]
Which to beholding gazers gives no light,
But rather doth with terror blindness strike.
If it do sigh or speak, 'tis like the wrath
890 Of an enragèd lion that would fight:
And not the skies alone, but even poor fields
Are blasted with the flames his lightning wields.
Whilst thou with lamps most sweet,
And with an amorous angelic light
895 Of two suns visible that never meet
Dost always the tempestuous troubled spright
Of thy beholder quiet and delight:[347]
Sound, motion, light, that beauty doth assume,
State, daintiness and value, do aright
900 Mix such a harmony in that fair sight
That skies themselves with vanity presume,[348]

[340] 871] Love is blind but sees, and corrects wisdom though he is mad.
[341] These two lines are rather confusing, but the gist of it is that love is both rational and irrational, a mixture of reason and desire.
[342] empery] dominance.
[343] Dymock strangely claims that love makes wonders 'yield and bow', where in the source love simply produces wonders by means of woman (III. Ch. 1371).
[344] take] All the editions have 'taken' here, but the clause only makes grammatical and metrical sense if one assumes that an additional n was printed by mistake (the clause means: your powers take root ('berth') and being from the virtue of a fair woman).
[345] 884] What qualities does the sky possess that are not surpassed by woman's beauty?
[346] The sky, like a Cyclops, only has one eye (the sun).
[347] quiet] quieten.
[348] with vanity] A slight mistranslation of Guarini's 'invan' ('in vain'; III. Ch. 1394). The skies contend with woman's beauty in vain.

If less than paradise those skies do shine,
To paragon with thee, thing most divine.
Good reason hath that sovereign creature, named
905 A man, to whom all mortal things do bow,
If thee beholding, higher cause allow
And yield to be.[349]
What though he rule and triumph truly famed?
It is not for high powers more worth do see
910 In him than is in thee,
Either of sceptre or of victory:
But for to make thee far more glorious stand,
Because the conqueror thou dost command:
And so't must be, for man's humanity
915 Is subject still to beauty's deity.
Who will not trust this, but contrary saith,
Let him behold Mirtillo's wondrous faith:
Yet, woman, to thy worth this is a stain,
Love is made love so hopelessly and vain.[350]

---

[349] And yield to be] And admits that it exists (the higher cause). It is, however, conceivable that the final 'bee' (in the original spelling) was a misprint for 'thee' — for in the source, man is said to bow and yield to woman ('t'inchina e cede'; III. Ch. 1402).

[350] Guarini's conclusion is more of a compliment than a rebuke (though there may be irony involved): 'Only this was missing from your virtues, | Woman, to produce love where there is no hope' ('E mancava ben questo al tuo valore, | donna, di far senza speranza amore'; III. Ch. 1412-13). It is to be noted that in S1591 a lack of punctuation makes the couplet somewhat confusing.

Act IV, Scene 1
CORISCA

So fixèd was my heart and whole intent
In bringing of this deer unto the bow,[351]
That I forgotten had my dearest hair
That brutish villain robbed me of:[352] Oh how I grieved
5 With such a price to purchase mine escape:
But 'twas of force to get out of the hands
Of that same senseless beast, who though he have
Less heart than any cony hath, yet might he do
Me many injuries and many scorns.
10 I always him despised: whilst he had blood
In any of his veins, like a horse-leech
I sucked him still. Now doth it grieve him that
I have giv'n o'er to love him still; just cause he had,[353]
If one could love a most unlovely beast.
15 Like herbs that erst were got for wholesome use,
The juice drawn out, they rest unprofitable,
And like a stinking thing we them despise,
So him: when I had whatsoe'er was good sucked out
From him, how should I use, but throw the sapless trunk
20 Unto the dunghill heap? Now will I see
If Coridon be gotten close into the cave.
What news is this I see? Sleep I or do I wake?
I am assured this cave's mouth erst was ope.
How close 'tis shut![354] How is this ancient stone
25 Rolled down? Was it an earthquake since?
Yet would I know if Coridon were there
With Amarillis, then cared I little for the rest.
Certain he's there, for 'tis a good while since
Lisetta gave him word. Who knows the contrary?
30 T'may be Mirtillo, movèd with disdain,
Hath done this deed; he, had he but my mind,
Could only have performed this rare exploit.
Well, by the mountain's way will I go see,
And learn the truth of all how it hath passed.

[351] deer] Amarillis ('la semplicetta', 'the simpleton', in the source; IV. 1. 1).
[352] Satyr, in II. 6.
[353] just cause he had] he would have just cause, if I had ever loved him in the first place.
[354] Probably, Dymock mistranslates Guarini's 'Com'ora è chiusa?' (IV. 1. 31; 'How come it's closed now?') as if it meant 'How closed it is!'.

Act IV, Scene 2
DORINDA, LINCO

DORINDA
35 Linco, I am assured thou knowst me not.

LINCO
Who would have thought that in these rusty rags[355]
Gentle Dorinda had been ever hid.
Were I some dog, as I but Linco am,
Unto thy cost I should thee know too well.
40 What do I see?

DORINDA
          Linco, thou seest great love
Working effects both strange and miserable.

LINCO
One like thyself, so soft, so tender yet,
That wert but now, as one would say, a babe,
And still methinks it was but yesterday
45 Since in mine arms I had thee, little wretch,
Ruling thy tender cries, and taught thee too
To call thy father dad, thy mother mam,
When in your house I was a servant hired.
Thou that so like a fearful doe wast wont
50 To fear each thing before thou felt this love —
Why, on a sudden thee would scare each blast,
Each bird that stirred a bush, each mouse that from
Her hole did run, each leaf would make thee start —
Now wandrest all alone by hills, by woods,
55 Fearing no beast that haunts the forests wild?

DORINDA
Wounded with love, who fears another hurt?

LINCO
Love had great power, that could not only thee
Into a man, but to a wolf transform.

DORINDA
Oh Linco, couldst thou but see here within,
60 There shouldst thou see a living wolf devour
My wretched soul like to a harmless lamb.

---

[355] rusty] Here and at the end of the scene, probably with the meaning of 'rough', 'rustic'.

LINCO
And who's that wolf? Silvio?

DORINDA
                              Ah, thou hast said.

LINCO
Thou, for he is a wolf, hast changed thyself
Into a wolf because no human looks
65 Could move his love; perhaps this beast's yet mought.[356]
But tell me, where hadst thou these clothes so ragged?

DORINDA
I'll tell thee true, today I went betime
There where I heard that Silvio did intend
A noble hunting to the savage boar.
70 At Erimantus' foot, where Elicet[357]
Puts up his head, not far off from the lawnd[358]
That from the hill is severed by descent,
I found Melampo, my fair Silvio's dog,
Whose thirst I think had drawn him to that place.
75 I that each thing of Silvio hold full dear,
Shade of his shape, and footsteps of his feet,
Much more the dog which he so dearly loved,
Him straightway took, and he without ado,
Like to some gentle cade,[359] came quietly with me:
80 Now whilst I cast this dog to reconvey
Home to his lord and mine, hoping to make
A conquest of his love by gift so dear,
Behold he comes seeking his footsteps out,
And here he stays. Dear Linco, I will not
85 Lose further time in telling every thing
That twixt us passed, but briefly to dispatch:
After a heap of feignèd vows and words,
The cruel boy fled from me straight away
In ireful mood with his thrice-happy dog,
90 And with my dear and sweetest sweet reward.

---

[356] because no human looks … this beast's yet mought] because human looks couldn't change his mind, perhaps dressing as a wolf might.

[357] Elicet] Dymock did not understand 'eliceto', Guarini's word for a holm-oak wood (IV. 2. 105). He probably decided it was the name of a hill. Again, the fact that in S1591 that common noun has a capital initial may explain his confusion.

[358] lawnd] glade.

[359] cade] pet lamb.

LINCO
Oh desperate Silvio! Oh cruel Boy!
What didst thou then? Disdaind'st thou not his deed?

DORINDA
As if the heat of his disdain had been
Of love unto my heart the greatest fire,
So by his rage increasèd my desire:
Yet still pursuing him unto the chase,
Keeping my broken way, I Lupus met;[360]
Here thought I good with him to change my clothes,
And in his servile habit me to hide,
That 'mongst the swains I for a swain might pass,
And at my pleasure see my Silvio.

LINCO
Went'st thou to hunt in likeness of a wolf,
Seen by the dogs, and yet returnèd safe?
Dorinda, thou hast done enough.

DORINDA
                        Linco,
No wonder 'tis, the dogs could do no harm
Unto their master's preordainèd prey.
There stood I by the toils amongst a sort
Of neighbour shepherds come to see the sport,
Rather to see the huntsman than the game.
At every motion of the savage beast
My heart did quake. At each of Silvio's acts
My soul stepped out, pushed on with all her will;
But my chief hope the fearful sight disturbed
Of that immeasurable boar in force.
Like as the ravenous strength of sudden storm
In little time brings trees and rocks to ground,
So by his tusks bedewed with blood and foam
We see dogs slain, staves broke, and wounded men.
How many times did my poor blood desire
For Silvio's blood to combat with the boar;[361]
How oftentimes would I have stepped to make
My breast a buckler for my Silvio's breast.

---

[360] Lupus] Lupino, her servant — 'Little Wolf' in Italian. The name is here shortened for metrical reasons.
[361] How many [...] boar] The construction is rather obscure, but it seems that Dorinda's blood desires to fight the boar to save Silvio's.

How often said I in myself, excuse,
Excuse the dainty lap of my dear love:[362]
125 So to myself spake I with praying sighs,
Whilst he his dog all armed with hardened skin
Lets loose against the beast, who waxèd proud
Of having made a wretched quarry's sight[363]
Of wounded shepherds and dogs slain outright:
130 Linco, I cannot tell this dog's great worth,
And Silvio loves him not without good cause.
Look how an angry lion entertains[364]
The pointed horns of some undaunted bull,
Sometime with force, sometime with policy,
135 And fastens at the last his mighty paws
So on his back as no power can remov't:
So strong Melamp' avoiding craftily
The boar's swift strokes and mortal wounding blows,
At last taints on his ear,[365] which first he shakes,
140 And afterward so firmly him he holds,
As his vast sides might wounded be at ease:
The dismal token of a deadly stroke.
Then Silvio, invocating Phoebe's name,[366]
Direct this blow (said he) and here I vow
145 To sacrifice to thee his ghastly head.
This said, from out his quiver of pure gold
He takes a speedy shaft, and to his ear
He draws his mighty bow, and straight the boar,
Between his neck and shoulder wounded, dies.
150 I freed a sigh, seeing my Silvio safe.
Oh happy beast that mightst thy life so leave,
By him that hearts from human breasts doth reave.[367]

LINCO
But what became of that same fearful beast?

---

[362] How often [...] love] A bizarre rendition, in which Guarini's 'Perdona' ('Forgive'; IV. 2. 191) turns into 'excuse', and 'sen' ('[Silvio's] breast'; IV. 2. 193) becomes 'lap'. In the source, Dorinda is praying for the boar to spare Silvio's breast.
[363] quarry's sight] Presumably, of having turned so many live bodies into dead meat ('quarry').
[364] entertains] A confusing translation of Guarini's 'incontri' ('meets'; IV. 2. 208).
[365] taints] hits (a tilting term).
[366] Phoebe] Diana as goddess of the moon (just 'Diana' in the source; IV. 2. 225).
[367] breasts] Both T1602 and T1633 have 'beasts' here, but Donno's correction is probably right (Guarini's Silvio robs human 'petti' of their hearts; IV. 2. 241).

DORINDA
I do not know, because I came away
For fear of being seen: But I believe
That solemnly they mean to carry it
Unto the temple, as my Silvio vowed.

LINCO
And mean you not to change these rusty clothes?

DORINDA
Yes wis,[368] full fain, but Lupin hath my gown,
And promisèd t'attend me at this spring,
But him I miss: dear Linco, if thou lov'st me,
Go seek him in these woods, he is not far;
I'll rest me in the meantime by this den,
For weariness makes me to sleep desire,
Nor would I home return in this attire.

LINCO
I go, and stir not you till I return.

Act IV, Scene 3
CHORUS, ERGASTO

CHORUS
Shepherds, have you not heard our demigod,
Montanus' worthy son, of Hercules' descent,
Hath slain the dreadful boar that did infest
All Arcady, and now he doth prepare
To satisfy his vows? If we will thankful be
For such a benefit, let's go and meet him,
And give him all the reverence that we can.[369]

ERGASTO
Oh doleful fortune! Oh most bitter chance!
Immedicable wound! Oh mournful day!

CHORUS
What voice of horror and of plaint hear we?

---

[368] wis] certainly.
[369] Here Dymock skips a rather difficult passage on how value does not care about honours, and yet it should be honoured.

ERGASTO
Stars, foemen to our good,[370] thus mock you us?
Did you so high our hopes lift up, that with
Their fall you might us plague the more?

CHORUS
180 This seems Ergasto, and 'tis surely he.

ERGASTO
Why do I stars accuse? Accuse thyself,
That brought'st the iron to love's anvil so,
Thou didst it strike, thou mad'st the sparks fly out
From whence this fire grows so unquenchable:
185 But heavens do know my pity brought me to't.
Oh hapless lovers, wretched Amarillis,
Unfortunate Titirus, childless father,
Sad Montanus, desolate Arcadia:
Oh miserable we; and to conclude,
190 All that I see, speak, hear, or think, most miserable.

CHORUS
What wretched accident is this that doth contain
So many miseries? Go'w, shepherds, go'w!
Let's meet with him: Eternal heavenly powers,
Will not your rage yet cease? Speak, good Ergasto,
195 What lamentable chance is this thou plainst?

ERGASTO
Dear friends, I plain us all the ruin of Arcadia.

CHORUS
What's this?

ERGASTO
        The prop of all our hopes is down.

CHORUS
Ah, speak more plain.

ERGASTO
        Daughter of Titirus,
The only branch of her decaying stock,
200 Hope of our health, which to Montanus' son
Was by the heavens promised and destined,
Whose marriage should have freed Arcadia,

---

[370] foemen] foes ('nemiche', with feminine termination; IV. 3. 286).

Wise Amarillis, nymph celestial,
Pattern of honour, flower of chastity —
205 My heart will not give me leave to speak.

CHORUS
                    Why, is she dead?

ERGASTO
Nay, doomed to death.

CHORUS
                    Ay me, what's this?

ERGASTO
Nay, worse, with infamy.

CHORUS
                    Amarillis infamous!

ERGASTO
Found with the adulterer, and if hence ye go not soon,
Ye may her see led captive to the temple.

CHORUS
210 Oh rare, but wicked valour of this female sex,[371]
Oh chastity, how singular thou art!
Scarce can a man say any woman's chaste,
Save she that ne'er was tried; unhappy age:
But courteous shepherd, tell us how it was.[372]

ERGASTO
215 This day betime you know Montanus came
With th'hapless father of the wretched nymph,
Both by one self devotion led, which was
By prayers to haste the marriage to good end:
For this the sacrifices offered were,
220 Which solemnly performed with good aspects.
For never were there seen entrails more fair,
Nor flames more bright, by which the blind divine,[373]
Movèd, did to Montanus say: this day
With Amarillis shall your son be wed.
225 Go quickly and prepare the marriage feast.

[371] wicked] This adjective contradicts the logic of the passage. Guarini's adjective is 'malagevole' (IV. 3. 348; difficult, hard to sustain).
[372] Here Dymock skips Ergasto's comment to the effect that if Honesty itself is found dishonest, every woman can be suspected (IV. 3. 355-58).
[373] divine] diviner, soothsayer: Tirenio.

Oh blindly done, blind prophets to believe.[374]
The fathers and the standers-by were glad,
And wept, their hearts made tender with this joy.
Titirus was no sooner gone, but straight we heard
230　And saw unhappy fearful signs, the messengers
Of sacred ire: at which, so sudden and so fierce,
Each stood amazed; the priests enclosèd were
Within the greater cloister, we without
Weeping were saying holy prayers, when lo,
235　The wicked satyr audience earnest craves
Of the chief priest: and for this was my charge,
I let him in, to whom he thus begins,
Fathers, if to your vows the incense and
The sacrifices be not answerable,
240　If on your altars purely burn no flames,
Wonder not, for in Ericina's cave
A treacherous nymph profanes your holy laws,
And in adultery her faith doth break.
Come ministers with me, we'll take in the fact.[375]
245　A while th'unhappy father breathes,[376] thinking he had
Found out the cause of these so dismal signs.
Straight he commands chief minister Nicander go
With that same satyr, and captived to bring
Them to the temple both. Him straight accompanied
250　With all our troupe of under-ministers[377]
The satyr by a dark and crooked way
Conducts into the cave: the young man,[378] scared
With our torchlight, so suddenly assailed,
Assays to fly unto that outward issue,
255　But it the satyr closèd hath too fast.

CHORUS
What did you then?[379]

---

[374] Actually, as will be discovered in Act v, Tirenio's prediction is correct.
[375] we'll take in the fact] A slightly misleading translation of 'prenderli sul fatto' ('catch them in the act'; IV. 3. 425).
[376] In the source, it is both fathers who hesitate (IV. 3. 430–31).
[377] under] minor.
[378] In the source it is Amarillis who tries to escape ('La giovane'; IV. 3. 445).
[379] The question in the source is about what the satyr was doing ('Ed egli, intanto, che facea?'; IV. 3. 453), but changing it allows Dymock to shorten Ergasto's reply.

ERGASTO
               I cannot tell you how
Amazed we were, to see her that we taken had
To be Titirus' daughter, whom no sooner we
Had laid hold on, but out Mirtillo steps
260 And throws his dart, thinking to wound Nicander:
And had the steel hit as he did direct,
Nicander had been slain: but shrinking back,
Whether by chance or wit, he shunned the harm.
But the strong dart piercèd his hairy clothes,
265 And there stuck fast; Mirtillo not being able
It to recover, captive taken was.

CHORUS
What's come of him?

ERGASTO
              He by an other way is led.

CHORUS
What shall he do?[380]

ERGASTO
             To get more out of him.
Besides, perhaps he shall not scot-free scape
270 For having so offended our high priest.
Yet would I could have comforted the wretch.

CHORUS
Why could you not?

ERGASTO
             Because the law forbids
Us under-ministers to speak with guilty folks:
For this I came about, and left the rest,[381]
275 Provoking heavens with tears and prayers devout,
To turn away this dreadful storm from us.
And so pray ye, and therewithal farewell.

---

[380] Here Dymock mistranslates the question 'E per far che?' ('And for what reason?'; IV. 3. 484), thus creating a non sequitur.

[381] Another passage is skipped here. In the source, Ergasto left the other priests but now intends to go to the temple via another route, in order to pray (IV. 3. 498–502).

CHORUS
So shall we do, had we but once performed[382]
Our duty unto Silvio. Eternal gods,
280 In pity, not in fury, show yourselves supreme.

Act IV, Scene 4
CORISCA

Now crown my temples with triumphant bays —
Victorious temples — this day happily
I combated have in the field of love,
And vanquishèd: this day both heaven and earth,
285 Nature and art, fortune and destiny,
Both friends and enemies have fought for me.
The wicked satyr whom I hated so
Hath helped me much: for it was better that
Mirtillo should, than Coridon, be ta'en,
290 To make her fault more likely and more ill:
What though Mirtillo taken be, he'll soon be free,
To her alone the punishment is due.
Oh solemn victory, oh famous triumph,
Dress me a trophy,[383] amorous deceits,
295 You in this tongue, in this same precious breast
Are above nature most omnipotent.
Why stay I now? 'Tis time for me to go:
Until the law have judged my rival dead,
Perhaps the priest may draw the truth from me.[384]
300 Fly then, Corisca, danger 'tis to lie
For them that have no feet wherewith to fly.
I'll hide me in these woods until I may
Return t'enjoy my joys: happy Corisca,
Who ever saw a braver enterprise?

Act IV, Scene 5
NICANDER, AMARILLIS

NICANDER
305 He had a heart most hard, or rather had
No heart at all, nor any human sense,

---

[382] had we but once performed] after performing our duty to Silvio.

[383] Dress me a trophy] Another translation-by-sound of 'Drizzatemi un trofeo' ('Erect my monument'; IV. 4. 534).

[384] A shortened simplification of the source, where Corisca reflects that Amarillis will probably blame her in order to save herself (IV. 4. 542–46).

ACT IV

That did not pity thee, poor wretched nymph,
And felt no sorrow for thy misery.
Only to see a damsel captivate[385]
Of heavenly countenance and so sweet a face,
Worthy the world should to thee consecrate
Temples and sacrifices, led to the temple
For a sacrifice, surely 'twere a thing
That with dry eyes I think none could behold:
But who knows how and wherefore thou wert born?[386]
Titirus' daughter, Montanus' daughter-in-law
That should have been, and that these two are they
Which do uphold Arcadia, and that thyself
A dainty nymph, so fair of form,
The natural confines of this thy life,[387]
Approachest now so near the bounds of death.
He that knows this, and doth not plain the same,
He is no man, but beast in human shape.

AMARILLIS
If that my fault did cause my wretchedness,[388]
Or that my thoughts were wicked as thou thinkst
My deed, less grievous would my death be then:
For it were just my blood should wash the spots
Of my defilèd soul, heaven's rage appease,
And human justice justly satisfy.
Then could I quiet my afflicted sprights,
And with a just remorse of well-deservèd death
My senses mortify, and come to death,
And with a quiet blow pass forth perhaps
Unto a life of more tranquillity.
But too, too much, Nicander, too much grieved
I am, in so young years, fortune so high,
An innocent, I should be doomed to die.

NICANDER
Ah pleased it heavens we had 'gainst thee offended,
Not thou offended 'gainst the heavenly powers:
For we, alas, with greater ease might have

---

[385] captivate] captive.
[386] But who knows] Let alone one who knows.
[387] Probably Dymock did not understand Guarini here. In the source, Amarillis is said to be 'so far | from the natural limits of your life' ('sì lontana | dal natural confin de la tua vita'; IV. 5. 575), i.e., too young to die.
[388] did cause] had caused.

Restored thee to thy violated name
Than thou appeased their violated powers.
But I see not who thee offended hath,
Saving thyself. Tell me, wert thou not found
345 In a close place with the adulterer, alone,
With him alone? Wert thou not promisèd
Unto Montanus' son? Hast thou not broke thy faith?
How art thou innocent?

AMARILLIS
                    I have not broke
The law, and I am innocent.

NICANDER
                        Thou hast not broke
350 The law of nature haply (love, if thou likest),
But human law and heaven's thou hast transgressed
(Love lawfully).

AMARILLIS
             Both heavens and men have erred to me:
If it be true that thence our haps do come,
For is it reason in my destiny,[389]
355 I bear the pain that's due to others' faults?

NICANDER
Peace, nymph; came up thy tongue in wilful rage.[390]
Let loose, do not condemn the stars, for we
Ourselves procure us all our misery.

AMARILLIS
I none accuse in heaven, but my ill fates.
360 And worse than them is she that me deceived.

NICANDER
Then blame thyself, that hast deceived thyself.

AMARILLIS
I was deceived, but by another's fraud.

NICANDER
'Tis no deceit, to whom deceit is dear.

---

[389] A confusing passage. In the source, Amarillis is saying that her fate appears to be to bear the pain for others' faults (IV. 5. 627–29).

[390] came up thy tongue in wilful rage] your words are motivated by wilful rage.

ACT IV

    AMARILLIS
    Then you I see condemn me for unchaste?[391]

    NICANDER
365 I say not so; ask but your deeds, they'll tell.

    AMARILLIS
    Deeds often are false tokens of the heart.

    NICANDER
    The deeds we see, we cannot see the heart.[392]

    AMARILLIS
    See what you will, I'm sure my heart is clear.

    NICANDER
    What led you then into the cave alone?

    AMARILLIS
370 Simplicity, and my too much belief.

    NICANDER
    Trust you your chastity unto your love?[393]

    AMARILLIS
    I trusted my false friend, and not my love.

    NICANDER
    What friend was that, your amorous desire?

    AMARILLIS
    Ormino's sister, who hath me betrayed.

    NICANDER
375 Sweet treachery, to fall into your love.

    AMARILLIS
    I knew not of Mirtillo's coming, I.

    NICANDER
    Why did you enter then? And to what end?

    AMARILLIS
    Let it suffice, not for Mirtillo's sake.

---

[391] Clearer in the Italian. Nicander has just insinuated that Amarillis *wanted* to be deceived, and Amarillis replies 'Do you then think me so indecent?' ('Dunque m'hai tu per impudica tanto?'; IV. 5. 644).

[392] Four more one-line repartees are omitted after this (IV. 5. 648–51).

[393] Trust you] Did you trust.

NICANDER
You are condemned, except y'have better proof.

AMARILLIS
380 Let her be askèd of my innocence.³⁹⁴

NICANDER
What, she that was the occasion of your fault?

AMARILLIS
She that betrayed me; will you not her believe?

NICANDER
What faith hath she that was so faithless then?

AMARILLIS
I by our goddess Cynthia's name will swear.

NICANDER
385 Thy deeds have marred the credit of thine oath:
Nymph, to be plain, these are but dreams, and waves
Of muddy water cannot wash clean, nor guilty hearts
Speak truth; thou shouldst have kept thy chastity
As dearly as the apple of thine eye.³⁹⁵

AMARILLIS
390 And must I then thus, good Nicander, die?
Shall none me hear, nor none my cause defend?
Thus left of all, deprived of every hope,
Only accompanied with an extreme
Unhappy funeral pity that not helps me?³⁹⁶

NICANDER
395 Nymph, be content, and since thou wert so fond
In sinning, be more wise in suffering punishment.
Direct thine eyes to heaven; thence art thou come,
And thence doth come all good or ill that haps,
As from a fountain doth a stream descend.
400 And though to us it ill do seem, as every good
Is mingled with some ill, yet there 'tis good.

---

³⁹⁴ In the source, Amarillis first proposes to ask Mirtillo (IV. 5. 664); Dymock either misread the personal pronouns or deliberately chose to simplify her line of defence. This, however, produces a slight incongruity, because it means that in the next line Nicander appears to accept that Corisca is to blame.
³⁹⁵ Another line is skipped here: 'Che pur vaneggi? A che te stessa inganni?' ('Why do you talk so wildly? Why do you deceive yourself?'; IV. 5. 678).
³⁹⁶ funeral] funereal, mournful.

ACT IV

Great Jove doth know, to whom all thoughts are known.
So doth our goddess whom we worship here
How much I grieve for thee: and if I have
405 Pierced with my words thy soul, like a physician I
Have done, who searcheth first the wound
Where it suspected is. Be quiet, then,
Good nymph, and do not contradict that which
Is writ in heaven above of thee.

AMARILLIS
410 Oh cruel sentence, whether writ in heaven
Or earth! In heaven it is not writ,
For there mine innocence is known: but what
Avails it since I needs must die? Ah too, too hard,
And too, too bitter cup. Ah, good Nicander,
415 For pity's sake make not such haste with me
Unto the temple! Stay, oh stay a little while!

NICANDER
Oh nymph, to whom death is so grievous now,
Each moment seems a death. It is thine ill to stay:
Death hath not so much harm, as fear thereof;
420 Thou sooner dead, thy pain is sooner past.

AMARILLIS
Some help may come, dear father: father,[397] now
Dost thou leave me, now leave thine only child?
Wilt thou not help me yet before I die?
Do not deny me yet thy latest kiss:
425 One blade shall wound both breasts, and out of mine
Thy blood must stream. Oh father! Oh sweet name
Sometime so dear which I ne'er called in vain,
Make you your only daughter's marriage thus,
A morning's bride, an evening's sacrifice?

NICANDER
430 Nymph, do not thus torment thyself and me.
'Tis time I lead you to the Temple now;
My duty 'tis, I may not slack it so.

AMARILLIS
Dear woods farewell, my dearest woods farewell,
Receive my latest sighs until my soul,

---

[397] The second 'father' is an invocation of her real father, Titirus (which creates some confusion).

435 By cruel wound from this my body free,
Return to seek your lovèd shadows out.
For innocents cannot be doomed to hell,
Nor 'mongst the blessèd can despairers dwell.
Oh Mirtillo, wretched was that day
440 That first I saw thee, and thy sight did please,
Since I my life must leave, more near to thee
Than thine, which proves the occasion of my death.
Wilt thou believe that she is doomed to death
For thee, that cruel ever was to thee
445 To keep me innocent? For me too bold,
For thee too little daring was my will:[398] however 'twas,
I faultless die, fruitless, and without thee,
My dear, I die, my dear Mirt —[399]

NICANDER
                              Surely she
Is dead, and in Mirtillo's lovèd name her life
450 Hath finishèd: her love and grief the blade
Prevented hath. Come help to hold her up,
She liveth yet, I feel her heart doth throb.
Carry her to the fountain here hard by,
Fresh water may restore her stonied sprights.[400]
455 But were it not a deed of pity, now,
To let her die of grief, and shun the blade?
No, let us rather succour now her life,
We do not know what heavens will do with her.

Act IV, Scene 6
CHORUS OF HUNTSMEN, CHORUS OF SHEPHERDS WITH SILVIO

CHORUS OF HUNTSMEN
Oh glorious child of great Alcides' race,[401]
460 That monsters killst, and wild beasts dost deface.

---

[398] Dymock skips her reflection to the effect that it was better either to sin or to fly away ('Era pur meglio | o peccar o fuggire'; IV. 5. 775).
[399] Mirt] Both T1633 and Donno normalize this to 'Mirtillo' — but the point is that Amarillis faints mid-word ('Mirti...', she manages to say in the source; IV. 5. 778).
[400] stonied] stupefied, stunned.
[401] Alcides'] Herculean. Here, for the sake of rhyme, Dymock finds it expedient to use the patronymic he eschewed in I. 1.

CHORUS OF SHEPHERDS
Oh glorious child, who Erimantus' boar
Hast overthrown, unconquerable thought.
Behold his head, that seems to breath out death:
This is the trophy of our demigod.
465 Help, shepherds, help to celebrate his name,
And with solemnity his deeds to grace.

CHORUS OF HUNTSMEN
Oh glorious child of great Alcides' race,
That monsters killst, and wild beasts dost deface.

CHORUS OF SHEPHERDS
Oh glorious child, by whom the fertile plains,[402]
470 Deprived of tillage, have their good regained.
Now may the ploughman go securely, and
Sow both his seed, and reap his harvest in:
These ugly teeth can now no more them chase.[403]

CHORUS OF HUNTSMEN
Oh glorious child of great Alcides' race,
475 That monsters killst, and wild beasts dost deface.

CHORUS OF SHEPHERDS
Oh glorious child, how thou dost couple still
Pity with fortitude. Cynthia, behold
Thy humble Silvio's vow; behold this head,
That here and here in thy despite is armed
480 With white and crooked tusks, envying thy horns.[404]
Thou puissant goddess, since thou didst direct
His shaft, the price of his great victory
Is due to thee: he famous by thy grace.

CHORUS OF HUNTSMEN
Oh glorious child of great Alcides' race,
485 That monsters killst, and wild beasts dost deface.

---

[402] There are five exchanges in the source, only two in the target play. Here Dymock skips a passage on the evils of idleness, and some praise of Silvio's valour as an active, courageous man. In general, the scene is shortened and simplified.
[403] chase] 'chace' in the original spelling, to underscore the rhyme with the antiphon.
[404] Diana, as goddess of the moon, was represented with the lunar crescent on her forehead.

Act IV, Scene 7[405]
CORIDON

      Until this time I never durst believe
      That which the satyr of Corisca said,
      Imagining his tale had been but forged
      Maliciously to work me injury:
490 Far from the truth it seemed to me that place
      Where she appointed I with her should meet
      (If that be true which was on her behalf
      Delivered me by young Lisetta late)
      Should be the place to take th'adulterer in.
495 But see a sign that may confirm the same,
      Even as he told me, so it is in deed.
      Oh what a stone is this, which shuts up thus
      The huge mouth of this cave? Oh Corisca,
      All in good time I have found out your guiles,
500 Which after so long use at last return
      With damage to yourself. So many lies,
      So many treacheries, must needs presage
      Some mortal disadventure at the least,
      To him that was not mad, or blind with love.
505 'Twas good for me I stayed away so long,
      Great fortune that my father me detained
      So with a tedious stay, as then methought.
      Had I kept time but as Lisetta bade,
      Surely some strange adventure had I had.
510 What shall I do? Shall I, attired with spleen,
      Seek with outrageous fury for revenge?
      Fie, no, I honour her too much:[406] so be
      The case with reason weighed; it rather would
      Have pity and compassion, than revenge.
515 And shall I pity her, that me betrays?
      She rather doth betray herself, that thus
      Abandons me, whose faith to her was pure,
      And give herself in prey
      To a poor shepherd stranger vagabond,
520 That shall tomorrow be more perfidous than she.
      Should I, according to the satyr's counsel, her accuse

---

[405] With forty-four lines for Guarini's seventy-seven hendecasyllables, this scene is heavily cut. In particular, Dymock skips a long passage which compares an inconstant, faithless woman to 'love's corpse' (IV. 7. 932–41).

[406] I honour her too much] I would do her too great an honour (by taking her so seriously).

Of the faith broken, which to me she swore?
Then must she die: my heart's not half so base.
Let her then live for me: or to say better,
525 Let her die unto me, and live unto others:
Live to her shame, live to her infamy;
Since she is such, she never can in me
Kindle one spark of fearful jealousy.

Act IV, Scene 8
SILVIO

Oh goddess, that no goddess art but of
530 An idle people, blind and vain: who with
Impurest minds and fond religion
Hallows the altars and great temples too.
What, said I temples? Wicked theatres
Of beastly deeds, to colour their dishonest acts
535 With titles of thy famous deity,
Because thy shames in others' shames made less
Let loose the rains of their lasciviousness.
Thou foe to reason, plotter of misdeeds,
Corrupter to our souls, calamity
540 To the whole world; thou daughter of the sea,[407]
And of that treacherous monster rightly born,
That with the breath of hope dost first entice
These human breasts, but afterward dost move
A thousand storms of sighs, of tears, of plaints:
545 Thou mayst be better called mother of tempests and
Of rage, than mother of love.[408]
To what a misery hast thou thrown down
Those wretched lovers? Now mayst thou vaunt thyself
To be omnipotent, if thou canst save
550 That poor nymph's life, whom with thy snares thou hast
Conducted to this miserable death.
Oh happy day I hallowed my chaste mind
To thee, my only goddess, Cynthia,
Such power on earth to souls of better sort
555 As thou art light in heaven above the stars.
Much better are those studious practices
Than those which Venus' unchaste servants use:

[407] Because Aphrodite, in Hesiod's *Theogony*, was said to have been born at sea from the foam generated by Uranus's genitals.
[408] A rare seven-syllable line.

Thy servants kill both bears and ugly boars,
Her servants are of bears and boars still slain.[409]
560 Oh bow and matchless shafts, my power and my delight!
Vain fantastive love,[410] come prove thine arms,
Effeminate, with mine: but fie, too much
I honour thee, poor weak and wreckling child,[411]
And for thou shalt me hear I'll speak aloud.
565 A rod to chastise thee will be enough. — *enough* —
What art thou, Echo, that so sounds again?
Or rather Love, that answerest loudly so? — *y so* —[412]
I could have wished no better match; but tell
Me then, art thou, by heaven, he — *even he* —
570 The son of her that for Adonis did
So miserably burn, in whom nought good is? — *goddess* —
A goddess? No, the concubine of Mars,
In whom lasciviousness doth wholly lie — *wholly a lye* —
Oh fine, thy tongue doth clack against the wind,
575 Wilt thou come forth? Thou dost but darkly dare — *y dare* —
I held thee for a coward still,[413] art thou a bastard or
Dost thou that title bravely scorn? — *y scorn* —
Oh God, then art thou Vulcano's son, by that
Lame smith begot. — *god* —
580 A god? of what? of winds, mad with base mearth[414] — *earth* —
God of the earth? Makes thou thy foes to rue? — *t'rue* —
With what dost thou still punish those that strive,
And obstinately do contend with love? — *with love* —
Nay soft, when shall crooked love (tell me, good fool)
585 Enter my breast? I warrant 'tis too straight. — *straight* —
What, shall I fall in love so suddenly? — *suddenly* —
What is her name that I must then adore? — *Dore* —
Dorinda, fool, thou canst not speak out yet,
But dost not thou mean her — *e'n her*[415] —

---

[409] The Italian Silvio only mentions boars — which makes perfect mythological and narrative sense, as Silvio just killed a dangerous boar, and a boar killed Aphrodite's lover Adonis in Greek myth (IV. 8. 1017).
[410] fantastive] Dymock's creation, to render Guarini's depiction of love as 'vana fantasima' ('immaterial phantom'; IV. 8. 1023).
[411] wreckling] weak, small. Only recorded as a noun in the *OED*.
[412] y] ay. Throughout the 'echo conversation', 'y' is used as either 'ay' or 'I'.
[413] I held thee for a coward still] I knew you were a coward.
[414] mearth] A graphological variant of 'mirth' (unrecorded by the *OED*, which notes, however, that Spenser rhymes 'merth(e)' with *e*-words). Used here for the sake of the echo-rhyme.
[415] e'n] even, precisely.

590 Dorinda whom I hate? But who shall force my will? — *I will* —
What weapons wilt thou use? Perhaps thy bow? — *thy bow* —
My bow? Not till it be by thy lewd folly broken. — *broken* —
My broken arms encounter me? And who
Shall break them? Thou? — *thou* —
595 Fie, fie, thou art drunk, go sleep, go sleep: but stay,
These marvels must be done: but where? — *here* —
Oh fool, and I am gone, how thou art laden with
Wit-robbing grapes that grew upon the vine. — *divine* —
But soft, I see, or else methinks I see
600 Something that's like a wolf in yonder grove.
'Tis sure a wolf. How monstrous great it is.
This day for me is destinèd to praise:
Good goddess, with great favours dost thou show
To triumph in one day over two beasts:[416]
605 In thy great name, I loose this shaft, the swiftest and
The sharpest which my quiver holds.
Great archeress, direct thou my right hand,
And here I vow to sacrifice the spoils
Unto thy name. Oh dainty blow, blow fallen
610 Even where my hand and eye it destinèd.
Ah that I had my dart, it to dispatch,
Before it get into the woods away.
But here be stones, what need I any else?
Here's scarcely one. I need none now: here is
615 Another shaft will pierce it to the quick.
What's this I see? Unhappy Silvio!
I've shot a shepherd in a wolvish shape.
Oh bitter chance! Oh ever miserable![417]
Methinks I know the wretch, 'tis Linco that
620 Doth hold him up. Oh deadly shaft! Oh most
Unhappy vow! I guilty of another's blood?
I thus the causer of another's death?
I that have been so liberal of my life,
So large a spender of my blood for others' health?
625 So, cast away thy weapons, and go live
All gloryless. But see where he doth come,[418]
A great deal less unhappy than thyself.

---

[416] 603–04] You show me great favour in allowing me to triumph.
[417] ever miserable] miserable forever ('da viver sempre misero e dolente'; IV. 8. 1122).
[418] Guarini's 'Ma ecco lo infelice' (IV. 8. 1136) is best interpreted as 'But here is the poor soul'. It makes no sense for the wounded Dorinda to 'come' towards Silvio.

Act IV, Scene 9
LINCO, SILVIO, DORINDA

LINCO
Lean thou thyself (my daughter) on this arm,
Unfortunate Dorinda.

SILVIO
                  Oh me! Dorinda? I am dead.[419]

DORINDA
630 Oh Linco, Linco, oh my second father!

SILVIO
It is Dorinda sure: ah voice, ah sight.

DORINDA
Dorinda to sustain, Linco, hath been
A fatal office unto thee: thou heardest
The first cries that I ever gave on earth,
635 And thou shalt hear the latest of my death.
And these thine arms, that were my cradle once,
Shall be my coffin now.

LINCO
                      Oh child more dear
Than if thou wer't mine own. I cannot speak,
Grief hath my words dissolvèd into tears.

SILVIO
640 Oh earth, hold ope thy jaws and swallow me.

DORINDA
Oh stay both pace and plaint, good Linco, for
The one my grief, my wound the other doth increase.

SILVIO
Oh what a hard reward, most wretched nymph,
Hast thou receivèd for thy wondrous love!

LINCO
645 Be of good cheer, thy wound not mortal is.

DORINDA
Aye, but Dorinda, mortal, will be quickly dead:
But dost thou know who 'tis hath wounded me?

---

[419] Silvio's comments in the first part of the scene are all asides.

LINCO
Let us care for the sore, not for the offence,
For never did revenge yet heal a wound.

SILVIO
Why stay I still? Shall I stay whilst they see me?[420]
Have I so bold a face? Fly, Silvio, fly
The punishment of that revengeful sight,
Fly the just edge of her sharp cutting voice.
I cannot fly, fatal necessity doth hold
Me here, and makes me seek whom most
I ought to shun.

DORINDA
                    Why Linco, must I die
Not knowing who hath given me my death?

LINCO
It Silvio is.

DORINDA
            Is't so?

LINCO
                    I know his shaft.

DORINDA
Oh, happy issue of my life's last end,
If I be slain by such a lovely friend.

LINCO
See where he is, with countenance him accusing.
Now heavens be praised, y'are at good pass,
With this your bow and shafts omnipotent:
Hast thou not like a cunning woodman shot?[421]
Tell me, thou that of Silvio liv'st; was it not I
That shot this dainty shoot?[422] Oh boy too wise,
Hadst thou believed this foolish agèd man,
Had it not better been? Answer me, wretch.
What can thy life be worth, if she do die?

---

[420] whilst] until. He has not been spotted yet.
[421] woodman] huntsman.
[422] of Silvio [...] shoot] Dymock seems to have missed Linco's sarcasm. The older shepherd is asking Silvio, or 'the one who lives like Silvio' (an echoic reference to I. 1), if this act is like Linco or like Silvio ('Dimmi, | tu che vivi da Silvio e non da Linco; | questo colpo, che hai fatto sì leggiadro, | è fors'egli da Linco o pur da Silvio?'; IV. 9. 1193–96).

670 I know thou'lt say thou thoughtst t'have shot a wolf,
    As though it were no fault to shoot
    Not knowing (careless wandering child) if 'twere
    A man or beast thou shotst at: what herdsman or
    What ploughman dost thou see attired in other clothes?
675 Ah Silvio, Silvio, who ever soweth wit so green,
    Doth ever reap ripe fruit of ignorance.
    Think you, vain boy, this chance by chance did come?
    Never without the powers divine did suchlike happen:
    Heaven is enraged at your supportless spite[423]
680 To love, and deep despising so human affects.
    Gods will not have companions on the earth,[424]
    They are not pleased with this austerity:
    Now thou art dumb, thou wert not wont t'endure.[425]

DORINDA
    Silvio, let Linco speak, he doth not know
685 What sovereign tie thou o'er Dorinda hast,
    In life and death by the great power of love.
    If thou hast shot me, thou hast shot thine own:
    Thou hitst the mark that's proper to thy shaft.
    These hands that wounded me have followed right
690 The aim of thy fair eyes. Silvio, behold her whom
    Thou hatest so, behold her as thou wouldst:
    Thou wouldst me wounded have, wounded I am.
    Thou wished me dead, I ready am for death.
    What wouldst thou more? What can I give thee more?
695 Ah cruel boy, thou never wouldst believe
    The wound by thee love made;[426] canst thou deny
    That which thy hand hath done? Thou never sawst
    The blood mine eyes did shed; seest thou this then,
    That gusheth from my side? But if with pity now
700 All gentleness and valour be not spent,
    Do not deny me, cruel soul, I pray,
    At my last gasp, one poor and only sigh:
    Death should be blest, if thou but thus wouldst say,
    Go rest in peace, poor soul, I humbly pray.

[423] supportless] intolerable.
[424] The implication being that by acting so proud and refusing all human contact, Silvio is behaving as if he were a god.
[425] 683] Now you do not speak, while before this you would not have endured my accusations without replying.
[426] The wound by thee love made] The wound love gave me for your sake.

SILVIO

705 Ah, my Dorinda, shall I call thee mine
That art not mine, but when I thee must lose?
And when thou hast thy death received by me,
Not when I might have giv'n thee thy life?
Yet will I call thee mine, that mine shalt be
710 Spite of my fortune: and since with thy life
I cannot have thee, I'll have thee in death.
All that thou seest in me is ready for revenge:
I killed thee with these weapons: with the same
I'll kill myself. I cruel was to thee:
715 I now desire nothing but cruelty.
I proudly thee despised: upon my knees
I humbly thee adore, and pardon crave,
But not my life. Behold my bow, my shafts.
Wound not mine eyes or hands, th'are innocent:
720 But wound my breast, monster to pity, foe
To love; wound me this heart, that cruel was
To thee. Behold, my breast is bare.

DORINDA

Silvio, I wound that breast? Thou hadst not need
Let it be naked to mine eyes, if thou desiredst
725 I should it wound.[427] Oh dainty beauteous rock,
So often beaten by the waves and winds
Of my poor tears and sighs in vain: and is it true
Thou pity feelst? Or am I, wretch, but mocked?
I would not this same alabaster skin
730 Should me deceive, as this poor beast's hath thee.
I, wound thy breast? 'Tis well love durst do so,
I ask no more revenge than thou shouldst love.
Blest be the day wherein I first did burn,
Blest be my tears and all my martyrdoms:
735 I wish thy praise, and no revenge of thee.
But courteous Silvio, that dost kneel to her
Whose lord thou art, since me thou needs wilt serve,
Let thy first service be, to rise when I thee bid;
The second, that thou liv'st. For me, let heavens
740 Work their will; in thee my heart will live.
As long as thou dost live, I cannot die.

---

[427] Thou hadst not need […] wound] You should not have bared it, if you wanted me to wound it ('Non bisognava agli occhi miei scovrirlo, s'avevi pur desio ch'io tel ferissi'; IV. 9. 1387–88). Dymock's use of 'need', mirroring Guarini's 'bisognava', is confusing here.

But if it seem unjust my wound should be
Unpunishèd, then break this cruel bow,
Let that be all the malice thou dost show.

SILVIO

745 Oh courteous doom: and so't shall be.
Thou, deadly wood, shalt pay the price of others' life.
Behold, I break thee, and I render thee
Unto the woods, a trunk unprofitable:
And you, my shafts, that piercèd have the side
750 Of my fair love, because you brothers be
I put you both together, and deliver you,
Rods armed in vain, and vainly featherèd.
'Twas true Love told me late in Echo's voice.[428]
Oh powerful tamer both of gods and men,
755 Late enemy, now lord of all my thoughts,
If thou esteemest it glory to have mollified
A proud obdurate heart, defend me from
The fatal stroke of death! One only blow
Killing Dorinda, will me with her kill.
760 So cruel death, if cruel death she prove,
Will triumph over thee, triumphant love.

LINCO

So wounded both, yet wounds most fortunate,
Were but Dorinda's sound. Let's soon go seek
Some remedy.

DORINDA

           Do not, good Linco, lead
765 Me to my father's house in this attire.

SILVIO

Shall my Dorinda go to other house
Than unto mine? No, sure: alive or dead
This day I'll marry thee.

LINCO

                    And in good time,
Since Amarillis hath lost life and marriage too.
770 Oh blessèd couple! Oh eternal gods!
Give two their lives, giving but one her health.

---

[428] 753] What love told me was true.

DORINDA
Silvio, I weary am, I cannot hold me on
My wounded side.

SILVIO
                    Be of good cheer,
Thou shalt a burden be to us most dear.
775 Linco, give me thy hand.

LINCO
                    Hold, there it is.

SILVIO
Hold fast, and with our arms we'll make a seat
For her. Sit there, Dorinda, and with thy right hand
Hold Linco's neck, and with thy left close mine.
Softly, my heart, for rushing of thy wound.[429]

DORINDA
780 Oh, now methinks I am well.

SILVIO
                    Linco, hold fast.

LINCO
Do not you stagger, but go forward right;
This is a better triumph than a head.

SILVIO
Tell me, Dorinda, doth thy wound still prick?

DORINDA
It doth; but in thine arms, my lovely treasure,
785 I hold even pricking dear, and death a pleasure.[430]

CHORUS

Oh sweet and golden age, when milk
Unto the tender world was meat,
Whose cradle was the harmless wood,

---

[429] rushing of] Obscure. In the source, Silvio is inviting Dorinda to move carefully, lest her wounded side feels the pain ('che'l ferito fianco | non se ne dolga'; IV. 9. 1382). Maybe 'brushing off' was intended here? Or is Silvio telling Dorinda not to make any sudden ('rushed') movements?

[430] The rhyming couplet is added by Dymock, but the sexual innuendo is in the source as well.

Their dearer parts⁴³¹ whose grass like silk
790 The flocks untouched did joy to eat.
Nor feared the world the spoil of blood,⁴³²
The troublous thoughts that do no good
Did not then make a cloudy veil
To dim our sun's eternal light.
795 Now reason being shut up quite,
Clouds do our wits' skies over-hail,⁴³³
From whence it is strange lands we seek for ease,⁴³⁴
Ploughing with huge oak trees the ocean seas.
This bootless superstitious voice,
800 This subject profitless then vain⁴³⁵
Of toys, of titles and of sleight,
Whom the mad world through worthless choice
Honour to name doth not disdain,
Did not with tyranny delight
805 To rule our minds, but to sustain⁴³⁶
Trouble for truth, and for the right
To maintain faith a firm decree
Amongst us men of each degree,
Desire to do well was of right,
810 Care of true honour, happy to be named,
Who what was lawful pleasure to us framed.
Then in the pastures' grovy shade
Sweet carols and sharp madrigals

---

⁴³¹ parts] It is not clear if Dymock means that the 'dearer parts' of the flocks ate the grass, or if the flocks ate the dearer (softer?) parts of the grass. He probably mistook Guarini's masculine 'parti' ('i parti': childbirths, i.e., the young; IV. Ch. 1397) for its feminine counterpart ('le parti': graphemically the same in the plural, but meaning parts). In the source, the flocks are allowed to cherish their newborns in peace.

⁴³² Dymock here skips 'tosco' ('poison'; IV. Ch. 1399), perhaps because he does not know the meaning of the word.

⁴³³ 796] Clouds pour hail over the skies of our minds. Dymock interprets rather strangely Guarini's two lines 'Or la ragion, che verna | tra le nubi del senso, ha chiuso il cielo' (IV. Ch. 1403–04; 'now reason, wintering | among the clouds of sense, has covered the sky'). In the source, it is not reason that is 'shut up'.

⁴³⁴ From whence it is] And that is why.

⁴³⁵ The spelling of this line in T1602, considering that 'then' might also stand for 'than', leaves a number of alternatives open, all of them obscure: 'This subject profit lesse then vaine'. Guarini simply writes that false honour is 'vain' and 'useless' ('vano [...] inutil'; IV. Ch. 1407–08).

⁴³⁶ Dymock gets lost in Guarini's complicated grammar. In the source, the verb 'sostenere' is the subject of a different clause to the effect that sustaining trouble for true sweetness, in the golden age, was the rule of happy honour ('Ma sostener affanno | per le vere dolcezze [...] fu di quell'alme [...] cura d'onor felice'; IV. Ch. 1413–18).

ACT IV

  Were flames unto dear lawful love:
815 There gentle nymphs and shepherds made
  Thoughts of their words, and in the dales
  Did Hymen joys and kisses move[437]
  Far sweeter and of more behove.[438]
  True lovers only did enjoy
820 Love's lively roses and sweet flowers,
  Whilst wily craft found always showers,
  Showers of sharp will, and will's annoy.[439]
  Were it in woods or caves for quiet rest,
  The name of husband still was likèd best.
825 False wicked world, that coverest still
  With thy base mercenary name
  The soul's chief good, and dost entice
  To nourish thought of newfound will,
  With likelihoods restrained again.[440]
830 Unbridling ever secret vice,
  Like to a net laid by device
  Among fair flowers and sweet spread leaves,
  Thou clothst wild thoughts in holy weeds,
  Esteeming seeming goodness deeds
835 By which the life with art deceives.
  Nor dost thou care (this honour is thy act)
  What theft it be, so love may hide the fact.
  But thou, great Honour, great by right,
  Frame famous spirits in our hearts,
840 Thou true lord of each noble breast,
  Oh thou that rulest kings of might,
  Once turn thee into these our parts,
  Which wanting thee, cannot be blest.
  Wake them from out their mortal rest[441]

---

[437] The Greek god presiding over marriage ceremonies. True honour, in Guarini's conservative ideology, is the one that inspires honest marital love.

[438] of more behove] more decent.

[439] Another obscure metaphor, based on the contrast between the sun and the rain. In the source, any 'stealthy lover' would find the roses of love 'hidden' ('furtivo amante ascose | le trovò sempre'; IV. Ch. 1428–29).

[440] likelihoods] Another obscure word in a rather obscure passage — though it is clear that Dymock, like Guarini, is here berating the present world for honouring false honour. Maybe 'likelihood' is intended as 'seemliness'.

[441] Wake] All the existing editions have 'Make' here, but it appears to be a misprint (the clause would be headless, and Guarini's chorus exhorts true Honour to issue a waking call to all those who follow base desires), perpetrated by the first printer and repeated across the centuries.

845 With mighty and with powerful stings
Who by a base unworthy will
Have left to work thy pleasure still,
And left the worth of antique things.
Let's hope our ills a truce will one day take,
850 And let our hopes not waver, no, nor shake:
Let's hope the setting sun will rise again,
And that the skies when they most dark appear,
Do draw, though covered, after wishèd clear.

Act v, Scene 1
URANIO, CARINO

URANIO
The place is ever good, where any thrives:
And every place is native to the wise.

CARINO
True, good Uranio, I by proof can tell,
That young did leave my father's house, and sought
5 Strange places out, and now turn home grey-haired,[442]
That erst departed hence with golden locks.
Yet is our native soil sweet unto him
That hath his sense: nature doth make it dear,
Like to the adamant,[443] whom though the mariner
10 Carry far hence, sometime where as the sun
Is born, and sometime where it dies; yet still
The hidden virtue wherewith it beholds
The northern pole it never doth forgo.
So he that goes far from his native soil,
15 And oftentimes in stranger land doth dwell,
Yet he retains the love he to it bore.
Oh my Arcadia, now I greet thy ground,
And welcome, good Uranio, for 'tis meet
You do partake my joys, as you have done my toil.

URANIO
20 I may partake your toil, but not content,
When I remember how far hence I left
My house and little household off: well may I rest
My limbs, but well I wot my heart will moan,
Nor, save thyself, could anything have drawn
25 Me from Elidis now: yet I know not
What cause hath made you travel to this place.

CARINO
Thou knowst my dear Mirtillo, whom the heavens
Have giv'n me for my son, came hither sick,

---

[442] turn] come back ('torno'; v. 1. 8). Dymock skips a couple of lines on young Carino's wish to see more than meadows and flocks. The whole scene is heavily abridged, though the general sentiments of the two characters are kept.
[443] adamant] lodestone.

Here to get health, according to the oracle,
30 Which said only Arcadia could restore it him.
Two months he hath been here, and I not able to
Abide that stay, went to the oracle
To know of his return, which answered thus:
Return thou to thy country, where thou shalt
35 Live merrily with thy Mirtillo dear.
Heavens have determinèd great things of him;
Nor shalt thou laugh but in Arcadia.[444]
Thou then, my dear companion, merry be,
Thou hast a share in all my good, nor will
40 Carino smile, if my Uranio grieve.

URANIO
All labours that I for Carino take
Have their reward: but for to short the way,
I pray you tell what made you travel first.

CARINO
A youthful love I unto music bore,
45 And greediness of foreign fame, disdaining that
Arcadia only should me praise, made me
Seek out Elide and Pisa famous so,
Where I saw glorious Aegon crowned with bays,[445]
With purple next to virtue evermore,
50 So that he Phoebus seemed:[446] when I devout
Unto his power did consecrate my lute.
Then left I Pisa and to Mycenae went,
And afterwards to Argos, where I was
At first adorèd like a god: but 'twill be too,
55 Too troublesome to tell the story of my life.[447]
I many fortunes tried, sometime disdained,
Sometime respected like a power divine:

---

[444] laugh] Dymock has probably mistaken Guarini's 'ridir' (say again, repeat) for 'rider' (laugh; 'Ma fuor d'Arcadia il ciò ridir non lice' ('but such things should not be repeated out of Arcadia'); v. 1. 70).

[445] Aegon] The Italian 'Egon' (v. 1. 92) may allude to an ancient athlete — but it is a covert allusion to Scipione Gonzaga, a nobleman, patron of the arts and versifier who later became a cardinal (hence the purple in the next line). The celebration of this figure stands in sharp contrast to Guarini's dissatisfaction with the Estense court of Ferrara (expressed by Carino immediately afterwards, by way of his references to Argos, Mycenae and the falsity of courtiers).

[446] Phoebus] The main epithet of Apollo, here invoked as the god of music and poetry.

[447] Another sign of Dymock's continuous elisions in this scene.

Now rich, then poor; now down, then up aloft;
But in the change of place, my fortunes never changed.
60 I learned to know and sigh my former liberty;
And leaving Argos I returnèd to
My homely bower I in Elidis had,
Where (gods be praised) I did Mirtillo buy,⁴⁴⁸
Who since hath comforted all mine annoys.⁴⁴⁹

URANIO
65 Thrice happy they who can contain their thoughts,
And not through vain and most immoderate hope
Lose the sweet-tasted fruit of moderate good.

CARINO
Who would have thought t'have waxèd poor in gold?
I thought t'have found in royal palaces
70 People of more humanity than here,
Which is the noble ornament of worthy sprights.
But I, Uranio, found the contrary:
People in name and words right courteous,
But in good deeds most scarce, and pity's foes.
75 People in face, gentle and pleasant still,
But fiercer than th'outrageous swelling sea.
People with countenance all of charity,
But thoroughly covetous, and fraught with envy.
The greater shows they make, the less truth they mean.
80 That which is virtue otherwhere, is there but vice:
Uprightest deeds, true love, pity sincere,
Inviolable faith of hand and heart,
A life most innocent; these they esteem⁴⁵⁰
But cowards still, and men of silly wits,
85 Follies and vanities that are ridiculous.
Cozenage,⁴⁵¹ lying, theft and rapine clad
In holiness, by others' downfalls and their loss
Rich still to grow,⁴⁵² to build their reputation
On others' infamy, to lay fine snares
90 To trap the innocent; these are the virtues of that place.
No merit, worth, reverence of age,

⁴⁴⁸ buy] acquire.
⁴⁴⁹ annoys] Guarini's 'noia' ('trouble'; v. 1. 124).
⁴⁵⁰ these] the men who display these.
⁴⁵¹ Cozenage] Cozening.
⁴⁵² by others [...] to grow] growing rich through the disgrace of others ('crescer col danno e precipizio altrui'; v. 1. 152).

Of law, or of degree, no reins of shame,
Respect of love or blood, nor memory
Of any good received: and to conclude,
95 Nothing so reverend, pure, or just can be
That seems forbidden to these gulfs of pride,
Of honour so ambitious, so covetous
Of getting still. Now I that always lived
Unwary of their snares, and in my forehead had
100 All my thoughts written, my heart discoverèd;
You well may judge, I was an open mark
To the suspicious shafts of envious folks.

URANIO
What can be happy in that caitiff land[453]
Where envy ever virtue doth command?[454]

CARINO
105 If since I travellèd my Muse had had
As good a cause to laugh as 't had to weep,
Perhaps my style would have been fit t'have sung
The arms and honours of my noble lord,[455]
So that he needed not to have envièd
110 The brave Maeonian trumpet of Achilles' fame.[456]
I might have made my country's brow been girt
With happy laurel too. But too inhuman is this age,
And too unhappy gift of poetry.
The swans desire a quiet nest, a gentle air,
115 Pernassus never knew this biting care.[457]
Who quarrels with his fate and fortune still,
His voice must needs be hoarse, his song but ill.
But now 'tis time to seek Mirtillo out.
Oh how this country's changed! I scarcely know't:
120 But strangers never want a guide that have a tongue.
We will enquire to the next harbour house,
Where thou thy weary limbs mayst well repose.

---

[453] caitiff] wretched.
[454] No rhyming couplet in the source.
[455] Probably a reference to Ariosto, Guarini's more fortunate predecessor as *Ferrarese* poet.
[456] Maeonian trumpet] Homer, who was thought by some to have hailed from Lydia (Maeonia).
[457] Mount Parnassus is home to the Muses, and the musical 'swans' here are poets.

Act v, Scene 2

TITIRUS, NUNTIO

TITIRUS
Which plain I first, my child, of thee? Thy life
Or honesty? I'll plain thine honesty,
125 Because thy sire, though mortal, honest was:
And in thy stead my life I'll plain and spend,
Of thy life and thine honesty to see an end.
Oh Montane, only thou with thy devices
And ill-cund oracles,[458] and with thy love,[459]
130 And proud despiser of my daughter, to this end
Hast brought my child. Oh doubtful oracles,
How vain you be? And honesty 'gainst love
In youthful hearts a weak defence doth prove.
A woman whom no match hath ever sought
135 Is evil guarded from this common thought.

NUNTIO
If dead he be not, or that through the air
No winds have carried him, him might I find:
But see him now, when least I thought I should:
Oh late for me, for thee too quickly found,
140 Except the news were better that I bring.[460]

TITIRUS
Bring thou the weapon that hath slain my child?

NUNTIO
Not this, but less. But how heard you this news?

TITIRUS
Why, lives she then?

NUNTIO
                    She lives, and may do still,
For in her choice it is to live or die.

TITIRUS
145 Oh blest be thou that lifts me up from death.
But how is she unsafe, since at her choice it is
To live or die?

---

[458] ill-cund] Either 'ill-conducted' (see 'cond | cund' in the *OED*) or 'studied badly' ('conned').
[459] and with thy love] A mistranslation. In the source, Montanus's son Silvio is said to be a despiser of Titirus's daughter and love in general ('d'Amore e di mia figlia | disprezzator superbo'; v. 2. 209).
[460] Except] Unless.

NUNTIO
           Because she will not live.

TITIRUS
She will not live? What madness makes her thus?

NUNTIO
Another's death; and if thou dost not move her,
150 She is so bent, as others send in vain
Their praying words.

TITIRUS
           Why stay we? Let us go!

NUNTIO
What, soft and fair, the temple's gates are shut,
And know you not how it unlawful is
For any one save sacerdotal foot
155 To touch the sacred ground, until such time
The sacrifice unto the altars come,
Adornèd with the sanctuary rites?

TITIRUS
How if she effect her purpose in the while?

NUNTIO
She cannot, for she's kept.

TITIRUS
                In the meantime,
160 Then tell truly how all this is come to pass.

NUNTIO
Thy mournful child now come before the priest
With looks of fear and grief that tears brought forth
Not only from us by, but by my troth,
Even from the pillars of the temple's self
165 And hardest stones, that seemed to feel the same,
Was in a trice accused, convict,[461] condemned.

TITIRUS
Oh wretched child, and why was she condemned?[462]

---

[461] convict] convicted ('convic't' in T1602).
[462] In the source, Titirus asks why she was condemned so hurriedly ('E perché tanta fretta?'; v. 2. 261), which makes more sense, because Titirus already knows about his daughter's crime.

NUNTIO
Because the grounds of her defence were small.
Besides, a certain nymph, whom she did call
170 In testimony of her innocence,
Was absent now, and none could find her out:
And fearful signs, and monstrous accidents
Of horror in the temple proved the doubt,
As dolorous to us, as strange and rare,
175 Not seen since we did feel heavenly ire
That did revenge Amintas' love betrayed,
The first beginning of our misery.
Diana sweat out blood,[463] the earth did shake,
The sacred cave did bellow out unwonted howling
180 And dire deadly cries.
Withal, it breathed out such a stinking mist,
As Pluto's impure kingdom hath no worse.
And now with sacred order goes the priest
To bring thy daughter to her bloody end,
185 The whilst Mirtillo (wondrous thing to tell)
Offered by his own death to give her life,
Crying, unbind those hands (unworthy strings),
And in her stead that should be sacrificed
Unto Diana, draw me to the altars,
190 A sacrifice to my fair Amarillis.

TITIRUS
Oh admirable deed of faithful love,
And noble heart.

NUNTIO
                    Now hear a miracle.
She that before so fearful was to die,
Changed on the sudden by Mirtillo's words,
195 Thus answers with a bold undaunted heart:
Thinkst thou, my dear, then by thy death to gain
Life to her death, that by thy life doth live?
Oh miracle unjust! On ministers, on, on, why do you stay?
Lead me forthwith unto mine end. I'll no such pity, I.
200 Mirtill replies, live, cruel piteous love,
My heart his spiteful pity doth reprove:
To me it longs to die.[464] Nay then to me

---

[463] sweat] sweated (it is Diana's statue, of course, that sweats out blood).
[464] longs] belongs (i.e., I should be the one who dies).

(She answers) that by law condemnèd am.
And here anew begins a wondrous strife,
205 As though that life were death, and death were life.
Oh souls well born, oh couple worthy of
Eternal honour, never dying praise:
Oh living, and oh, dying glorious lovers.
Had I so many tongues, so many voices,
210 As heaven hath eyes, or ocean sea hath sands,
All would be dumb and hoarse in setting out
Their wondrous and incomprehended praise.
Eternal child of heaven, oh glorious dame[465]
That mortal deeds enchroniclest to time,
215 Write thou this history, and it enfold
In solid diamond with words of gold.

TITIRUS
But what end had this mortal quarrel then?

NUNTIO
Mirtillo vanquisheth![466] Oh rare debate,
Where dead on living gets the victory.
220 The priest speaks to your child: be quiet, nymph,
We cannot change this doom, for he must die
That offers death. Our law commands it so.
And after bids your daughter should be kept
Lest grief's extreme should bring her desperate death.
225 Thus stood the state when Montane sent me for thee.

TITIRUS
In sooth 'tis true, sweet scented flowers shall cease
To dwell on riverbanks, and woods in spring
Shall be without their leaves, before a maid
Adorned with youth shall set sweet love at naught.[467]
230 But if we stay still here, how shall we know
When it is time unto the church to go?[468]

NUNTIO
Here best of all, for in this place, alas,
Shall the good shepherd sacrificèd be.

---

[465] glorious dame] Fame.
[466] All previous editions have a confusing question mark here.
[467] In the source, Titirus exclaims that riverbanks and hills will be without flowers in spring before a beautiful young woman has to live without (someone else's) love (v. 2. 349–52).
[468] church] Unlike Guarini ('tempio'; v. 2. 354), Dymock drops the Arcadian veil here.

TITIRUS
And why not in the church?

NUNTIO
Because there where
235 The fault is done, the punishment must be.

TITIRUS
And why not in the cave? There was the fault.

NUNTIO
Because to open skies it must be hallowed.

TITIRUS
And how knowst thou all these mysterial rites?

NUNTIO
From the high priest, who from Tireno had them,
240 For true Amintas and untrue Lucrine[469]
Were sacrificèd so. But now 'tis time to go.
See where the sacred pomp softly descends:[470]
'Twere well done of us by this other way,
To go unto the temple to thy daughter.

Act v, Scene 3
CHORUS OF SHEPHERDS, CHORUS OF PRIESTS, MONTANUS, MIRTILLO

CHORUS OF SHEPHERDS
245 Oh daughter of great Jove, sister of Phoebus bright,
Thou second Titan,[471] to the blinder world that givest light.

CHORUS OF PRIESTS
Thou that with thy well-tempered vital ray
Thy brother's wondrous heat doth well allay,
Which mak'st sweet nature happily bring forth
250 Rich fertile births of herbs, of beasts, of men:
As thou his heat dost quench, so calm thine ire
That sets Arcadia's wretched hearts on fire.

CHORUS OF SHEPHERDS
Oh daughter of great Jove, sister of Phoebus bright,
Thou second Titan, to the blinder world that givest light.[472]

---

[469] Lucrine] Lucrina, shortened for metrical reasons.
[470] pomp] ceremony.
[471] Thou second Titan] Diana, i.e., the moon, sister of Phoebus (Apollo as the sun) and second giver of light.
[472] Dymock (or his printer) shortens all reiterations of the antiphon.

MONTANUS

255 Yea, sacred priests, the altars ready make,
Shepherds devout, reiterate your sounds,
And call upon the name of our great goddess.

CHORUS OF SHEPHERDS

Oh daughter of great Jove, sister of Phoebus bright,
Thou second Titan, to the blinder world that givest light.

MONTANUS

260 Now shepherds stand aside, nor you my servants
Come not near, except I call for you.
Valiant young man, that to give life elsewhere
Abandonest thine own, die comforted thus far:
'Tis but a speedy sigh which you must pass;
265 For so seems death to noble-minded sprights,
That once performed, this envious age,
With thousands of her years shall not deface
The memory of such a gentle deed:
But thou shalt live the example of true faith.
270 But for the law commands thee, sacrificed,
To die without a word, before thou kneelst,
If thou hast ought to say, say it, and hold thy peace
Forever after that.

MIRTILLO

Father, let it be lawful that I call thee so,
275 For though thou gav'st not, yet thou tak'st my life:
My body to the ground I do bequeath, my soul
To her that is my life. But if she die,
As she hath threatenèd to do, ay me,
What part of me shall then remain alive?
280 Oh, death were sweet, if but my mortal parts
Might die, and that my soul did not desire the same.
But if his pity ought deserves that dies,
For sovereign pity then, courteous father,
Provide she do not die; and with that hope
285 More comforted I'll pay my destinies.
Though with my death you me from her disjoin,
Yet make her live, that she may me retain.

MONTANUS
Scarce I contain from tears: oh, frail mankind![473]
Be of good cheer, my son,[474] I promise thy desire,
290 I swear it by this head, this hand take thou for pledge.

MIRTILLO
Then comforted, I die all comforted:
To thee, my Amarillis, do I come.
Soul of the faithful shepherd as thine own
Do thou receive, for in thy lovèd name
295 My words and life I will determine straight:
So now to death I kneel, and hold my peace.

MONTANUS
On, sacred Ministers, kindle the flame
With frankincense and myrrh, and incense throw thereon
That the thick vapour may on high ascend.

CHORUS OF SHEPHERDS
300 Oh daughter of great Jove, sister of Phoebus bright,
Thou second Titan, to the blinder world that givest light.

Act v, Scene 4
CARINO, MONTANUS,[475] NICANDER, MIRTILLO, CHORUS OF SHEPHERDS

CARINO
What countrymen are here, so bravely furnishèd
Almost all in a livery?[476] Oh, what a show
Is here? How rich, how full of pomp it is!
305 Trust me, I think it is some sacrifice.

MONTANUS
Reach me, Nicander, the golden basin[477]
That contains the juice of Bacchus' fruit.

NICANDER
Behold, 'tis ready here.

---

[473] This line is spoken as an aside in the source.
[474] Of course 'father' and 'son' are used generically here, but they are (ironically) biologically right.
[475] With characteristic inconsistency, here Dymock turns Montano/Montanus into 'Montanio'.
[476] Guarini's Carino comments on the Arcadians' dwellings before the ceremony. Also, in the source all of Carino's speeches are given as asides until he interrupts the sacrifice; here he sounds as if he is talking to his absent friend, Uranio.
[477] basin] Spelled 'bason' in all the editions.

MONTANUS
                So may this faultless blood
Thy breast, oh sacred goddess, mollify,
310 As do these falling drops of wine extinguish
This blazing flame. So, take the basin, there;
Give me the silver ewer now:[478]

NICANDER
                       Behold, the ewer.

MONTANUS
So may thine anger cease, with that same faithless nymph
Provoked,[479] as doth this fire this falling stream extinguish.

CARINO
315 This is some sacrifice, but where's the holocaust?

MONTANUS
Now all is fit, there wants nought but the end.
Give me the axe.

CARINO
                If I be not deceived,
I see a thing that by his back seemeth a man.
He kneels: he is perhaps the holocaust.
320 Oh wretch, 'tis so, the priest holds him by the head.[480]
And hast thou not, unhappy country, yet
After so many years heaven's rage appeased?

CHORUS OF SHEPHERDS
Oh daughter of great Jove, sister of Phoebus bright,
Thou second Titan, to the blinder world that givest light.

MONTANUS
325 Revengeful goddess that for private fault
Dost public punishment on us inflict,
(Whether it be thy only will, or else
Eternal providence's immutable command),
Since the infected blood of Lucrina false
330 Might not thy burning justice then appease,
Drink now this innocent and voluntary sacrifice,
No lesser faithful than Amintas was,
That at thy sacred altar in thy dire revenge I kill.

---

[478] ewer] jug.
[479] Lucrina (see I. 2).
[480] the head] To be read as a single syllable ('th'ead' in T1602 and T1633).

CHORUS OF SHEPHERDS
Oh daughter of great Jove, sister of Phoebus bright,
335 Thou second Titan, to the blinder world that givest light.

MONTANUS
Oh how I feel my heart wax tender now,[481]
Binding my senses with unusual maze:[482]
So both my heart not dares, my hands unable are
To lift this axe.

CARINO
              I'll see this wretch's face
340 And then depart, for pity will not let me stay.

MONTANUS
Perhaps against the sun my strength doth fail,
And 'tis a fault to sacrifice against the sun.
Turn thou thy dying face toward this hill.
So now, 'tis well.

CARINO
              Oh wretch! What do I see?
345 My son Mirtillo! Is not this my son?

MONTANUS
So now I can.

CARINO
              It is even so.

MONTANUS
              Who lets my blow?[483]

CARINO
What dost thou, sacred priest?

MONTANUS
              Oh man profane,
Why hast thou held this holy axe? how darest
Thou thy rash hands impose upon the same?

---

[481] Again, all of Montanus's comments up until 'So now I can' ('Or posso...'; v. 4. 524) are asides in the source, except when he asks Mirtillo to turn.
[482] maze] amazement.
[483] A strange translation of the aside 'e 'l colpo libro' (v. 4. 524; 'here I go', 'here's the blow'), possibly caused by a misreading of 'libro' (from the expression 'librare il colpo', 'to deal the blow') as 'libero' ('free').

CARINO
350 Oh my Mirtillo, how cam'st thou to this?

NICANDER
Go, dotard, old and foolish insolent.

CARINO
I never thought t'have thee embracèd thus.

NICANDER
Patch,[484] stand aside, thou mayst not handle things
Sacred unto the gods with hands impure.

CARINO
355 Dear to the gods am also I, that by
Their good direction hither came even now.

MONTANUS
Nicander, cease, hear him, and turn him hence.

CARINO
Then, courteous priest, before thy sword doth light
Upon his neck, why dies this wretched boy?
360 I, by the goddess thou ador'st, beseech thee tell.

MONTANUS
By such a heavenly power thou conjur'st me,
That I were wicked if I thee denied:
But what will't profit thee?

CARINO
                   More than thou thinkst.

MONTANUS
Because he for another willing is to die.

CARINO
365 Die for another? Then I for him will die.
For pity, then, thy falling blow direct,
Instead of his, upon this wretched neck.

MONTANUS
Thou dotest, friend.

CARINO
              And will you me deny
That which you grant another man?

---

[484] Patch] Fool.

MONTANUS
                    Thou art
A stranger, man.

CARINO
          How if I were not so?

MONTANUS
Nor couldst thou, for he dies but by exchange.[485]
But tell me, what art thou? Thy habit shows
Thou art a stranger, no Arcadian born.

CARINO
I an Arcadian am.

MONTANUS
                I not remember
That I ever saw thee erst.

CARINO
                    Here was I born,
Carino called, and father of this wretch.

MONTANUS
Art thou Mirtillo's father then? Thou com'st
Unluckily, both for thyself and me.
Stand now aside, lest with thy father's tears
Thou makest fruitless, vain our sacrifice.

CARINO
If thou a father wert!

MONTANUS
                  I am a father, man,
A tender father of an only son.
Yet were this same my Silvio's head, my hand
Should be as ready for't as 'tis for this:
For he this sacred habit shall unworthy wear
That to a public good his private doth prefer.

CARINO
Oh let me kiss him yet before he die.

MONTANUS
Thou mayst not, man.

---

[485] A shortened form of Montanus's exposition of the law: 'campar per altrui | non può chi per altrui s'offerse a morte' (v. 4. 557–58; 'saved by someone else | cannot be those who offered themselves to save someone else').

CARINO
                    Art thou so cruel, son?
Thou wilt not answer thy sad father once.

MIRTILLO
390 Good father, hold your peace.

MONTANUS
                             Oh wretched, we
The holocaust contaminate, oh gods.

MIRTILLO
The life you gave, I cannot better give,
Than for her sake, who sole deserves to live.

MONTANUS
Oh, thus I thought his father's tears would make
395 Him break his silence.

MIRTILLO
                     Wretch, with error have
I done; the law of silence quite I had forgot.

MONTANUS
On, ministers, why do we stay so long?
Carry him to the temple, back to th'holy cell,
There take again his voluntary vow.
400 Then bring him back, and bring new water too,
New wine, new fire. Dispatch, the sun grows low.

Act v, Scene 5
MONTANUS, CARINO, DAMETAS

MONTANUS
But thank thou heavens, thou agèd impudent,
Thou art his father! If thou wert not, well,
I swear by this same sacred habit on my head I wear,
405 Thou shouldst soon taste how ill I brook thy boldness.
Why, knowst thou who I am, knowst thou that with
This rod I rule affairs both human and divine?

CARINO
I cry you mercy, holy sacred priest.

MONTANUS
I suffered thee so long, till thou growst insolent.
410 Knowst thou not rage that justice stirreth up,
The longer 'tis delayed, the greater 'tis?

CARINO
Tempestuous fury never wainèd rage[486]
In breasts magnanimous, but that one blast
Of generous affect could cool the same.
415 But if I cannot grace obtain, let me
Find justice yet; you cannot that deny.
Lawmakers be not freèd from the laws:
I ask you justice, justice grant me then.
You are unjust, if you Mirtillo kill.

MONTANUS
420 Let me then know how I can be unjust.

CARINO
Did you not tell me it unlawful was
To sacrifice a stranger's blood?

MONTANUS
                                I told you so,
And told you that which heavens did command.

CARINO
He is a stranger you would sacrifice.

MONTANUS
425 A stranger, how? Is he not then thy son?

CARINO
Let it suffice, and seek no further now.

MONTANUS
Perhaps because you not begot him here.

CARINO
Oft he least knows, that most would understand.

MONTANUS
Here we the kindred mean, and not the place.

CARINO
430 I call him stranger, for I got him not.

MONTANUS
Is he thy son, and thou begotst him not?

CARINO
He is my son, though I begot him not.

---

[486] wainèd] brought (i.e., 'rage never caused tempestuous fury').

MONTANUS
Didst thou not say that he was born of thee?

CARINO
I said he was my son, not born of me.

MONTANUS
435 Extremity of grief hath made thee mad.

CARINO
If I were mad, I should not feel my grief.

MONTANUS
Thou art or mad, or else a lying man.

CARINO
A lying man will never tell the truth.

MONTANUS
How can it be son, and not son at once?

CARINO
440 The son of love, and not of nature he's.

MONTANUS
Is he thy son? He is no stranger then:
If not, thou hast no part at all in him:
Father or not, thus thou convincèd art.

CARINO
With words and not with truth I am convinced.

MONTANUS
445 His faith is doubted that his words contraries.[487]

CARINO
Yet do I say thou dost a deed unjust.

MONTANUS
On this my head, and on my Silvio's head,
Let my injustice fall.

CARINO
                You will repent it.

MONTANUS
You shall repent, if you my duty hinder.

---

[487] Whose words contradict his faith.

CARINO
450 I call to witness men and gods.

MONTANUS
                         Gods you
To witness call that you despisèd have.

CARINO
Since you'll not hear me, hear me heaven and earth.
Mirtill a stranger is, and not my son,
You do profane your holy sacrifice.

MONTANUS
455 Heavens aid me from this bedlam man.[488]
Who is his father since he's not your son?

CARINO
I cannot tell you. I am sure, not I.

MONTANUS
See how he wavers; is he not of your blood?

CARINO
Oh no.

MONTANUS
    Why do you call him son?

CARINO
                        Because
460 I from his cradle have him nourished still,
And ever loved him like my son.

MONTANUS
Bought you him? Stole you him? Where had you him?

CARINO
A courteous stranger in Elidis gave me him.

MONTANUS
And that same stranger, where had he the child?

CARINO
465 I gave him.

---

[488] bedlam] mad. A very English, London-centred touch for the Italian 'importuno' ('annoying'; v. 4. 568).

MONTANUS
    Thou mov'st at once disdain and laughter.
First thou him gav'st, and then hadst him in gift?

CARINO
I gave him that which I with him had found.

MONTANUS
And where had you him?

CARINO
      In a low hole
Of dainty myrtle trees upon Alpheios' bank:
470 And for this cause Mirtillo I him called.

MONTANUS
Here's a fine tale. What, have your woods no beasts?

CARINO
Of many sorts.[489]

MONTANUS
    How scaped he being devoured?

CARINO
A speedy torrent brought him to this hole,
And left him in the bosom of a little isle,
475 On every side defended with the stream.

MONTANUS
And were your streams so pitiful they drowned him not?[490]
Your rivers gentle are that children nurse.

CARINO
Laid in a cradle like a little ship,
With other stuff the waters wound together,
480 He was safe brought by chance unto this hole.

MONTANUS
Laid in a cradle?

CARINO
    In a cradle laid.

MONTANUS
And but a child?

[489] Of many sorts] A phonetic translation of 'e di che sorte!' (v. 5. 709; 'and what [terrible] beasts!').

[490] In this part of the exchange, Dymock eliminates some of Montanus's sarcastic comments. In general, the translator reproduces all the lines of the scene, but in rather compressed form.

CARINO
             Aye, but a tender child.

MONTANUS
How long was this ago?

CARINO
                  Cast up your count:
Is it not nineteen years since the great flood?
485 So long 'tis since.

MONTANUS
              Oh how I feel a horror shake
My bones.

CARINO
         He knows not what to say:
Oh wicked act, o'ercome yet will not yield.
Thinking t'outstrip me in his wit, as much
As in his force, I hear him murmur,
490 Yet he nill bewray that he convincèd is.

MONTANUS
What interest had the man you speak of in
That child? Was he his son?

CARINO
                           I cannot tell.

MONTANUS
Had he no better knowledge then of it than thus?[491]

CARINO
Nor that know I.[492]

MONTANUS
              Know you him if you see him?[493]

CARINO
495 He seemed a shepherd by his clothes and face,
Of middle stature, of black hair; his beard
And eyebrows were exceeding thick.

---

[491] In the source, Montanus asks whether Carino knows anything else about the stranger ('Né mai di lui | notizia avesti tu maggior di questa?'; v. 5. 746–47).
[492] Not that I know.
[493] Know you him if you see him?] Would you recognize him?

MONTANUS
                        Shepherds,
Come hither soon.

DAMETAS
                Behold we are ready here.

MONTANUS
Which of these did he resemble then?

CARINO
500 Him whom you talk withal he did not only seem,
But 'tis the same, who though't be twenty years ago,
Hath not a whit altered his ancient look.[494]

MONTANUS
Stand then aside. Dametas, stay with me.
Tell me, knowst thou this man?

DAMETAS
                        Me seemeth so,
505 But yet I know not where.

CARINO
                Him can I put in mind.

MONTANUS
Let me alone. Stand you aside a while.

CARINO
I your commandment willingly obey.

MONTANUS
Now answer me, Dametas, and take heed
You do not lie; 'tis almost twenty years
510 Since you returned from seeking out my child
Which the outrageous river bare away.
Did you not tell me you had searched in vain
All that same country which Alpheios waters?

DAMETAS
Why ask you this?

MONTANUS
                Did not you tell me him
515 You could not find?

---

[494] In the source, Carino adds that Dametas's hair, unlike his, has not gone white.

ACT V

DAMETAS
             I grant I told you so.

MONTANUS
What child then was it, tell me, which you gave
Unto this stranger which did know you here?

DAMETAS
Will you I should remember what I did
So long ago? Old men forgetful are.

MONTANUS
520 Is not he old? Yet he remembers it.

DAMETAS
Tush, he doth rather dote!

MONTANUS
                That shall we see.
Come hither, stranger, come.

CARINO
               I come.

DAMETAS
                    Oh that
Thou wert as far beneath the ground.[495]

MONTANUS
                Tell me,
Is this the shepherd that gave thee the gift?

CARINO
525 This same is he.

DAMETAS
           What gift is't thou speakst of?

CARINO
Dost not remember in the temple of Olympic Jove,
Having had answer of the oracle,
And being ready to depart, I met with thee,
And asked thee of the oracle, which thou declaredst;
530 After I took thee home unto my house,
Where didst thou not give me an infant child,
Which in a cradle thou hadst lately found?

---

[495] Spoken as an aside.

DAMETAS
And what of that?

CARINO
                  This is that very child,
Which ever since I like mine own have kept,
535 And at these altars must be sacrificed.

DAMETAS
Oh force of destiny![496]

MONTANUS
                Yet wilt thou feign?
Is it not true which he hath told thee here?

DAMETAS
Oh were I dead as sure as it is true.

MONTANUS
And wherefore didst thou give another's goods?

DAMETAS
540 Oh, master, seek no more, let this suffice.

MONTANUS
Yet wilt thou hold me off and say no more?
Villain, thou diest if I but ask again.

DAMETAS
Because the oracle foretold me that the child
Should be in danger on his father's hands[497]
545 His death to have, if he returnèd home.

CARINO
All this is true, for this he told me then.

MONTANUS
Ay me, it is too manifest, the case is clear.[498]

CARINO
What resteth then, would you more proof than this?

MONTANUS
The proof's too great, too much have you declared,
550 Too much I understand. Oh Carino, Carino,
How I change grief and fortunes now with thine,

[496] Another aside in the source.
[497] on his father's hands] at his father's hand.
[498] Dymock eliminates Montanus's reference to the prophetic dream related in I. 4 (v. 5. 823).

How thy affections now are waxen mine.
This is my son, oh, most unhappy son
Of a more wretched father. More savage was
555 The water in him saving, than in running quite away,
Since at these sacred altars by thy father's hands
Thou must be slain, a woeful sacrifice,
And thy poor blood must wash thy native soil.

CARINO
Art thou Mirtillo's father then? How lost you him?

MONTANUS
560 The deluge ravished him, whom when I lost,
I left more safe; now found, I lose him most.

CARINO
Eternal providence which with thy counsel hast
Brought all these occurrents to this only point,[499]
Th'art great with child of some huge monstrous birth:
565 Either great good or ill thou wilt bring forth.

MONTANUS
This 'twas my sleep foretold, deceitful sleep.
In ill too true, in good too lying still.
This was th'unwonted pity and the sudden horror that
I felt to stay the axe and shake my bones:
570 For nature sure abhors a stroke should come
From father's hands, so wild abominable.

CARINO
Will you then execute the wicked sacrifice?

MONTANUS
By other hands he may not at these altars die.

CARINO
Why, will the father murder then the son?

MONTANUS
575 So bids our law, and were it piety to spare
Him since the true Amintas would not spare himself?

CARINO
Oh wicked fates, me whither have ye brought?

---

[499] occurrents] occurrences.

MONTANUS
To see two fathers' sovereign pity made a homicide,
Yours to Mirtillo, mine unto the gods.
580 His father you denying for to be,
Him thought to save, and him you lost thereby.
Thinking and seeking, I, to kill your son,
Mine own have found, and must mine own go kill.

CARINO
Behold the monster horrible this fate brings forth.
585 Oh cruel chance, Mirtillo, oh, my life.
Is this that which the oracle told of thee?
Thus in my native soil hast thou me happy made!
Oh son of me poor old and wretched man,
Lately my hope, my life, now my despair and death.

MONTANUS
590 To me, Carino, leave these woeful tears.
I plain my blood: my blood, why say I so,
Since I it shed? Poor son, why got I thee?
Why wert thou born? Did the mild waters save thy life
The cruel father might the same bereave?
595 Sacred immortal powers, without whose deep insight
No wave doth stir in seas, no blast in skies,
No leaf upon the earth: what great offence
Have I committed, that I worthy am
With my poor offspring for to war with heaven?
600 If I offended have, oh yet my son
What hath he done you cannot pardon him?
Oh Jupiter, thy great disdainful blast[500]
Would quickly suffocate my agèd sense,
But if thy thunderbolts will not, my weapons shall.
605 The dolorous example I'll renew
Of good Amintas, our belovèd priest.
My son amazed shall see his father slain,
Ere I a father will go kill my son.
Die thou, Montane, 'tis only fit for thee.
610 Oh powers, I cannot say whether of heaven or hell,
That agitate with grief despairful minds,[501]
Behold your fury; thus it pleaseth you.
I nought desire save only speedy death;

---

[500] thy] 'the' in both T1602 and T1633.
[501] despairful] despairing.

A poor desire my wretched life to end
615 Some comfort seems to my sad spright to send.

CARINO
Wretched old man, as greater flames do dim
The lesser lights, even so the sorrow I
Do of thy grief conceive hath put out mine.
Thy case alone deserveth pity now.

Act v, Scene 6
TIRENIO,[502] MONTANUS, CARINO

TIRENIO
620 Softly,[503] my son, and set thy feet secure,
Thou must uphold me in this ruggèd way.
Thou art my body's eye, I am thy mind's,
And when thou com'st before the priest, there stay.

MONTANUS
Is't not the reverend Tirenio which I see,
625 Who blind on earth, yet seeth all in heaven?
Some great thing moves him thus; these many years
I saw him not out of his holy cell.

CARINO
God grant he bring us happy news.

MONTANUS
Father Tirenio, what's the news with you?
630 You from the temple? How comes this to pass?

TIRENIO
To you I come for news, yet bring you news.[504]
How oft blind eyes do aid the inward sight,
The whilst the mind, untroubled with wild sights,
Withdraws into itself, and linceous eyes[505]
635 Doth set awork in sightless senses blind.
We may not, Montane, pass so lightly o'er

---

[502] Tirenio's name, as pointed out in Guarini's 'Annotationi' (p. 439 of the 1602 Ciotti edition), harks back to that of the blind Theban seer Tiresias.
[503] Softly] The Italian Tirenio also asks his unnamed helper to hurry up ('Affrettati'; v. 6. 936).
[504] Here Montanus's reply is suppressed, and two of Tirenio's speeches compressed into one. The whole scene is shortened.
[505] linceous] A curious nonce word derived from the Italian 'lincèi' ('lynx-like', i.e., sharp-sighted; v. 6. 966).

The unexpected things that heavenly mixture tempers with human,[506]
Because the gods do not converse on earth,
Nor parley hold with mortal men at all.[507]
640 But all these works so great, so wonderful,
Which the blind world to blinder chance ascribes,
Is nothing but celestial council talk:
So speak th'eternal powers amongst themselves,
Whose voices, though they touch not deafened ears,
645 Yet do they sound to hearts that understand.
Oh four, oh six times happy he that understands it well.
The good Nicander, as thou didst command,
Stays to conduct the holy sacrifice,
But I retained him by an accident
650 That's newly fall'n: the which (I know not) all
Unwonted and confused, twixt hope and fear
Dulleth my sense. I cannot understand, and yet the less
I comprehend, the more I do conceive.

MONTANUS
That which you know not, wretch,[508] I know too well.
655 But tell me, can the fates hide ought from thee,
That piercest to the deep'st of destinies?

TIRENIO
If, son, the use divine of light prophetical
Were nature's gift, and not the gift of heaven,
Then mightst thou see, as well as I, that fate's
660 Secrets sometime deny our working minds,
This only 'tis that makes me come to thee,
That I might better be informed who 'tis
That is discovered father to the youth
That's doomed to die, if I Nicander understand.

MONTANUS
665 That father you desire to know am I.[509]

TIRENIO
You father of our goddess' sacrifice?

---

[506] The longest line in the whole translation — though 'tempers' is 'temps' in T1602.
[507] parley] 'partly' in 1602. Emended to 'parly' in T1633, but reprinted as 'partly' by Donno.
[508] wretch] In the English text the term seems to apply to Tirenio, which is rather inappropriate, considering the awe which the blind priest inspires in Montanus.
[509] Two more turns at talk are skipped here: the English characters go straight to the point.

MONTANUS
I am the wretched father of that wretched son.

TIRENIO
Of that same faithful shepherd, that to give
Life to another, gives himself to death?

MONTANUS
670 His that by death giveth another life,[510]
Yet by that death kills him that gave him life.

TIRENIO
And is this true?

MONTANUS
                  Behold my witness here.

CARINO
That which he saith is true.

TIRENIO
                  And who art thou?

CARINO
I am Carino, his father thought till now.

TIRENIO
675 Is this the child the flood so bare away?

MONTANUS
The very same.[511]

TIRENIO
                  And for this then dost thou,
Montanus, call thyself a wretched father?
Oh monstrous blindness of these earthly minds,
In what a dark, profound and misty night
680 Of errors be they drowned, when thou, oh heavenly sun,
Dost not enlighten them? Montanus, thou
Art blinder in thy mind than I of eyes,
That dost not see thyself the happiest father
And dearest to the gods that ever yet did child beget.
685 This was the secret which the fates did hide.
This is that happy day, with so much blood,

---

[510] His] His father — i.e., I am the father of that shepherd who…
[511] Throughout the exchange, Dymock's characters display a more conversational, concise style (here the Italian Montanus exclaims 'Ah! Tu l'hai detto, | Tirenio'; 'Ah! You said it, Tirenio'; v. 6. 1036–37).

So many tears, we did expect.
This is the blessèd end of our distress.
Oh thou, Montanus, turn into thyself!⁵¹²
690 How is the famous oracle forgot,
Printed i' the hearts of all Arcadia?
No end there is for that which you offends,
Till two of heaven's issue love unite —
The tears of joy so satisfy my heart
695 I cannot utter it. No end there is,
No end there is to that which you offends,
Till two of heaven's issue love unite,
And for the ancient fault of that false wight
A faithful shepherd's pity make amends.
700 Tell me, Montanus, is not this thy son
Heaven's issue? Is not Amarillis so?
Who hath united them but holy love?⁵¹³
Silvio by parents' force espousèd was
To Amarillis, whom he hated still.
705 If thou the rest examine, you shall plainly see
The fatal voice only Mirtillo meant.
For since Amintas' chance where have we seen
Such faith in love that might coequal this?
Who since Amintas willing was to die
710 For any nymph, only Mirtill except?⁵¹⁴
This is that faithful shepherd's pity which deserves
To cancel that same ancient error of Lucrine.
With this deed is the heavens' ire appeased,
Rather than with the shedding human blood,
715 Rendering unto th'eternal justice that
Which female treachery did take away.
Hence 'twas no sooner he unto the temple came,
There to renew his vow, but straight did cease
All those prodigious signs; now did
720 The holy image sweat out blood no more,⁵¹⁵
Nor shook the ground, nor any noise nor stench
Came from the cave, save gracious harmony
And odours. Oh sweet mighty providence,
Oh heavenly gods, had I all words, all hearts,

---

⁵¹² turn into thyself] A calque of 'Torna in te stesso' (more 'pull yourself together' than 'become yourself'; v. 6. 1064).
⁵¹³ holy] From T1633, accepted by Donno. T1602 has 'onely'.
⁵¹⁴ Mirtill except] except Mirtillo.
⁵¹⁵ holy image] The statue of Diana.

725 All to thy honour would I consecrate.
But to my power I'll render you your due.[516]
Behold, upon my knees, oh heavenly powers,
I praise your name, how much am I obliged
That you have let me live until this day!
730 An hundred years I have already worn,
And never yet was life so sweet as now:
I but begin to live, now am I born again.
Why lose I time with words that unto deeds is due?
Help me up, son, without thee can I not
735 Upraise these weak and feeble members, son.[517]

MONTANUS
Tirenio hath waked such joy in me,
United yet with such a miracle,
As I scarce feel I joy,[518] nor can my soul
Confounded show my[519] high retainèd mirth.[520]
740 Oh gracious pity of the highest gods,
Oh fortunate Arcadia, oh earth[521]
More happy than all earths beneath the sun,
So dear's thy good, I have forgot mine own,
And my beloved son's, whom twice I lost,
745 And twice again have found; these seem a drop
To the huge waves of thy great good. Oh dream,
Oh blessèd dream, celestial vision rather.
Arcadia, now thou waxest bright again.

TIRENIO
Why stay we, Montane, now? Heavens not expect
750 A sacrifice of rage, but thanks and love.
Instead of death, our goddess now commands
Of marriage knot a sweet solemnity:
But say, how far's tonight?

MONTANUS
                    Not past one hour.

---

[516] to my power] to the best of my powers.
[517] members] 'membra' (the limbs, or, by extension, the whole body).
[518] The repetition of 'I' seems involuntary, though dictated by metrical constraints.
[519] my] 'me' in all the editions.
[520] retainèd] 'ritenuta' in the source, meaning 'long repressed' (v. 6. 1140).
[521] earth] The Italian 'terra' in this case means 'land', 'country' (v. 6. 1148).

TIRENIO
Then to the temple turn, where let thy son
755 Espousèd be to Amarillis straight, whom he may lead
Unto his father's house before the sun be set.
So heavens command. Come, go'w, Montanus, go'w.

MONTANUS
Take heed, Tirenio, we do not violate
Our holy law. Can she her faith now give
760 Unto Mirtillo, which she Silvio gave?

CARINO
And unto Silvio may she give her faith.
So, said thy servant, was Mirtillo called,
Though I more liked Mirtillo him to name.

MONTANUS
That's very true, I did revive his name
765 In this my younger son.

TIRENIO
That doubt's well cleared; now let us go.

MONTANUS
Carino, go with us; this day Mirtillo hath
Two fathers found, Montane a son, and thou a brother.

CARINO
In love Mirtillo's father, and your brother,
770 In reverence a servant to you both.
And since you are so kind to me, I pray you then
Bid my companion welcome for my sake.

MONTANUS
Most welcome both.

CARINO
                        Eternal heavenly powers,
How diverse are your high untrodden ways
775 By which your favours do on us descend
From those same crooked deceitful paths whereby
Our thoughts would fain mount up into the sky!

Act v, Scene 7
CORISCA, LINCO

CORISCA
Linco, belike the spiteful Silvio
When least he meant a lover is become,
But what became of her?

LINCO
                    We carried her
To Silvio's house, whose mother her embraced
With tears of joy or grief I know not whether,
Glad that her son is waxed a loving spouse,
But sorry for the nymph's mishap, and that
She is a stepdame evil furnishèd
Of two daughters-in-law: plaining one dead,
Another wounded.

CORISCA
                Is Amarillis dead?

LINCO
She must die straight, for so doth fame report.
For this I go to comfort old Montanus,
Who losing one son's wife, hath found another.

CORISCA
Then doth Dorinda live?

LINCO
                    Live? It were well
Thou wert so well.

CORISCA
              Her wound not mortal was?

LINCO
Had she been dead, yet Silvio's cunning would
Have her revived.

CORISCA
            What art her healed so soon?

LINCO
From top to toe I'll tell the wondrous cure.
About the wounded nymph stood men and women,
Each with a ready hand, but trembling heart.
But fair Dorinda would not any should

Save Silvio touch her, saying that the hand
800 Which was her hurt should be her remedy.
Silvio, his mother and I stayed there alone,
Working with counsel two, one with his hand.[522]
Silvio, when gently he had wiped away
The bloody streams that stained her ivory flesh,
805 Assays to draw the shaft out of the wound,
But the wild steel, yielding unto his hand,
Left hidden in the wound the harmful head.
Hence came the grief, for 'twas impossible,
With cunning hand or dainty instrument
810 Or other means, to draw it out from thence.
Opening the wound perhaps with wider wound,
He might have found the steel with other steel.
So mought he do, or so he must have done,
But too, too piteous, and too loving now
815 Was Silvio's hand, for suchlike cruel pity:
By such hard means love never healeth wounds,
Although it seemed to her that pain itself
Was pleasant now between her Silvio's hands.
He not amazed says thus: this head shall out,
820 And with less pain than any will believe.
I put it there, and though I be not able straight
To take it out, yet with the use of hunting
I will restore the loss I have by hunting.
I do remember now an herb that is well known
825 Unto the savage goat, when he is wounded
With some huntsman's shaft: this they to us,
Nature to them bewrayed, and 'tis hard by.
All suddenly he parts unto a neighbour hill,[523]
And there a bundle gathers; straight to us
830 He comes, and out he draws the juice thereof,
And mingles it with vervain seed, and root
Of centaur's blood,[524] making a plaster soft
Which on the wound he lays. Virtue miraculous,
The pain straight ceased, the blood was quickly staid,
835 The steel straightway, without or toil or pain,
The workman's hand obeying, issues out.

---

[522] 802] Amarillis's mother and Linco are only giving advice, while Silvio is using his hands.
[523] neighbour] neighbouring.
[524] centaur's blood] *Centaurium*, or (in English) centaury, a plant considered by the ancient Greeks to have curative properties. The addition of blood appears to be Dymock's invention.

And now her strength returns to her again,
As though she had not suffered wound at all:
Nor was it mortal, for it had untouched
840 Both left the bones and belly's outward run,
And only pierced into the musculous flank.

CORISCA
Great virtue of an herb, but much more great
For fortune of a woman hast thou told.

LINCO
That which between them passed when this was done
845 Is better to be guessed at than be told.
Dorinda sure is well, and with her side
Can serve herself to any use she likes.
Thou thinkst she hath endured more wounds by this,
But as the piercing weapons diverse are,
850 So are the wounds: of some the grief is sharp,
Of some 'tis sweet; one healing waxeth sound,
The less another heals, the sounder 'tis.
In hunting he to shoot such pleasure found
That, now he loves, he cannot choose but wound.

CORISCA
855 Still thou wilt be that amorous Linco.

LINCO
In mind but not in force, my dear Corisca.
Green blooms desire within this agèd trunk.

CORISCA
Now Amarillis hath resigned her life,
I will go see what dear Mirtillo doth.

Act v, Scene 8
ERGASTO, CORISCA

ERGASTO
860 Oh day of wonders, day all love, all grace,
All joy, oh happy land, oh heavens benign.

CORISCA
See where Ergasto is, he comes in time.

ERGASTO
Now all things joyful are, the earth, the air,
The skies, the fire, the world, and all things laugh.

865 Our joys have pierced the lowest hell, nor is
　　 There any place that not partakes our bliss.

CORISCA
How jocund is this man!

ERGASTO
　　　　　　　　　　　Oh happy woods
That often sighed and wept our woeful case,
Enjoy our joys, and use as many tongues
870 As leaves that leap at sound of these sweet winds,
Which filled with our rejoicings calmly smile;
Sing they the sweet adventures of these friends.

CORISCA
He speaks of Silvio and Dorinda sure.
Well, we must live, tears are no sooner ebbed
875 But straight the flood of joy comes huffing in.[525]
Of Amarillis not a word he speaks,
Only takes care to joy with them that joy.
Why, 'tis well done, for else this human life
Would still be full of sighs: whither away,
880 Ergasto, gost so pleasantly, unto some marriage?

ERGASTO
Even so, but hast thou heard the happy chance
Of the two fortunate lovers? Is't not rare, Corisca?

CORISCA
To my contentment even now I heard it all
Of Linco, and 't doth somewhat mitigate
885 The grief I for my Amarillis feel.

ERGASTO
Why Amarillis? Of whom thinkst thou I speak?

CORISCA
Of Silvio and Dorinda, man.

ERGASTO
What Silvio? What Dorinda? Thou knowst nought!
My joy grows from a higher, nobler root.
890 I Amarillis and Mirtillo sing,
The best contented subjects of love's ring.

---

[525] huffing] swelling.

CORISCA
Why, is not Amarillis dead?

ERGASTO
How dead?
I tell thee she's a bright and merry bride.[526]

CORISCA
Was she not then condemnèd unto death?

ERGASTO
895 She was condemned, but soon released again.

CORISCA
Tellst thou me dreams? Or dreaming do I hear?

ERGASTO
Thine eyes shall tell thee if thou'lt stay a while.
Soon shalt thou see her with her faithful friend
Come from the temple, where they plighted have
900 Their marriage troth, and so go to Montanus' house
To reap sweet fruit of their long amorous toils.
Oh, hadst thou seen, Corisca, the huge joy,
The mighty noise of joyful voices, and
Th'innumerable troupes of men and women;
905 Thou shouldst have seen, old, young, sacred and profane,
But little less than mad or drunk with mirth.
With wonder who ran not to see the lovers?
Each reverence, to each them embracèd were.[527]
Some praised their pity, some their constancy.
910 Some praised the gifts that Jove, and some that nature gave.
The hills, the dales, the meadows did resound
The glorious name of faithful shepherd.
From a poor shepherd to become so soon
A demigod, and in a moment pass
915 From life to death, the neighbour obsequies[528]
To change for unexpected and despairèd nuptials!
This is somewhat, Corisca, but not half

---

[526] Two turns at talk are erased here — she accuses him of making fun of her; he assures her that is not the case (v. 8. 1372–73).

[527] were] 'there' in T1602 and Donno. Simply turning 'them' into 'they' would make the line clearer (in the source, Ergasto is telling Corisca that everybody was paying their homage to and embracing the lovers; v. 8. 1391–93).

[528] neighbour obsequies] imminent funeral rites ('le vicine esequie'; v. 8. 1402).

Her to enjoy, for whom he sought to die,[529]
Her that disdained to live if he had died.
920 This is fortune, this is such a sweet
As thought prevents,[530] and yet thou art not glad.
Is not thy Amarillis then as dear to thee
As my Mirtillo is to me?

CORISCA
Yes, yes, Ergasto, see how glad I am.

ERGASTO
925 Oh hadst thou seen but Amarillis when
She gave Mirtill her hand for pledge, and took
His hand again, thou easily hadst perceived
A sweet but unseen kiss: I could not say
Whether she took it, or she gave it him.
930 Her cheeks would have the purest colour stained[531]
Purple or roses, art or nature brings.
How modesty was armed in dainty shield
Of sanguine beauty, with force of that stroke
Unto the striker turned, whilst she all nice
935 Seemèd as though she fled, but to recover force
She might more sweetly encounter that same blow,
Leaving it doubtful if this kiss were given or ta'en,
With such a wondrous art it granted was.
This taken sweet was like an action mixed
940 With rapine and with yielding both at once,
And so courteous that it seemed to crave
The very thing that it denying gave:
Such a retreat, and such a speedless flight,
As mend the pace of the pursuers might.
945 Oh sweetest kiss. I cannot stay, Corisca,
I go directly, I, to find a wife:
For mongst the joys there is no pleasure sure
If gentle love do not the same procure.[532]

CORISCA
If he say true, then thou, Corisca, hast lost all.

---

[529] 917–18] This is a lot, but still very little if compared with the happiness of enjoying the woman for whom he wanted to die — the woman who did not want to live if he had died.
[530] As thought prevents] It passeth understanding ('ch'ogni pensiero avanza'; v. 8. 1414).
[531] Rather obscure. In the source, the colour of her cheeks is simply better than any colour in nature or art ('Ogni colore o di natura o d'arte | vincean le belle guance'; v. 8. 1428–29).
[532] There is no rhyming couplet in the source.

Act v, Scene 9
CHORUS OF SHEPHERDS, CORISCA, AMARILLIS, MIRTILLO

CHORUS OF SHEPHERDS

950 Come, holy Hymenaeus, come this even
According to our vows and to our songs.
Dress thou these lovers as them best belongs.
Both th'one and th'other of the seed of heaven,
Knit thou the fatal knot this blessèd even.

CORISCA

955 Ah me, it is too true; this is the fruit
Thou from thy store of vanities must reap.
Oh thoughts, oh my desires, no less unjust
Than false and vain. Thus of an innocent
I sought the death to have my beastly will;
960 So bloody cruel was I then, so blind.
Who opens now mine eyes? Ah wretch, I see
My fault most foul that seemed felicity.

CHORUS OF SHEPHERDS

Come, holy Hymenaeus, come this even
According to our vows and to our songs.
965 Dress thou these lovers as them best belongs.
Both th'one and th'other of the seed of heaven,
Knit thou the fatal knot this blessèd even.[533]
See, faithful shepherd, after all thy tears,
All thy distresses, whither thou art come;
970 Is not this she from thee was ta'en away
By law of heaven and earth? By cruel fate?
By her chaste will? And by thy poor estate?
By her faith given another man, and by her death?
Behold, Mirtillo, now she's only thine.
975 This face, these eyes, this breast, these dainty hands,
All that thou seest, hearst, and feelst, so often sought
In vain by thee, are now rewards become
Of thine undaunted faith, yet thou art dumb.

MIRTILLO

How can I speak? I scarce know if I breathe,
980 Nor what I see, I scarce believe I see:
Let Amarillis you that pleasure give,
In her alone my soul's affections live.

---

[533] In Guarini's intention, after the repeated lines of each chorus a single actor would utter the rest.

CHORUS OF SHEPHERDS
Come, holy Hymenaeus, come this even
According to our vows and to our songs.
985 Dress thou these lovers as them best belongs.
Both th'one and th'other of the seed of heaven,
Knit thou the fatal knot this blessèd even.

CORISCA
What do ye now with me, treacherous toys,
Wild frenzies of the body, spots of the soul?[534]
990 You long enough have me betrayèd here.
Go get you to the earth, for earth you are;
You were th'arms erst of lascivious love,
Trophies of chastity now may you prove.

CHORUS OF SHEPHERDS
Come, holy Hymenaeus, come this even
995 According to our vows and to our songs.
Dress thou these lovers as them best belongs.
Both th'one and th'other of the seed of heaven,
Knit thou the fatal knot this blessèd even.

CORISCA
Why triflest thou, Corisca? Now's fit time
1000 Pardon to impetrate.[535] Fearst thou thy pain?
Be bold, thy pain cannot be greater than thy fault.
Beauteous and blessèd couple, of the skies
And earth beloved, since to your glorious fate
This day hath meekly bowed all earthly force,
1005 Good reason she do bow that 'gainst the same
Hath set a work all of her earthly force.
Now, Amarillis, I will not deny
I did desire the same which you desired,
But you enjoy it, for you worthy were.
1010 You do enjoy the loyalest man alive.
And you, Mirtillo, do enjoy the chastest nymph
That e'er the world hath bred. Believe you me,
For I a whetstone was unto your faith,[536]

---

[534] A reference to her makeup, though the metaphorical significance is clear enough.
[535] impetrate] beg for.
[536] whetstone] In his 'Annotationi' (p. 479 of the 1602 Ciotti edition), Guarini points out that though some readers had interpreted 'cote' (v. 9. 1542) as 'touchstone', what was meant here was 'flint'. Through her actions, Corisca made the lovers burn even more. Dymock modifies the metaphor.

And to her chastity. But courteous nymph, before
1015 Your anger do descend on me, behold
Your husband's face; there shall you find the force
Both of my fault, and of your pardon too.
For in the virtue of such worthiness,
You cannot choose but cause of pardon find.
1020 Besides, you felt, alas, the selfsame fire
That did inflame unfortunate desire.

AMARILLIS
I do not only pardon thee, Corisca, but
I count thee dear, th'effect beholding, not the cause.
For fire and sword, although they wounds do bring,
1025 Yet those once healed, to us so whole th'are dear.
Howsoever now thou prov'st,[537] or friend, or foe,
I am well pleased the destinies did make
Thee the good instrument of my content:
Happy deceits, fortunate treacheries.
1030 And if you please merry with us to be,
Come then, and take part of our joys with us.

CORISCA
I have sufficient mirth you pardon me,
And that my heart is healed of her disease.

MIRTILLO
And I, Corisca, pardon all thy harms,
1035 Save this delaying of my sweet content.

CORISCA
You and your mirth I to the Gods commend.

CHORUS OF SHEPHERDS
Come, holy Hymenaeus, come this even
According to our vows and to our songs.
Dress thou these lovers as them best belongs.
1040 Both th'one and th'other of the seed of heaven,
Knit thou the fatal knot this blessèd even.

---

[537] now thou prov'st] In the source Amarillis speaks in the past tense (whether you were a friend or foe, it does not matter now; v. 9. 1560–61).

Act v, Scene 10
MIRTILLO, AMARILLIS, CHORUS OF SHEPHERDS

MIRTILLO
I am so tied to pain, that in the midst
Of all my joys I needs must languish still:
Is't not enough this ceremonious pomp
1045 Doth hold us thus, but that Corisca must
Come in to hinder us?

AMARILLIS
                    Th'art too quick, my dear.[538]

MIRTILLO
Oh, my sweet treasure, I am not secure,
Yet do I quake for fear of losing thee.[539]
This seems a dream, and still I am afraid
1050 My sleep should break, and thou, my soul, shouldst fly away.
In better proof my senses would I steep
That this sweet sight is not a dreaming sleep.

CHORUS OF SHEPHERDS
Come, holy Hymenaeus, come this even
According to our vows and to our songs.
1055 Dress thou these lovers as them best belongs.
Both th'one and th'other of the seed of heaven,
Knit thou the fatal knot this blessèd even.

CHORUS
Oh happy two,
That plaints have sowed and reapèd smiles.
1060 In many bitter grievous toils[540]
Have you embellished your desires.
Henceforth prepare your amorous fires,[541]
And bolden up your tender sprights
Unto your true sincere delights.
1065 You cannot have a sounder joy,

---

[538] quick] hasty.
[539] Yet] Still.
[540] toils] 'foils' in all the editions (but it is quite probably a misprint: the source has 'doglie', 'griefs'; v. Ch. 1605).
[541] Dymock's chorus continues to address the two fictional lovers, while in the source their faithfulness and chastity are held up as examples to the reader ('Quinci imparate voi, | o ciechi e troppo teneri mortali'; 'Now learn from this, | you blind and frail mortals'; v. Ch. 1607–08).

There is no ill can you annoy.
This is true joy, true pleasure and true mirth,
T'which virtue got,[542] in patience giveth birth.

FINIS

---

[542] T'] That.

BIBLIOGRAPHY

Primary sources

Battista Guarini, *Il pastor fido*

Early modern editions:

Il Pastor Fido: Tragicomedia Pastorale (Venice: Giovanni Battista Bonfadino, 1589; date on title page 1590)
Il Pastor Fido: Tragicomedia Pastorale [...] *Aminta: Favola Boschereccia* (London: John Wolfe for Giacomo Castelvetro, 1591)
Il Pastor Fido, Tragicommedia Pastorale [...] *Ora in questa XX. Impressione di curiose, & dotte Annotationi arricchito* [...] *Con un Compendio di Poesia tratto da i duo Verati* (Venice: Giovanni Battista Ciotti, 1602)

Modern edition:

Il pastor fido, ed. by Elisabetta Selmi, with an introduction by Guido Baldassarri (Venezia: Marsilio, 1999)

Early modern translations:

Le Berger Fidelle. Pastorale, trans. by Roland Brisset (Tours: Iamet Mettayer, 1593)
Il Pastor fido: Or The faithfull Shepheard. Translated out of Italian into English [trans. by Tailboys Dymock] (London: [Thomas Creede for] Simon Waterson, 1602)
Il pastor fido, The faithfull Shepherd, trans. by Richard Fanshawe (London: R. Raworth, 1647)
Il pastor fido. Le Berger fidelle. [...] *En vers*, trans. by Antoine de Torche (Paris: Gabriel Quinet, 1664)
Der Teutsch-Redende Treue Schaeffer des berühmten Welschen Guarini, trans. by Hans Assmann von Abschatz (n.p.: 1672)
Pastor Fido: Or, the Faithful Shepherd, trans. by Elkanah Settle (London: William Cademan, 1677)

Modern editions of early modern translations:

A Critical Edition of Sir Richard Fanshawe's 1647 Translation of Giovanni Battista Guarini's 'Il Pastor Fido', ed. by Walter F. Staton Jr. and William E. Simeone (Oxford: Clarendon Press, 1964)
Three Renaissance Pastorals: Tasso-Guarini-Daniel, ed. by Elizabeth Story Donno (Binghamton: Medieval & Renaissance Texts & Studies, 1993) [contains an edition of the 1602 Dymock translation]
El Pastor Fido de Battista Guarini, Ediciones de Nápoles 1602 y Valencia 1609, trans. by Cristóbal Suárez de Figueroa, ed. by Enrique Suárez Figaredo (Madrid: Centro Virtual Cervantes, 2006–2007)

Critical Works

AMMIRATI, LUIGI, *Nola nella luce della Rinascenza: La prima rappresentazione del Pastor Fido col Prologo di G. B. Marino nel 1599* (Nola: printed by G. Scala, 1980)

ANDREWS, RICHARD, '*A Midsummer Night's Dream* and Italian Pastoral', in *Transnational Exchange in Early Modern Theater*, ed. by Robert Henke and Eric Nicholson (Aldershot: Ashgate, 2008), pp. 49–62

BELLE, MARIE-ALICE, 'Rhetorical *Ethos* and the Translating Self in Early Modern England', in *Trust and Proof: Translators in Renaissance Print Culture*, ed. by Andrea Rizzi (Leiden: Brill, 2018), pp. 62–84

—— and Brenda M. Hosington (eds), *Thresholds of Translation: Paratexts, Print, and Cultural Exchange in Early Modern Britain (1473–1660)* (Basingstoke: Palgrave Macmillan, 2018)

BLISS, LEE, 'Defending Fletcher's Shepherds', *Studies in English Literature*, 23 (1983), 295–310

BRAZEAU, BRYAN, 'London Calling: John Harington's Exegetical Domestication of Ariosto in Late Sixteenth-Century England', *History of European Ideas*, 42 (2016), 640–50

BROWN, F. C., *Elkanah Settle: His Life and Works* (Chicago: The University of Chicago Press, 1910)

BURKE, PETER, 'Translations into Latin in Early Modern Europe', in *Cultural Translation in Early Modern Europe*, ed. by Peter Burke and Ronnie Po-Chia Hsia (Cambridge: Cambridge University Press, 2007), pp. 65–80

CAEMMERER, CHRISTIANE, 'Die Schäferliteratur und die Frauen', in *'Wenn sie das Wort ich gebraucht': Festschrift für Barbara Becker-Cantarino*, ed. by John Pustejovsky and Jacqueline Vansant (Amsterdam: Rodopi, 2013), pp. 221–47

CARRARA, ENRICO, *La poesia pastorale* (Milan: Vallardi, 1909)

CHISHOLM, DUNCAN, 'The English Origins of Händel's "Pastor fido"', *The Musical Times*, 115.1578 (1974), 650–54

CLUBB, LOUISE GEORGE, *Italian Drama in Shakespeare's Time* (New Haven: Yale University Press, 1989)

—— 'Pastoral Jazz from the Writ to the Liberty', in *Italian Culture in the Drama of Shakespeare & His Contemporaries: Rewriting, Remaking, Refashioning*, ed. by Michele Marrapodi (Aldershot: Ashgate, 2007), pp. 15–26

COLDIRON, A. E. B., 'Commonplaces and Metaphors', in *The Oxford History of Literary Translation in English, vol. 2: 1550–1660*, ed. by Gordon Braden, Robert Cummings and Stuart Gillespie (Oxford: Oxford University Press, 2010), pp. 109–17

—— *Printers without Borders: Translation and Textuality in the Renaissance* (Cambridge: Cambridge University Press, 2015)

—— 'Visibility Now: Historicizing Foreign Presences in Translation', *Translation Studies*, 5.2 (2012), 189–200

COTTEGNIES, LINE, 'La traduction anglaise du *Pastor Fido* de Guarini par Richard Fanshawe (1647): Quelques réflexions sur la naturalisation', *Études Épistémè*, 4 (2003), 30–49

CUMMINGS, BRIAN, 'Encyclopaedic Erasmus', *Renaissance Studies*, 28.2 (2014), 183–204

DALLA VALLE, DANIELA, *Pastorale barocca: Forme e contenuti dal Pastor Fido al drama pastorale francese* (Ravenna: Longo, 1973)

DUTTON, RICHARD, *Ben Jonson: Authority, Criticism* (Houndmills, Basingstoke: Palgrave Macmillan, 1996)

ECCLES, MARK, 'Samuel Daniel in France and Italy', *Studies in Philology*, 34.2 (1937), 148–67

FRODELLA, SHEILA, 'La migrazione del *Pastor fido* in Inghilterra', in *Studi di Anglistica e Americanistica. Percorsi di ricerca*, ed. by Fiorenzo Fantaccini and Ornella De Zordo (Firenze: Firenze University Press, 2012), pp. 105–61

GADD, IAN, 'The Stationers' Company in England before 1710', in *Research Handbook on the History of Copyright Law*, ed. by H. Tomás Gómez-Arostegui and Isabella Alexander (Cheltenham: Elgar, 2016), pp. 81–95

GATTO, MARISTELLA, 'Sulla "scena" della storia: traduzione e riscrittura in *The Faithfull Shepherd* di Sir Richard Fanshawe', in *Forme del tragicomico nel teatro elisabettiano e giacomiano*, ed. by Vittoria Intonti (Napoli: Liguori, 2004), pp. 217–46

GIAVARINI, LAURENCE, 'La reception du *Pastor Fido* en France au XVIIe siecle: bref état des lieux de la recherche', *Études Épistémè*, 4 (2003)

GREG, WALTER W., *Pastoral Poetry & Pastoral Drama: A Literary Inquiry, with Special Reference to the Pre-Restoration Stage in England* (London: A. H. Bullen, 1906)

HALASZ, ALEXANDRA, 'The Stationers' Shakespeare', in *Shakespeare's Stationers: Studies in Cultural Bibliography*, ed. by Marta Straznicky (Philadelphia: University of Pennsylvania Press, 2013), pp. 17–27

HENKE, ROBERT, *Pastoral Transformations: Italian Tragicomedy and Shakespeare's Late Plays* (Newark: University of Delaware Press, 1997)

HERMANS, THEO, 'Images of Translation: Metaphor and Imagery in the Renaissance Discourse on Translation', in *The Manipulation of Literature: Studies in Literary Translation*, ed. by Theo Hermans (London: Croom Helm, 1985), pp. 103–35

HERNÁNDEZ-PECORARO, ROSILIE, 'Cristóbal Suárez de Figueroa and Isabel Correa: Competing Translators of Battista Guarini's *Il Pastor Fido*', *Romance Notes*, 46.1 (2005), 97–105

HOLDSWORTH, W. S., 'Press Control and Copyright in the 16th and 17th Centuries', *The Yale Law Journal*, 29.8 (1920), 841–58

JAVITCH, DANIEL, 'Introduction to Giovan Battista Giraldi Cinthio's "Discourse or Letter on the Composition of Comedies and Tragedies"', *Renaissance Drama*, 39 (2011), 197–206

JONES, RICHARD FOSTER, *The Triumph of the English Language: A Survey of Opinions Concerning the Vernacular from the Introduction of Printing to the Restoration* (Stanford: Stanford University Press, 1953)

KRETSCHMER, F. A., 'The "res/verba" Dichotomy and "copia" in Renaissance Translation', *Renaissance and Reformation / Renaissance et Reforme*, 11.1 (1975), 24–29

LAGAE-DEVOLDÈRE, DENIS, 'L'Adaptation du *Pastor Fido* de Fanshawe par Elkannah Settle (1676)', *Études Épistémè*, 4 (2003), 50–60

LAWRENCE, JASON, '"The Whole Complection of Arcadia Chang'd": Samuel Daniel and Italian Lyrical Drama', *Medieval and Renaissance Drama in England*, 11 (1999), 143–71

LAZZARINI, ANDREA, 'Una polemica attorno al *Pastor fido* in lingua Napolitana di Domenico Basile', *Studi secenteschi*, 44 (2013), 187–203

LEFEVERE, ANDRÉ, 'Translation Practice(s) and the Circulation of Cultural Capital:

Some *Aeneid*s in English', in *Constructing Cultures: Essays on Literary Translation*, ed. by Susan Bassnett and André Lefevere (Clevedon: Multilingual Matters, 1998), pp. 41–56

LESLIE, ROBERT W., 'Shakespeare's Italian Dream: Cinquecento Sources for *A Midsummer Night's Dream*', *Comparative Drama*, 29.4 (1995-1996), 454–65

LYNE, RAPHAEL, 'English Guarini: Recognition and Reception', *Yearbook of English Studies*, 36.1 (2006), 90–102

MATTHIESSEN, F. O., *Translation: An Elizabethan Art* (New York: Octagon Books, 1965 [1931])

MOORE, J. L., *Tudor-Stuart Views on the Growth Status and Destiny of the English Language* (Halle a.S.: Max Niemeyer, 1910)

MORINI, MASSIMILIANO, 'Goths and Greeks: The Rise of Anglo-Saxon England and Germanic English in Early Modern Britain', *Filologia Germanica / Germanic Philology*, 12 (2020), 171–90

—— 'Restoration Theatre, Indirect Translation and the Canon: Settle's Guarini', *Theatralia*, 24.1 (2021), 34–42

—— 'Shakespeare's Language and the Restoration', in *The Shakespeare Apocrypha*, ed. by Douglas A. Brooks (Lewinston: Edwin Mellen Press, 2007), pp. 339–88

—— 'The Superiority of Classical Translation in Sixteenth-Century England: Thomas Hoby and John Harington', *Philological Quarterly*, 98.3 (2019), 273–95

—— '"To reforme a frame"': The 1602 Translation of *Il pastor fido* and Elizabethan Theatrical Publishing', *Cahiers Élisabeéthains*, 104.1 (2021), 42–60

—— *Tudor Translation in Theory and Practice* (Aldershot: Ashgate, 2006)

—— 'Virgil in Tudor Dress: In Search of a Noble Vernacular', *Neophilologus*, 97.3 (2013), 591–610

NERI, NICOLETTA, *Il pastor fido in Inghilterra* (Torino: Giappichelli, 1963)

NICCOLI, GABRIELE, 'Modalità metamorfiche nella figura e funzione del maggior satiro ferrarese del tardo Cinquecento', *Quaderni d'Italianistica*, 29.2 (2008), 5–16

PERELLA, NICOLAS J., 'Amarilli's Dilemma: The *Pastor Fido* and Some English Authors', *Comparative Literature*, 12.4 (1960), 348–59

—— *The Critical Fortune of Battista Guarini's "Il pastor fido"* (Firenze: Olschki, 1973)

PETRINA, ALESSANDRA, 'Introduction: The Definition of Cultural Identity through Translation', in *Acquisition through Translation: Towards a Definition of Renaissance Translation*, ed. by Alessandra Petrina and Federica Masiero (Turnhout: Brepols, 2020), pp. 17–32

PIERI, MARZIA, *La scena boschereccia nel Rinascimento italiano* (Padova: Liviana Editrice, 1983)

—— 'Selve e giardini nella scena europea di Ancien Régime', *Italies*, 8 (2004), 189–207

PIGMAN III, G. W., 'Pastoral Drama', in *The Oxford History of Literary Translation in English, vol. 2: 1550-1660*, ed. by Gordon Braden, Robert Cummings and Stuart Gillespie (Oxford: Oxford University Press, 2010), pp. 293–98

POZZI, FRANCESCO, 'La prima rappresentazione del "Pastor Fido" di Battista Guarini a Crema: Carnevale 1595 o 1596', *Insula Fulcheria*, 36 (2006), 265–82

RHODES, NEIL, GORDON KENDAL and LOUISE WILSON, eds, *English Renaissance Translation Theory* (London: The Modern Humanities Research Association, 2013)

Riccò, Laura, *'Ben mille pastorali': L'itinerario dell'Ingegneri da Tasso a Guarini e oltre* (Roma: Bulzoni, 2004)

Rossi, Vittorio, *Battista Guarini ed il pastor fido: Studio biografico-critico* (Torino: Loescher, 1886)

Sampson, Lisa, 'The Mantuan Performance of Guarini's *Pastor fido* and Representations of Courtly Identity', *Modern Language Review*, 98.1 (2003), 65–83

—— *Pastoral Drama in Early Modern Italy: The Making of a New Genre* (Abingdon: The Modern Humanities Research Association and Routledge, 2006)

Sánchez García, Encarnación, '"Salientes acquae". Due edizioni poetiche napoletane in lingua spagnola: "El pastor fido" di Cristóbal Suárez (1602) e le "Obras" di Garcilaso de la Vega (1604)', in *Cancioneros del Siglo de Oro: Forma y formas / Canzonieri dei Secoli d'oro: Forma e forme*, ed. by Andrea Baldissera (Como: Ibis, 2019), pp. 183–204

Schlueter, June, 'Samuel Daniel in Italy: New Documentary Evidence', *Huntington Library Quarterly*, 75.2 (2012), 283–90

Schneider, Federico, *Pastoral Drama and Healing in Early Modern Italy* (Farnham: Ashgate, 2010)

Schurink, Fred, 'Introduction', in *Tudor Translation*, ed. by Fred Schurink (New York: Palgrave Macmillan, 2011), pp. 1–17

Schwartz, Alba, *Der Teutsch-redende treue Schäfer: Guarinis'Pastor fido' und die Übersetzungen von Eilger Mannlich 1619, Statius Ackermann 1636, Hofmann von Hoffmannswaldau 1652, Assmann von Abschatz 1672* (Bern: Peter Lang, 1972)

Selmi, Elisabetta, *'Classici e Moderni' nell'officina del 'Pastor Fido'* (Alessandria: Edizioni dell'Orso, 2001)

Smith, Robert A. H., 'Thomas Creede, *Henry V* Q1, and *The Famous Victories of Henrie the Fifth*', *The Review of English Studies*, 49.193 (1998), 60–64

Straznicky, Martha, 'Introduction: What is a Stationer?', in *Shakespeare's Stationers: Studies in Cultural Bibliography*, ed. by Marta Straznicky (Philadelphia: University of Pennsylvania Press, 2013), pp. 1–16

Sukic, Christine, 'Samuel Daniel et les traductions anglaises du *Pastor Fido* au XVIIe siècle en Angleterre: du voyage d'Italie à la naturalisation', *Études Épistémè*, 4 (2003), 18–29

Syme, Holger Schott, 'Thomas Creede, William Barkley, and the Venture of Printing Plays', in *Shakespeare's Stationers: Studies in Cultural Bibliography*, ed. by Marta Straznicky (Philadelphia: University of Pennsylvania Press, 2013), pp. 28–46

Taylor, Andrew, 'Introduction: The Translations of Renaissance Latin', *Canadian Review of Comparative Literature / Revue Canadienne de Littérature Comparée*, 41.4 (2014), 329–53

Toury, Gideon, *Descriptive Translation Studies and Beyond* (Amsterdam: John Benjamins, 1995)

Verkuyl, P. E. L., *Battista Guarini's 'Il pastor fido' in de Nederlandse dramatische literatuur* (Assen: Van Gorcum, 1971)

Wiggins, Martin, and Catherine Richardson, *British Drama 1533–1642: A Catalogue. Volume IV: 1598–1602* (Oxford: Oxford University Press, 2014)

Yamada, Akihiro, *Thomas Creede: Printer to Shakespeare and His Contemporaries* (Tokyo: Meisei University Press, 1994)

MODERN HUMANITIES RESEARCH ASSOCIATION
TUDOR AND STUART TRANSLATIONS

A SELECTION OF RECENTLY PUBLISHED TITLES

Anne Cooke's Englishing of Bernardino Ochino
Edited by Patricia Demers

Erasmus in English 1523–1584
Volume I: 'The Manual of the Christian Soldier' and Other Writings
Edited by Alex Davis, Gordon Kendal and Neil Rhodes

Erasmus in English 1523–1584
Volume II: 'The Praise of Folly' and Other Writings
Edited by Alex Davis, Gordon Kendal and Neil Rhodes

Plutarch in English, 1528–1603
Volume I: Essays
Edited by Fred Schurink

Plutarch in English, 1528–1603
Volume II: Lives
Edited by Fred Schurink

Petrarch's 'Triumphi' in English
Edited by Alessandra Petrina

Thomas May: Lucan's 'Pharsalia' (1627)
Edited by Emma Buckley and Edward Paleit

William Barker: Xenophon's 'Cyropaedia'
Edited by Jane Grogan

www.tudor.mhra.org.uk

www.ingramcontent.com/pod-product-compliance
Lightning Source LLC
Chambersburg PA
CBHW051643230426
43669CB00013B/2420